Advance Praise

GRANDPARENTING: A SURVIVAL GUIDE

by Margery Fridstein, MA, LPC

"This is a wise and helpful book which will guide grand-parents of all ages and situations through the rewards and challenges of their vital role in the lives of their children and grandchildren."

"A must-read book for first-time grandparents as well as for those who already have grandchildren. Easily readable and well organized, this book offers valuable information and resources."

"When I was a young father, my wife and I had Dr. Spock to guide us in child care. As our children grew older, we turned to Louise Bates Ames and her books on various ages of children and their development to help us better understand our children. As a grandfather of ten grandchildren, each with a different personality and talents, I wondered where a grandparent could turn for guidance.

"Margery Fridstein's *Grandparenting: A Survival Guide* is the answer. At a time when divorce, single parent homes and an increasingly complex society have intruded on grand-parenthood, I now have a guide to what was once a simple, loving task and what has now become, for some grand-parents, a complex relationship."

"I can think of no one more qualified to write a book on grandparenting than Margery Fridstein. As a wife, mother, grandparent, therapist, educator and an unusually sensitive human being, Margery writes from a unique personal and professional perspective. Her book is a warmly-crafted educational guide ... Certainly this book will help the reader be a *grand*-parent."

"Sensitive to the needs of grandparents, parents and grand-children ... useful insight and approaches to divorce, blended families and working mothers as well as the traditional family ... Well-written, warm and humorous, it covers the important points of grandparenting (and parenting) well."

"This book is not only a gift to grandparents, but a wonderful resource for parents and others who work with children. The information is comprehensive, the suggestions are practical, and the list of resources is invaluable. Margery Fridstein tells it like it is by acknowledging all the variations of family constellations and dynamics in the '90s, while creating safety for grandparents' feelings about their role ... never overly clinical as it is flavored lovingly, honestly and humor-ously by Margery's experience in her cherished role of grand-parent. Her words comfort and inspire."

GRANDPARENTING:
A Survival Guide

How Better to Understand Yourself,
Your Children, and Your Children's Children

Margery Fridstein, MA, LPC

Tageh Press
Glenwood Springs, Colorado

Library of Congress Card Number Pending.
ISBN 0-9638385-2-0

First printing 1997.

Manufactured in the United States of America.

Tageh Press
P.O. Box 401
Glenwood Springs, CO 81602

Graphic Design and Production: Lori Rattan, Tageh Press
Cover Illustration: David Apatoff
Printing: Publishers Press, Salt Lake City, UT
Cover Printing: Gran Farnum Printing, Glenwood Springs, CO
Author Photo: Chaz Evans, Crystal River Photography, Carbondale, CO

Library of Congress Cataloging-in-Publication Data

Fridstein, Margery.
    Grandparenting: A Survival Guide - how better to understand your-
        self, your children, and your children's children / Margery Fridstein.
    Includes bibliographic references and index.
    ISBN 0-9638385-2-0
    1. Grandparenting 2. Parenting 3. Child Development

QUANTITY DISCOUNTS: Associations, Societies, Schools and Universities, Health Clinics and Hospitals – this book is available at quantity discounts on bulk purchases for educational, premiums and sales promotion use. For information, please contact: Special Sales Dept., Tageh Press, P.O. Box 401, Glenwood Springs, CO 81602; or e-mail: *tageh@rof.net.*

Dedication

To Amanda, Carly, Darcie, Douglas, Dylan, Eric, Graham,
Heather, Jessica, Melissa, and Sarah.

*I find the great thing in this world is
not so much where we stand,
as in what direction we are moving.*
– Goethe

Contents

Introduction

Aging baby boomers are becoming grandparents. This closely analyzed segment of the population has changed the rules in the past, and there is no doubt you baby boomers will be different grandparents. Characteristic of boomers is a demanding, want-to-know attitude. Now, after spending years working to better understand yourselves, your marriages and your children, you are entering a new developmental stage: Grandparenthood. This book isn't only for boomer grandparents – it's for grandparents of all ages and stages.

Grandparenting: A Survival Guide began when my son and his wife were expecting their first *two* babies. They asked me to be there to help out when they brought their twins home from the hospital. This book was conceived during those never-ending night feedings that I took over to give them some rest. I no sooner finished with Jessica then Darcie began to cry. I put Darcie down, and Jessica was ready to eat again. I probably never worked harder in my life, but it was a tremendous joy to be with my son and his wife as they became a family.

During that week of grandparent care, I reflected on how dramatically ideas, attitudes and life situations had changed since my parenting days. I considered the many new questions I received from grandparents in my clinical practice: how to relate to their children in this new role, what is helpful and what is not, how to become more involved, what limits to set, and what books to read? Perhaps with my professional experience as a psychotherapist and child development specialist, as well as my own personal grandparenting experience, I could produce a book offering useful, practical insights for grandparent survival as we approach the millennium.

Every time a child is born, two grandparents are born. Grandparents range in age from 30 to 110, and their ranks grow as we live longer. Grandparenthood is parenthood, one step removed. Unlike parenting, grandparents have no control over *when* or *if* it happens. Most grandparents want to be involved, some are ambivalent, and others are not prepared at all. Involvement as grandparents is a luxury for some, and a necessity for others.

The dramatic changes in today's modern family life have parents worried and uncertain. Conditions have changed, and the rules (if, in fact, there are any *rules*) have changed beyond recognition from past generations. The lack of societal and institutional supports to help raise children is alarming. Grandparents are also confused in their role, and overwhelmed by these societal changes. Yet we have a very real need for informed, effectively attuned and devoted grandparents who can offer a safety net for their children, and their children's children. In addition, grandparents need to learn to support, nurture and guide their changing families (as grandparents have always done) without appearing old-fashioned and irrelevant, and with a minimum of interference.

Two elements make this handbook unique among other grandparenting books available. The first section, *A New Life Begins*, examines the changing role of grandparenthood from a *child development perspective*. Chapters flow chronologically from the news of impending grandparenthood, to the birth of the grandchild, through the child's development until the age of 10 (by which time grandparents will likely be comfortable in their role). A minor note: to avoid the distracting need to refer to *he or she* or *him or her* at every gender reference, I alternate throughout the text with reference to infants, toddlers and children as *him* or *her.*

The second section, *Grandparenting Today's Families*, addresses critical issues that other sources flinch at in discomfort or prefer to gloss over. Here you will find frank, helpful information, including chapters about working mothers and children; divorce, death and mourning; remarriage; child abuse and teen pregnancy; infertility, adoption and other choices; and children with special needs. Some of these controversial issues are often avoided because they may be unpleasant to face, but they must be addressed because they are realities of our time. There is little need for a grandparenting survival guide when life is rosy; it is when difficulties arise that grandparents and other family members are most in need of help. This book provides useful strategies families can put to use at once on their own. As you will see, in the end we survived — and *thrived!*

Case studies and personal vignettes illustrate and elaborate on factual information and ideas. Helpful tips are provided throughout the book. Each chapter concludes with a topic-appropriate summary of recommendations and reading lists for adults and children. However, this is *not* a recipe book. There is seldom a single right or wrong answer to the issues raised. Rather, this is an opportunity to become familiar with those issues and consider options and choices.

The basic goal is to provide information to enable grandparents to be *good enough grandparents,* following the model of D.W. Winnicott's "good enough mother."

My personal aims in writing this book are:

1. To encourage readers to examine the changed relationships brought about by the new baby: the parent/adult-child relationship, the parent/adult-child/baby relationship, and the grandparent/grandchild relationship. By examining these relationships, grandparents can gain a clearer understanding about family dynamics and respond with more sensitivity to issues that arise between generations.
2. To alert grandparents to appreciate the magnitude of societal changes that have taken place since their parenting days, and consider how these changes affect them. My goal is to help grandparents be better informed and more supportive for their adult children, and become the kind of grandparents children need as we enter the 21st century.
3. To emphasize that grandfathers are every bit as important to grandchildren as grandmothers! Most grandparent writing focuses on the grandmother. This is an error, in my opinion, and one that stands corrected in this survival guide.

I am indebted to many people who helped make this book possible. In particular I want to thank my children, their spouses, and their children for allowing me to use bits and pieces of their lives to illustrate and expand on points I make in the text. In the same vein, I am forever grateful to my many grandparent friends who have shared their experiences — some humorous, others sad, and some highly conflictual. While I have altered identities and circumstances to safeguard privacy, some may recognize themselves. I pray I have not offended anyone in the ways I may have modified certain stories for purposes of guidance and enlightenment to benefit others.

Lastly, let me thank all the families with whom I have had the privilege of working professionally over the last 25 years. You have taught me a great deal about the important issues covered in this book. I have made every effort to protect the privacy of all those whose situations I have borrowed for educational and anecdotal purposes. To all of you, my collaborators, my heartfelt thanks.

By and large, my personal and professional experience has been with white middle-class families, and it is from this vantage point that I have drawn most of my examples. However, I believe there is a universality to the experiences I have cited, and I consider this material pertinent to all ethnic groups. My readers may draw their own conclusion.

Several wonderful people have been instrumental in bringing this book to publication through what seemed at times a gestation period more elephant-like than human. The book actually drew its first breath when literary agent Steve Cogil said, "Yes, go for it – it's a good idea!" Later, literary agent Susan Golomb entered the picture, and although we never met face to face, we spent many hours working together on the phone. Enter Rose Brandt, writer and collaborator for a brief period of time. While our paths eventually went separate ways, she was a great help to me.

In a roundabout way, my proposal reached Harlan Feder, whose enthusiasm for the project led me to completion. Harlan, as my editor and publisher, has been the one to *really* make it happen. It is to Harlan that I owe the greatest thanks. I also wish to express my gratitude to David Apatoff for his delightful original cover illustration, to art director Lori Rattan for her exceptional production and design, and to Dana Knipe for proofreading.

I want to thank three people who have had considerable impact on my life and who helped make this book possible by their presence and example: Mary Giffin, M.D.; David Dean Brockman, M.D.; and Bob Fridstein, my husband, co-grandparent, friend and support forever.

My four adult children Peggy, Thomas, Kathy and Nancy, have each contributed their time and energy as well as their unique skills and talents to support my writing with their ideas and input. My friends Barry Kayes and Jane Anderson, and my husband Bob Fridstein, have all offered me helpful editorial advice. I thank you all!

Additional thanks to my computer consultant, Bill Boineau, who comes running when my wonderful machine starts giving me a hard time and I grow frantic. Also my thanks to Helen Palmer of the Pitkin County Library, who always finds the materials I need.

Margery Fridstein
Snowmass Village, Colorado

GRANDPARENTING:
A Survival Guide

SECTION ONE

A New Life Begins and Grows

1

Anticipating Grandparenthood

Old age is always 15 years older than I am.
  – Bernard Baruch

"Hi, grandma!"

Diane described the unexpected telephone call she received from her daughter Gwen in Phoenix with a mixture of surprise and wonder. Diane initially assumed her daughter had misdialed and meant to reach her grandmother, and told Gwen her mistake.

"No mistake, Mom. You're going to be my baby's grandmother!"

My goodness, a grandparent at age 48. "I'm too young for this," Diane said, dazed.

For all of us, this is the most important event in our lives that we have absolutely no control over. Whether we love the idea or hate it – whether we choose to become involved or not – whether our lifestyle accommodates being a grandparent or not – when our offspring becomes pregnant or impregnates someone, we begin our journey along the path of grandparenting.

Consider that every time a child is born, a grandparent is also born. Accepting the title of grandparent, while dreaded by some, is an event cherished and embraced by most adults. It is a common misconception, especially among younger people, that the types of situations, problems and solutions described in *Grandparenting: A Survival Guide* are strictly for senior citizens. Not only are all grandparents *not* necessarily senior citizens, some of us are young enough to still be producing our *own* babies. Others of us have about given up on the prospect of our busy career-minded children ever becoming parents themselves.

Many texts are available to help new parents better understand their role and to recognize and respond to the various stages of child development. Parents have long had access to a host of books on parenting; now grandparents have a source of assistance and advice in the form of *Grandparenting: A Survival Guide.* This comprehensive handbook is filled with useful information for 21st century grandparents to help us better understand *ourselves* as we experience this new developmental stage, as well as our adult children as parents, and all the complicated relationships with our grandchildren.

Some of the material contained in this text may remind you of your own experiences with your grandparents and your children's grandparents. Whether you are thrilled to become a grandparent ("Finally!"), shocked ("I can't be that old!") or just plain confused ("What am I supposed to do now?"), you will find useful answers, suggestions, strategies and resources.

We will discover that much of the grandparenting terrain has changed dramatically from past generations. Today, when half of our nation's children grow up directly affected by divorce, single-parent households and blended families, the role of grandparents is more complex and vital than ever before. For some families, grandparents are crucial for survival.

What Are Grandparents Like?

In her book *Funny, You Don't Look Like a Grandmother,* Lois Wyse writes that she was shocked to become a grandmother. She thinks of her own grandmothers as the *real* grandmothers. They made soup and wore dresses big enough to hide the consequences of their own cooking.

"They didn't know from gyms, exercise or second marriages," she writes. "Today's grandmother does. And more: she is selling real estate, working out and zapping around Paris with or without a husband."

Chicago Tribune columnist Bob Greene offers another amusing perspective on grandparenthood. In a column about his 25th high school reunion, he wrote:

> *"A lot of people will tell you there is not much difference between a 20th high school reunion and a 25th high school reunion. These people are wrong. At your 25th high school reunion you will find some of your classmates are grandparents. Grandparents .. I don't care how mature you are; I don't care how serious about life you are; I don't care how responsible a citizen you are. When you walk into the first house at which this guy chugging beer next to you is a man who is referred to as 'Grandpa' by a child somewhere in this land of ours, it gives reason for pause ... So here at your 25th reunion, when this wonderfully attractive woman who has flown in from Wyoming walks up to you wearing cowboy boots and a dazzling, friendly smile, and you ask her what has been going on, and she says not much, except that she's a grandmother now ..."*

There are lots of us grandparents, and our numbers are increasing daily. Today's grandparents are more active than past generations and, on average, have more disposable income. In addition, we live longer, healthier lives thanks to medical and scientific advances. It is not unusual for grandparents to know their grandchildren as teenagers and adults, as well as to become great-grandparents some day.

As the baby boomer generation become grandparents, they are expected to have a huge impact on our society. The first of the 80 million baby boomers turned age 50 in 1996. By 2030 the oldest boomers will be age 84 and the youngest age 65.

Given their sizeable percentage of the population, this group is predicted to exert an unprecedented influence on retirement programs and health care.

The experts have not yet predicted future grandparenting trends, but we can speculate that baby boomers will handle grandparenting and great-grandparenting roles and duties very differently from the way their parents did. A demanding, "want-to-know-everything" attitude is a primary characteristic of the boomers. They should find this survival guide most useful!

How People Adapt to Grandparenthood

Newly informed grandparents-to-be adapt to their role in as many unique ways as there are individual personalities:

- *Surprise*: Margaret and Stan celebrated Margaret's 65th birthday with their California-based son and his wife. Margaret and Stan still waited and longed to become grandparents. The California couple handed their mom a most unique birthday gift: a sonogram picture of their three-month intrauterine fetus sucking its thumb. It was the perfect birthday present!

- *Free*: In becoming grandma and grandpa, parents are often freed up to be more loving, indulgent, patient and generous than they ever were as mother and father. They are no longer responsible for instilling moral values, nor are they in charge of discipline and rules. Now free from ambition, free from the need to control, free from anxiety – they are at last free to enjoy.

- *A New Lease on Life*: The special love from their grandparents gives the child a valuable sense of security in being loved without always deserving it. In turn, the child conveys a message to grandparents that they are needed, wanted and loved. This is a new lease on life, cherished by all.

- *Open-Mindedness:* Mike and Jane's daughter Amy was

divorced and raising her son as a single parent. She met Pete and they had a wonderful romance. One day she called Jane to tell her she was pregnant. According to Jane, Amy made no mention of marriage, abortion or single parenting two children, and Jane refrained from asking, although she was very concerned.

A few months later, Amy phoned to tell her parents she and Pete were getting married and asked them to come to the wedding. The proposed wedding kept being postponed and again Jane worried. Jane finally learned that the wedding postponement was related to Pete's delay in finalizing his divorce. When the date was set, the bride was visibly pregnant. Jane and Mike attended the wedding of their daughter, tummy and all in her white wedding dress.

Now Amy and Pete, their baby, Grant, Amy's son Todd and Peter's daughters Jessica and Loren all form a wonderful family, and Mike and Jane are delighted.

- *Unusual*: According to a news report, a grandmother carried her daughter's unborn baby in her uterus because the daughter was medically unable to bear the pregnancy (perhaps the ultimate grandparenting role, and one that nearly all of us will thankfully be spared!)

What Is Our Role As Grandparents?

The father of a 5-year-old, in therapy to deal with some personal problems, admitted at one point that he chose me as his therapist because I was a grandmother and "grandmothers are the matriarchs of the world."

Researchers are full of statistics about us:

- Women who become grandmothers when they are age 45 or younger are unlikely to discuss the fact – they say it makes them feel old.

- Divorced women tend to keep their status as grandmothers quiet – they fear it somehow makes them less attractive in the marriage market.
- Men feel less negative talking about becoming a grandparent than women.
- Grandfathers over age 65 tend to be more physically affectionate with their grandchildren than they were with their own children.
- Contemporary grandparents, in contrast to past generations, are more likely to experience tension between their place in the extended family and their quest for independence.

In some family constellations today, grandparents are the primary care parent. This is particularly true when teenagers become parents. The time between a divorce and remarriage is often another period when grandparents may become primary care parents. The important issues these roles bring up will be discussed in later chapters. In some cultures, the grandmother is typically the primary nurturer and caretaker of the children.

As a 40-something couple recently told me, "We told our teen daughters, 'Remember, if you get pregnant, dad and I are not planning to take care of your single-parent baby!'" They may be wise to establish such parameters.

What Kind of Grandparent Will *You* Be?
Once you have entered the process of becoming a grandparent, it is time to ask – and answer – an important question: "What kind of grandparent do *you* want to be?"

In 1964, Bernice Neugarten and Carol Weinstein, sociologists at the University of Chicago, completed a landmark study of the style of grandparenting among 70 pairs of middle-class grandparents. They defined five different types of grandparents. Their research remains the reference point on grandparenting styles today.

- *The Formal*: Those who follow what they regard as the proper prescribed role for grandparenting. (I'm not sure there *is* any proper prescribed role today!)

  Example: A woman in therapy expressed anger that her grandchildren called her by her first name, which she did not at all encourage. She also complained that her grandchildren did not act as respectful of her as she thought they should. These comments were very significant in her treatment; they led us to explore the rigidity of her own upbringing as well as the unrealistic demands she made on her children.

- *The Fun Seeker*: Their relationship to the grandchild is characterized by informality and playfulness. My husband Bob and I try to fit in this category – I hope our children and grandchildren agree!

  Example: During the Christmas holidays, our whole family – 21 members in all – gather from near and far to spend the holiday together. The grandchildren range in age from 6 months to 20 years. In my opinion, only *fun loving* grandparents could live with the crowding, disorder, excitement and sometimes chaotic interaction of such a large group. Everyone loves the week together, and I am glad we are of the temperament that we can enjoy this annual get-together joyfully without stressing out.

- *The Surrogate Parent*: This occurs more frequently for the grandmother, usually initiated by the younger generation, often a working mother, who turns actual care of her baby over to her mother. (These numbers have increased greatly in the past several decades.)

  Example: Molly's daughter-in-law was not a working mom, but she was in drug rehabilitation, so their son and grandson Jeremy, age 5, moved in with Molly and Ben. Jeremy's grandma cared for him while his dad went to work until the boy's mother was back on her feet and they could return home.

- *The Reservoir of Family Wisdom*: The grandfather is usually the dispenser of special skills or resources.

     Example: Children love stories of the olden days before VCRs, computers, video games and the Internet. Grandparents can describe, through words and images, relatives who have died or who live far away, so they exist for the child. They are official biographers of the children's parents, and family archivists in general. They help transmit ethnic heritage, religious faith and moral and cultural values. They can preserve those family rituals which mean so much to a continuing sense of community.

- *The Distant Figure*: The grandparents who emerge as if from the shadows on holidays and special occasions.

     Example: Max had just completed his second divorce. He was alone and lonely. He had pretty much lost contact with his children and their children, his grandchildren. He began seeing Ellen, who had also had two marriages, but in contrast to Max, Ellen remained close to her three adult children. Ellen and Max decided to live together; no more marriages for either of them. As Max became involved with Ellen's family, she encouraged him to reconnect with his family. Today, with Ellen's help, Max is no longer a *distant figure;* he is a happily involved grandfather.

It Was Never Like *This* In Our Parents' Day

     Times have changed, and the real-life twists and turns of our children's lives are often beyond the most fertile imaginations of fiction writers. Imagine how your parents might have reacted to the following situation described by a woman who came for counseling:

"My 42-year-old son is going to be a father with his 42-year-old girlfriend. He's a very busy surgeon, and he doesn't have time to think about marriage. I think I had better go out and meet the girl. I hope it's true. She has had two

previous marriages, but no children. This is her first pregnancy. I want to be a grandmother."

You are probably as curious about the outcome of this scenario as I was. Unfortunately, I never learned any more details. But the story illustrates the often surreal extremes of modern-day love, life and parenting.

Joan's 36-year-old son is marrying a woman with three children. Joan exclaims with good-natured optimism, "This is sure an easy way to become a grandparent."

Our parents usually became grandparents of one child at a time. But even this is changing. The number of multiple births in the U.S. hit a record high in 1991: almost 24 in every 100 births delivered twins, triplets or more – the highest rate in 50 years, according to the Metropolitan Life Insurance Company. The trend is probably the result of increased use of fertility drugs, which can promote multiple births among couples experiencing difficulty conceiving.

Greg, fiftyish, related, "I remember my grandparents as too frail or too fat to ever drop to the floor and try somersaults with their grandchildren. If such a thing had occurred, we would have assumed it was a heart attack and phoned 911 (if 911 had existed). My mother is 70-something, has eight grandchildren and plays tennis three times a week."

Yes, it was never like this in the *olden* days. A growing number of grandparents must balance the competing demands of work, play and family life, just as their adult children do. Others are dealing with the aftermath of divorce and the challenges of step-grandparenthood as they and their children move from one marriage to the next. Some manage to welcome grandchildren born to gay and lesbian couples or unmarried parents. Some grandparents need help dealing with all the new realities of modern family life.

The Decision to Become A Grandparent

As I mentioned earlier, we do not make the decision to become grandparents. It is made for us, whether we like it or not. Accepting the title of *grandparent* for the first time is an event that is embraced by most adults and avoided by a few. If you feel as if you have been taken by surprise, the material in this text will help prepare you for this exciting new experience, just as first-time parents assemble information about what they can expect.

What about those who dread becoming grandparents, or perhaps fear some part of the transformation? Typical negative reactions include:

- They have their lives and we have ours.
- I don't want to meddle or interfere.
- It is probably best for all of us to be independent.
- I don't want to get into child care and baby-sitting – it would tie me down.
- I consider it an imposition on my time and space.
- I think it would be bondage to get involved with grandchildren.
- I have established a nice life of order, and this will bring in all sorts of chaos.
- I hate the label *grandmother/grandfather;* it makes me feel too old.

These are expressions of the *distant figure* grandparents. They might not have much initial interest in a grandparents survival guide – but they may need it most of all.

I am not ready to give up on these distant figure grandparents. While they may feel this way as they anticipate grandparenthood, they may respond very differently once they have held and caressed their new baby grandchild. In the same way Max reconnected with his grandchildren with Ellen's help, the option for connection remains present for most grandparents.

Connecting with grandchildren is emotional rather than cognitive, and I suspect the distant figure grandparent will not always be so distant as he or she enters this new developmental stage of grandparenthood.

As adults grow older, they may not program grandparenthood into their lives. The husband retires and wants to travel. The older couple develop activities, routines and enjoy hobbies and new interests.

Then they learn they are going to become grandparents. Frequently the expectant grandmother is very excited and wants to be available to the couple. The retiring grandfather-to-be is reluctant. He has planned this future for a long time and does not want the kids to mess up his plans. This situation is conflictual, to say the least, and also fairly common. When these grandparents seek help, I proceed from this checklist:

1. First I obtain a family history, and a history of the couple, because each situation is different.
2. What is the grandparent couple's true relationship with each other? Are they as compatible as is necessary to participate in extensive travel together? How do their interests and activities compare and contrast?
3. Is this an older, long-established marriage, or a newer one in which only one of them is biologically related to the expectant couple? This can make a significant difference in how each spouse greets the news.
4. Do they have other grandchildren? Does grandpa find new babies boring? Often men are not as interested in infants as women.
5. Do each of them have preconceived notions of their impending grandparenthood? Are they positive, negative, or some of each? Have they discussed their thoughts with each other? Do their concerns match up or contrast with each other?

Short of extreme circumstances, I typically recommend compromise. But the compromise should relate to the variables mentioned here. As with most questions and answers in grandparenting issues, there is no easy-bake cookbook recipe. Each question and answer, every choice or decision, is idiosyncratic to that particular situation.

Yet many standard guidelines do apply, and can help serve as signposts along the way. Encourage discussion of the issues at hand among everyone involved, and listen to each other as well as express thoughts and feelings. This process of trying to understand how everyone really feels usually leads to a workable solution.

Planning For the Birth

Baby birthing has changed considerably in recent times, along with much else. It is hard to believe that only 20 years ago, fathers were not allowed to accompany moms into the delivery room. That was the *sterility* era, with its fears of infection during childbirth. Nurses were afraid the father might faint, requiring their attention when the mother needed their care. Prenatal education for both father and mother has changed all that. Both parents are now well prepared for childbirth before the first labor pains occur.

The birthing procedure is very different today. Many uncomplicated births are attended by a midwife. Some expectant parents prefer to give birth at home rather than at a hospital. These changes are due in part to the shift from the use of more toxic anesthetics to natural childbirth (or close to it) with the assistance of an epidural or saddle block to ease pain. Maternity rooms have been completely redesigned in most hospitals so that the whole experience happens in one room which includes a bed or couch for dad. With this new informality, birthing parents are free to invite whomever they wish to attend the delivery. An OB/GYN friend recalled a recent delivery at which the whole extended family was present – 16 people, including little children. They called this *the birthday party*. My friend assured me this is not commonplace.

Nurses and doctors welcome the presence of grandmothers, but are reluctant to include grandfathers. It appears the feeling is mutual, because grandfathers are more reluctant to accept an invitation to attend the delivery. My friend thinks grandfathers need more prenatal education so they will feel more comfortable attending the delivery if they want to. The father's possible anxiety about seeing his daughter exposed is misplaced. The birthing mother is much more covered than her father might imagine. Once the doctor encouraged a grandfather-to-be to join the grandmother-to-be at the birth. He did so – reluctantly. After the delivery, he thanked the doctor for encouraging him, and found the experience "beautiful." My friend finds it very moving to witness grandparent bonding as he delivers their grandbaby.

Because of the mother's position during delivery, she may be the only one in the room who cannot see the baby being born. If this is important to her, the doctor can connect a TV monitor for her to watch the delivery. With this capability, waiting grandparents may watch the birth by remote TV.

Sometimes the parents do not want their parents attending or viewing the delivery. They may view this as a very special experience for the two of them. Grandparents-to-be need to be respectful of these wishes and not impose. As I repeat throughout this book, in most situations grandparents must wait to be asked!

Your New Name

My first grandchild was born when I was age 49. The parents had been married a few years, they had completed their education, and they were ready to begin a family. I thought I was ready, too.

As their baby began to use words, the parents asked me what I wanted their child to call me.

"Why don't you have her call me 'Margy,'" I said, assuring myself that some cute baby talk derivative would develop. My mother's name was Edith and her friends called her Edie. She offered *Edie* to her first grandchild, which became *Deedee,* a wonderful name that we all used – her children, all her grandchildren and her step-grandchildren.

It didn't happen quite the same way with me. One day I was in the supermarket and I heard a cute, loud voice from a grocery cart calling out "Margy!" to me, and *Margy* I have remained to all my succeeding grandchildren. I can make all kinds of rationalizations, but if I am honest with myself now, I asked to be called Margy because emotionally I was not ready to be called Grandma, or Nanna, or Granny.

Give some serious thought to what name you want your grandchildren to call you when the time comes. You will be living with your name for a long time, and you will be addressed by it in public and among your friends and acquaintances. Choose wisely: the name you help select now may also reflect your present comfort (or discomfort) level with becoming a grandparent well into the future.

A State of Expectancy

Being expectant grandparents is a new experience. Freed from the responsibility of parenthood, you can prepare to unabashedly enjoy your grandchildren. Your love is unburdened by the doubts and anxieties you experienced when your own children were young, because you do not have the responsibility for raising them.

As expectant grandparents:

- You have almost as much to learn as your children do about all the new developments and information regarding prenatal care.
- You will find that your relationship with your adult child begins to shift during the pregnancy.
- Prepare yourself for the big day – and read on.

Recommendations

- Be mindful that you have *no say* in the decision to become a grandparent.
- Grandparenthood will be more meaningful for you if you are better informed and prepared – thus the purpose of this guide.
- Think about the kind of grandparents you want to be, as well as the kind of grandparents that will best suit your children's needs.
- Use visits, the telephone, fax, e-mail and airlines for close communication and contact with the expectant parents, whether they live near by or far away.
- Be prepared for, or at least empathic to, the varieties of contemporary parenting. These may include: an older father who already has grandchildren and a young wife; a couple with other children by previous marriages; single parent births; or even same-sex parenting partners.
- Remember as you use this guide that it is difficult to generalize about these complex relationships, and that every situation is unique and every family is different.

Reading List

Cherlin, Andrew J., and Frank F. Furstenberg, Jr. *The New American Grandparent: A Place in the Family, A Life Apart.* Harvard University Press, 1992.

Kornhaber, Arthur, M.D., with Sondra Forsyth. *Grandparent Power! How to Strengthen the Vital Connection Among Grandparents, Parents, and Children.* New York: Crown, 1994.

LeShan, Eda. *Grandparenting in a Changing World.* New Market Press, 1993.

2

Congratulations – You're a Grandparent!

A baby is God's opinion that the world should go on.
– Carl Sandburg

Joe and Peggy were so excited when Angie told them that they were about to become grandparents. It did not occur to them until later that she had also said rather nervously, "You've got to come help me when the baby's born! I don't know the first thing about babies!"

Joe fretted to his wife, "I sure hope you remember what to do." When Peggy realized the whole family was relying on her to guide them with the newborn, she began to worry. After all, it had been 35 years since she had cared for a newborn. "I don't think I can do it, it's been so long," she confessed to her best friend.

Brad and Sarah married young and decided to have a family right away so Sarah could continue her career as soon as possible. They made a firm commitment to share household tasks and child care on an equal basis. As Sarah's delivery date approached, Brad asked his widowed father if he could come and help when the baby was born. "What for?" his father said. "Won't her mother be there? Taking care of babies is women's work." Brad was crushed.

Grandparent Gestation

You've been through nine months of grandparent gestation and now the baby is here. Nobody has asked you if you are ready for this. You have little influence over the choices you see the new parents making. Life is clearly more complicated than it was in your grandparents' day, and nobody seems to know how a grandparent is supposed to behave now. A generation ago, my children's grandparents came to our house for weekly Sunday dinner. Today you may not even live in the same country as your new grandchild.

You may have waited a long time to become a grandparent. (Marriage and childbearing now occur much later than they did in our generation.) Your daughter could well be age 40 before she has a child, and your son could be over age 50. On the other hand, your teenager might become pregnant and decide to keep the baby while you are still raising your other children. Far more variations exist in parenting and grandparenting now than there used to be.

The grandparents' role in the family no longer fits any of the former stereotypes. When I grew up, I remember friends who had either one or both grandparents living with them. That is rare today. Yet many grandparents have found themselves in the situation of practically being forced into raising their grandchildren because of the inability of one or both parents to handle the task.

Families are far more spread out geographically than they used to be. Attitudes toward grandparenting vary widely. Some grandparents ache for a grandchild. Others think it is nice, but they wonder if it will interfere with the rest of their lives. Many grandparents today are healthy, independent and financially stable with busy lives of their own.

These days there are no rules about the *correct* role of a grandparent – it will be up to you to form your own *grandparent identity*. There are many considerations:

- What kind of lifestyle do you have?
- Are you fully employed and as busy as ever?
- Do you have the time and the desire to care for your grandchild on a regular basis?
- What are your spouse's needs?
- Are you in a new marriage, with *his-and-her* grandchildren?
- Are you realistically able to actively help with a new baby? If so, to what extent?
- How are your physical health and strength?
- How close do you live to your grandchild's home?
- How well have you interacted with your adult children in the past?

Some grandparents may need to reduce their emotional identification with their child. If you find yourself wanting to be involved in every detail of your child's life, this may be a good time to find or develop new outlets. Some mother/daughter bonds are so close that they can lead to conflicts as the daughter seeks to free herself from her mother's influence.

Other grandparents may need to put their own interests temporarily aside to be more available (in person or on the telephone) to listen and be supportive. Occasionally, some grandparents are best advised to leave the new family alone at this time. If there are festering, unresolved emotional antagonisms between you and your adult child, the baby's interests are bound to suffer when you offer to help. Explain your feelings to your children, then back away and hope that circumstances will change so you will be able to have a healthy relationship with the young family in the future.

When Baby Arrives

You may be eager to be present at the hospital, if not in the delivery room itself, when the baby is born. Yet babies are notoriously unpredictable and their arrival can confound even the most experienced grandparent. In my own family, although we had cared for all the newborns, we had never been present at the birth of grandchildren. When Nancy, our youngest daughter, asked if we wanted to attend her upcoming delivery of their second child, I was thrilled to accept her invitation (her dad declined).

Nancy lived four hours away, and was due May 30. Her first baby had been late and, as an old hand with babies, I was fairly blasé about the due date. None of our grandchildren had come early. Bob and I went camping over the Memorial Day weekend, and we called Nancy on Monday to let her know we were on our way home. To our surprise, a babysitter answered and informed us that she was already in the delivery room. We raced home, unloaded the car and I sped to the hospital, but by the time I arrived, the baby had been born. While I wasn't at the actual birth, I was with her when the baby was only six hours old and that was wonderful for both of us.

If you are determined, you might make it in time – even from across the country. My friend Carol was expecting her first grandchild, and Carol's daughter, who lived in California, really wanted her parents at the delivery. She called as soon as she began to feel labor pains. "Get on a plane! The baby's coming!" Carol and her husband caught a flight out of Aspen, changed planes in Denver, flew to San Francisco, rented a car, drove to the hospital and got there in time to witness the delivery!

My friend Gerri was unexpectedly invited into the delivery room when her first grandchild was being born. She commented later that if she had only known, she wouldn't have gotten dressed up – because while watching the delivery she moved in a little too close and the afterbirth sprayed onto her best wool sweater!

To avoid possible disappointments and upset, discuss with your children in advance if it is a priority for you to attend the delivery, and whether or not you will be attending (or are expected to attend) the delivery. Let the parents know that you want to be there, if that is the case, but also respect their wishes if they prefer that you come visit afterward instead. Find out if attending is more important to them than it is to you, and whether or not they may be disappointed if you express little interest in being present. From that understanding, you can make well-informed arrangements.

Should you visit right away after the baby is born? The answer can depend on several factors. In general, there is nothing nicer for the new parents than to have help after the birth. New mothers are not pampered in the hospital the way they once were. For a normal vaginal delivery, most insurance companies previously did not cover a hospital stay longer than 24 hours. The American Academy of Pediatricians (AAP) lobbied insurance companies to increase the covered stay to 48 hours in the best interest of the newborn. (As reported in *Pediatric Journal*, Vol. 96, No. 4, Oct. 1995, "Hospital Stay for Healthy Term Newborns," by the Committee on Fetus and Newborns.)

According to the AAP, the timing for discharging mother and newborn from the hospital should be decided by the physician caring for the baby, not by arbitrary policy established by third-party payers. Each mother and infant should be evaluated individually to determine the optimal time for discharge. After 24 hours, mothers are seldom ready to resume their home routine immediately. As of September 9, 1996, President Clinton signed into law a bill requiring insurance companies to cover at least a 48-hour stay in the hospital for maternity.

Despite being allowed an additional day in the hospital, mothers are normally still tired when they come home and need all the help they are offered. They will continue to tire easily for weeks as child care, emotional adjustment and hormonal shifts require their energy and effort. The new mother needs help with baby care and household chores, and the baby's father and the grandparents are usually her primary sources of support. Even when the father is able to stay home and assist, an experienced pair of hands can be very reassuring. Grandparents sometimes say, "I don't think I'd know what to do, it's been so long," but it will all come back – you'll remember what to do because you've done it before.

However, if the relationship between you and the new parents is strained, your presence may only increase their stress. You will still want to see and acknowledge the new baby, but you might want to wait a little while before visiting. Sometimes the parents simply do not want their parents around. The new parents may have researched the baby topic so thoroughly that they do not feel the grandparents have anything useful to contribute right away.

Tensions may also develop because your professional, independent adult children are not used to having anyone help them. This may have less to do with whether or not they actually need help than with their own issues about asking for help from you, or a reluctance to acknowledge that they might benefit from help.

Being Helpful

If you do visit the new parents, you will be most helpful if you can sublimate your own needs to theirs. In the extreme, unreasonable behavior includes the out-of-town grandparents who arrived just after the birth and expected to be partied and entertained by the couple, or the grandparents who carried a big chip on their shoulder because the other grandparents happened to visit the baby first. These grandparents could not have considered how their behavior would affect their children at this sensitive time.

Grandparents commonly consider how they can provide the most help with the least stress for the new family. It may work best for the grandparents to visit separately. This often reduces family tension by limiting the number of visitors in close quarters. We used this approach successfully with our children. I visited first for a week, then Bob went for another week, providing the family with help for two weeks. By the second week, the new father was usually back at work and the mother was more comfortable with baby care. Bob ran errands, shopped for groceries and pitched in with household chores, all of which were greatly appreciated. It is useful to coordinate with the other set of grandparents to cover this special time without crowding each other.

Caring for a new baby is a big adjustment for everyone. Remember what it was like for you? Your children are just as eager and determined to be good parents. They have high expectations for themselves. Yet they live in a culture that does little to prepare or support them in child raising. Early development is a most important stage of life. It forms the underpinnings for future growth, a kind of safety net. The more support new parents receive in the beginning, the stronger your grandchild's safety net can be. So whether or not you can visit the new family, your goal should be to do whatever you can to help the parents develop their parenting skills.

The first requirement for good parenting is self-confidence. To nurture her baby, a new mother needs to feel good about herself. If she feels unappreciated, isolated or afraid, she will have little emotional energy for the baby. The same principle applies to the baby's father. If he is ignored and shut out of baby care at the beginning, he may feel defeated and abandon the child care to the mother. Yet a child needs all the nurturers he or she can get. Let the father know that he is needed, and encourage him to be involved right from the start.

Ask the parents what kind of help they want, and invite them to continue to tell you as their wishes change. They may plan things one way, then discover after the birth that something very different is required. A mother may ask you to prepare her meals, and then realize that what she *really* needs is your help with the night feedings. If you are unable to be present in person, ask the parents if they would like you to call frequently to stay in touch, or if they would prefer to call you when it is more convenient. In some situations, offering to pay for a domestic helper may be the best possible assistance you can provide.

When Help Becomes Interference

"I *know* you're the baby's mother, and I *don't* want to interfere, *but* ..." Is there a mother alive who has never heard this phrase? You may remember how much you hated hearing it. At the time, you may have sworn that you would *never* say anything like that to your children. Can you still remember how vulnerable you used to feel over your mother or mother-in-law's slightest criticism? Sometimes even the most diplomatic, well-meaning suggestion can undermine a new parent's confidence. And when parents grow anxious, the baby becomes fretful, which makes the parents even more anxious, and so on.

Grandparents can avoid contributing to this vicious cycle by offering their suggestions about child care only when requested. If the parents describe a current problem, you can offer, "I understand. Would you like to hear what worked best for me?" If they say yes, carefully refrain from suggesting that your way is the way they should do things now. Remain discreet and tactful, even over the phone. You may often find yourself silently biting your tongue. It can be difficult to stand by and see problems occurring when you feel you could help but have not been asked. There's no point in pushing your opinions on them – in reality, most new parents are not going to follow their parents' suggestions anyway, no matter how considerately they are offered.

There are rare situations when the parents are unable to function and you will need to be actively involved with baby care, but as a rule it is best to refrain from telling the new parents how to care for their baby. Child care recommendations have changed greatly over the last 20 years (we'll explore these changes more fully in the next chapter). Even when you are certain that you know better, the way the parents prefer to handle the baby may be different from your way. The last thing anyone needs at this sensitive time is a heated debate between parents and grandparents over conflicting child care advice.

If you still feel the need to speak up, consider first how vulnerable the new parents are to anything that sounds even remotely like criticism, especially from you. Phrase all comments and suggestions as diplomatically as possible, and don't take it personally if they become upset anyway. They have just stepped into an entirely new role, and no matter how many books they have read, they will still be anxious and insecure when the baby actually arrives. Although they desperately need your understanding and support, anything resembling interference or unsolicited advice will feel like an attack on their already shaky self-esteem. Your first task as a grandparent will be a balancing act: providing emotional and physical support with no strings attached!

Learning Grandparenting Skills

Chances are you will learn most of your grandparenting skills the old-fashioned way, by trial and error – the same way you learned parenting skills. When my oldest daughter had her first child, it was quite a learning experience for me. Since we lived in the same town, I felt I could help her sufficiently without taking time off from my work. But she unexpectedly had a cesarean section delivery, and her activity was quite limited for several days. Because I had not scheduled time off from work, I was only able to manage quick visits early in the morning and late in the day. I was unable to provide the support she needed and wanted. It would have been much better for everyone involved if I had cut back on my work commitments, and in retrospect I wish I had taken that time off.

Sometimes when grandparents arrive to lend a hand, they fill a greater need by caring for an older child than helping with the newborn or performing household chores. That can be a great help! If the older child receives special attention from the grandparents while his parents are busy with the new baby, it hastens his healthy adjustment to the new arrival. Sometimes parents want to send the older child away to stay with the grandparents at this time. In my experience, this makes it much harder for the child to accept the baby. No matter how wonderful the visit away from home is, children of all ages feel left out and unwanted if they are sent away from home. Their fantasies can run wild: "Mommy and Daddy will never love me again now that they have the *baby*! The new baby will take all *my* toys! They'll forget *me*!"

Healy, age 3, stayed with her out-of-town grandparents during the last month of her mom's pregnancy, when Lee was confined to bed to avoid premature delivery. Healy returned home just before her brother's birth, and was able to visit with mom in the hospital and help choose Josh's name. After Healy's return from a wonderful, fun-filled visit with her grandparents, her parents became aware that she refused to use the words *please* or *thank you*. Initially her parents were unconcerned and assumed this was a reaction to Josh's birth. As time went on and the impolite behavior continued, Healy's parents and her preschool teacher tried a number of interventions, all without success. Her parents came to see me the summer before Healy began kindergarten because they knew that her refusal to say please or thank you would not be so easily tolerated. We decided I would see Healy for a few sessions and see if we could find her lost words of politeness.

Psychotherapy is not always a cause-and-effect science. While I can theorize that Healy was angry about leaving home during her mom's pregnancy, and in some way her behavior was a punishment to her parents, explaining all that to her was not the cure. In our sessions we talked about needing to find her pleases and thank yous. Enlisting the help of the stuffed animals, we searched my office for her lost words. We talked about leaving the words at grandma and grandpa's house. With the animals, we made up a play about Healy being with her grandparents and Mom being pregnant with Josh. I suggested how she might have felt at that time: lonely, left out, sad, angry, worried. She was never able to verbally acknowledge these negative feelings.

However, after a few sessions together, she arrived at her appointment one afternoon to inform me that she had found her pleases and thank-yous, and she could now say them. Her mom concurred.

What happened? Something in our work together freed Healy up enough to get past whatever it was that had her stuck. She found her pleases and thank-yous and was ready to start kindergarten.

This story is not unusual. Even under the most ideal circumstances, it is normal for an older child to feel displaced by a new baby, and to feel anger about it. As adults, we would become angry if someone suddenly moved into our home and took over *our* place in the family. If we were sent away for this intruder's arrival, or before the intruder's arrival as in Healy's case, those feelings would be greatly reinforced. A child that has been sent away, even to the most loving grandparents, may respond with behavior problems. When the parents bring the child to see a counselor, they may insist, "Oh, no, she just *loves* the baby, it *can't* be that." Indeed, she loves the baby and at the same time she hates the baby. She is appropriately ambivalent. I usually find that the older child's behavior problems improve rapidly when their anger about the new baby is addressed.

Communicating with the Parents

The period just after the baby's birth can be a particularly confusing time for parents and grandparents. Especially with a first grandchild, the family may need to figure out how to work together to support each other. At this vulnerable time, there is great opportunity for support or insensitivity, meaningful communication or misunderstanding, warm emotional bonding or chilly, long-lasting resentments.

As a grandparent, you will quickly realize how little influence you exert over your grandchildren's lives unless you can communicate effectively with their parents. We all think we know how to communicate, but communication is far more than an exchange of words and ideas. Most of us do not find it easy to clearly convey to others our feelings, needs and desires, or to ask others for help. Often we say one thing, but think or feel otherwise. Our verbal and nonverbal messages may be completely different. Sometimes this habit is so ingrained that we cannot recognize it even when it is pointed out by others. It is often forgotten that communication is an exchange, a two-way, two-part skill which involves being able to identify and verbally express your thoughts and feelings, then stop talking and *listen* to the other person respond with their thoughts and feelings.

Over the years, ineffective communication between family members can easily form patterns of miscommunication. If this applies to your family, seriously examine how and what you say to each other. If you are unwilling to speak up and share what you truly think and feel, other people are likely to behave the same. Then you may all end up feeling upset, misunderstood or manipulated. Conversely, sharing what you truly feel, even when those emotions or opinions are unpopular, makes it easier for others to respond on a deeper level of emotional honesty.

Edna and Paul were excitedly planning their retirement dream, a long-awaited trip to East Africa, when their daughter June announced that she was expecting her first baby. June's due date was right in the middle of the projected trip. Edna and Paul had already helped their other children with several babies. They really wanted to take the trip anyway, but they thought June would be upset if they did not come to help her. Without mentioning it to anyone, they reluctantly canceled their trip. When they arrived to help June after the baby's birth, they were still resentful about passing up their dream vacation. These unspoken feelings gave the visit an underlying tension. June, in a vulnerable state already and not knowing what was wrong, felt hurt and somehow responsible.

A lot of unnecessary family conflict could have been avoided if Edna and Paul had simply told June of their long-awaited travel plans in the beginning. Instead, they decided to cancel their plans without sharing their dilemma with June and her husband. An open, honest evaluation of the situation might have prevented hurt feelings all around during what should have been a joyful time for everyone.

In another ticklish situation, the grandparents were able to resolve a possible conflict through honest communication with the parents. Fran and Jack were delighted when Laurie announced that she was pregnant. They were eager to come and help her care for the new baby. However, when the ultrasound indicated she was carrying twins, they grew concerned. They had not cared for a newborn since Laurie's birth 30 years ago, and now there were going to be two of them.

They sought out books and courses to help allay their anxiety, without success. Finally they decided to delay their participation with child care until the babies were older, and apprehensively explained their decision to the expectant parents. To their surprise, the couple was very understanding and simply made other arrangements for help after birth. Without this open discussion, the grandparents might have avoided the new family out of desperation with no clear explanation, leaving the parents to wonder at their seeming lack of interest and involvement. As the twins grew older, Fran and Jack became quite comfortable caring for them and often baby-sat when the parents had to travel on business.

Encourage the new parents to share their concerns with you. If they have a problem with how you are helping them, it's up to them to speak up about it, and when they do, don't take it personally. It isn't easy for them, either.

Jean was a wonderful cook. She loved to help when her grandchildren were born by bringing over huge quantities of the hearty, traditional Jewish food that she had raised her kids on. The only problem was that her children had changed their diets, and hardly touched the food she brought over. At first it was hard for them to speak up. "Won't Mom be hurt?" they thought. "She really means well." But finally they got up the courage to tell her that they did not eat that way anymore. Although initially disappointed, Jean soon discovered other ways to direct her energy so that everyone felt better.

Sometimes family communication is complicated by incompatible personalities. The most common situation seems to be conflict with in-laws. A typical dilemma: "My daughter is having a baby and wants my help, but I can barely stand to be in the same room with her husband! What should I do?" This situation requires honest communication and creative thinking.

- Some grandparents find they can stay more comfortably at a nearby motel or hotel and come to help at the house when the husband is at work.
- Encourage the couple to invite his parents in the beginning, and offer to host the mother and baby when they are able to travel.
- Simply put up with the *unpleasant* son-in-law temporarily for the sake of the mother and baby.
- Take the opportunity of a new child to try to improve relations with the son-in-law.
- When your daughter-in-law, who is a thorn in your side, really needs your help, for the sake of your new grandchild overlook all the issues and help her.

We are all quite honest with each other in my family. When our daughter and son-in-law were expecting their most recent baby, our 11th grandchild, they shared the names they were considering for the baby. One particular name on their list raised very unpleasant associations for me. At first I resisted commenting, but after realizing how uncomfortable that name made me, I decided to share my feelings. The expectant parents were receptive to my comments and simply scratched the name from their list.

In maintaining healthy relationships with your children, be particularly careful in your wording about sensitive issues:

- When you communicate how you feel with someone, begin what you say with *I* statements. For example, start your sentence with "I feel ..." rather than, "You made me feel ..." or "You caused me to feel ..."
- Avoid being judgmental.
- Respect the person you are speaking with in order to allow them to *hear* what you are trying to say.
- Be aware of old or unresolved anger that can result in holding grudges, feeling unappreciated or general resentment, and withdrawing from family members in times of need.

The Mother/Daughter Relationship

When Gloria brought Noah home from the hospital, Betty dropped everything to be with her daughter. Her mother's obvious pride made Gloria feel affirmed in her mother's eyes for the first time in her life, but their relationship soon began to deteriorate. Noah was a fussy baby, and Betty's way of helping was to take over completely. Gloria felt inadequate because she could not comfort her own baby.

In response to her sense of failure with the baby, she became very demanding of her mother. Gloria was unpleasant no matter how much Betty did for her. After her mother had left and Gloria began to settle in with her baby, she felt ashamed of how demanding and unappreciative she had been. She called her mother and apologized, and by talking it out they were both able to understand and forgive each other.

Gloria's story illustrates the tension that can arise between mother and daughter with the arrival of the first baby. During this emotionally charged time, both mother and daughter seek to become adept in new roles. They have both imagined that this will be a time of great joy that draws them closer, but it often proves instead to be quite stressful.

The new mother wants to learn and be affirmed by her mother in her new role, but she may also want to regress and be nurtured by her mother. The new grandmother's emotions may be just as ambivalent. Even the most longed-for grandchild will remind her of her aging. Then she may suddenly fear that she has not adequately prepared her daughter for motherhood, and had better do some quick on-the-spot training. Some mothers and daughters already know they do not do well in close quarters, but they may be reluctant to discuss this honestly because of expectations about their proper role. For all these reasons, this joyous visit can easily become a disaster.

Some relationships cannot be forced to fit our fantasies. Ginger found it hard to be a mother in a community far from her widowed mother. She was envious of her friends who had their mothers living nearby. It seemed to Ginger that her friends' mothers were always within reach for support and help. Ginger and her baby often joined her friends and their mothers for lunch. If only she, her baby, and her mother could have weekly lunches like that!

But whenever her mother came to visit, they had a terrible time. Her mother still smoked and Ginger would not allow smoking in the house or near the baby. Ginger disapproved of the foods that her mother fed baby Todd when she took him out by herself. Ginger felt that her mother constantly criticized her. They did not get along. Each time her mother visited, Ginger could not wait for her to leave – only to immediately begin longing for the next reunion.

Social shifts can make mother/daughter relations even more difficult. Attitudes toward childbirth, recovery, breast-feeding and baby care have changed greatly in the last 20 years. Typically, your daughter is not particularly interested in how you did things when she was young. She has an array of books on her bed table, which she may or may not have read. Forget how you did it – those books are her bibles.

One new mother announced at her baby shower, "You know, I would ask my friends for advice – even those who don't have children – before I would ask my mother." Her mother was sitting right there and laughed along with the others. How painful it must have been for her mother to hear her lifetime of experience so lightly dismissed!

Despite the potential for stress between mother and grandmother, the birth can be the beginning of a wonderful new relationship between them. They are both entering unfamiliar new roles, and may be more willing to reach out to each other than ever before. They now share the common bond of *motherhood* which can profoundly deepen their relationship. Also, the daughter may be eager to hear about her mother's child raising experiences, even if she swears that she would never raise her baby that way.

The Psychodynamics of Grandparenting

Although you may be completely unaware of it, by the time your first grandchild is born, your *grandparent identity* has largely been formed already. This *identity* – a synthesis of feelings, attitudes, beliefs and experiences – is influenced by many factors. Your health, finances, marital status, family relationships and geographical proximity will all affect how you relate to your grandchildren. (The many choices you make now will determine how you express it.)

Perhaps the most powerful influence on your grandparenting style is how your parents and grandparents treated you as a child. Give some serious thought and consideration to how you were raised, to the family rules that governed your own childhood, and the childhood experiences that stand out most clearly in your memory. Do you remember your grandparents with love and affection? Do you hope that you will be as good to your grandchildren as they were to you? If so, then you probably will be.

What if these relationships lacked in affection, safety, appropriate behavior, or other qualities important to you? Perhaps you do not even remember why, but you feel fear or anger (or other emotions) when you think of your grandparents. If your childhood experiences were unhappy, make sure that your grandchildren do not remember you the same way. Sometimes a difficult childhood makes us especially determined not to repeat the mistakes of the past.

How did your parents and your spouse's parents treat your children? Are they role models for you now that you are grandparents, or, in reviewing their relationship with your family, are you seeing much that you don't want to replicate? Use them, good or bad, as a frame of reference.

Marcia's parents had always been cold and selfish. After she married Jim and had children of her own, her parents cut off all contact with the young family. Although they lived nearby, they never saw or spoke with their grandchildren again. This was so painful that Marcia vowed she would never behave that way. When her grandchildren were born, Marcia and Jim were there to help in every way. No need was left unfilled. When the young mothers went back to work, Marcia arranged her life so that she could provide plenty of child care. Her friends criticized her for sacrificing her life to her grandchildren, but they did not understand how much it meant to Marcia to be a caring grandmother.

We know we internalize our childhood experiences – they become a part of our adult identity. Even when we do not consciously remember these early events, they continue to influence our attitudes and behavior, sometimes without our awareness. Thus the adult who was once an unloved grandchild often finds it difficult to spontaneously show love to his or her own grandchildren. In Marcia's case, as a mother she was deeply hurt by her parent's lack of interest in her children, and she was determined not to let this happen to her children now that they were parents.

People from dysfunctional families are not inextricably bound to the past. They can become excellent parents and grandparents, but it generally requires a willingness and determination on their part to confront the past and develop a resolve to do things differently in the future. If this issue applies to you, I strongly advise you to seek counseling to *free the ghosts in the nursery* and come to terms with the past. Do not pass on your unresolved feelings, even indirectly, to another generation. As you begin to confront and resolve those difficult memories, both you and your family will benefit.

Happiness is Being A Grandparent!

In her entertaining book, *Funny, You Don't Look Like a Grandmother*, Lois Wyse points out that "A mother becomes a true grandmother the day she stops noticing the terrible things her children do because she is so enchanted with the wonderful things her grandchildren do."

The opportunity to care for the newest generation of your family is one of life's greatest joys. Freed from the never-ending demands of parenthood, you can approach these children more robustly and with less hesitation than you did your own children. Some grandparents take full advantage of the opportunity.

Shortly after my friend Anna's granddaughter was born, I asked her casually, "How's the baby doing?" Anna's face lit up with pride. "She's fine! And I can't stop talking about her! I can't believe how preoccupied I am with such a tiny person. She can't even walk or talk!" Anna was overjoyed to be a grandmother.

This attitude is not universal among grandparents. A healthy, retired middle-class couple described how their grandson had been placed in a foster home because their daughter had been unable to care for him. When asked how they felt about this, they replied, "We were just so relieved that we weren't asked to take care of him." It was clear they did not want grandparenting to turn into parenting – regardless of whether or not it might have been better for their grandson to be raised by his family rather than in a foster home.

Grandchildren can keep you young, and bless you again with the simple joys of childhood – without the stresses of parenthood. They are a great healing agent for those who may have begun to wonder if life has any remaining purpose or value. There is nothing more moving than a grandchild who gives you a big hug and whispers, "I love you, grandma!" or "I love you, grandpa!" It is rewarding to know that you are a link between the generations. In the words of Margaret Mead, "The society that cuts off older people from meaningful contact with children is greatly endangered. In the presence of grandparent and grandchild, past and future merge in the present."

Recommendations

Pre-delivery planning can avoid many clashes. Raise these questions with your children during the last trimester:

- What kind of maternity leave will they be taking?
- Do they want you to help or visit? If so, when and for how long?
- Would they prefer you to come as a couple or individually?
- Would they like you to attend the delivery?
- What kind of help do they need? Do they want you to care for the baby so the mother can get some rest, or do they want you to manage the household so that she can look after the baby herself? If there is an older child, who will care for him?
- Can you coordinate your help with that of the other grandparents?
- If you cannot help them, or if there are any restrictions on your activities and availability, discuss this up front. Ask in what other ways you can support them.

- When you help, be considerate and tolerant. The new parents are under a lot of stress. You want to make things as easy for them as possible, rather than create further tension in the household. Keep your comments supportive and affirming of their efforts.
- If your child is the father, consider that most women prefer to have their mother around when they have a baby – but sometimes it does not work out that way. What role would they like you to play?
- If you and your child have been bickering for years, accept that this will not magically change after the baby's birth. Discuss your differences openly and look for the least stressful approach.
- If there is a proposed name that creates bad feelings for you, let the parents know in a tactful way.
- You may feel that grandparenthood is coming too soon or too late, or that your situation is too complicated or unconventional. Relax, be happy and proud. Congratulations!

Reading List for Adults

Berenstain, Jan and Stan Berenstain. *What Your Parents Never Told You About Being a Mom or Dad.* New York: Crown Publishers, 1995. Creators of the popular Berenstain Bears childrens books offer practical advice with a breezy, humorous tone.

Erickson, Erik H., Joan M. Erikson and Helen Q. Kivnick. *Vital Involvement in Old Age.* New York: W.W. Norton, 1994. A discussion of aging by a famous psychologist.

LaShan, Eda. *Grandparents – A Special Kind of Love.* New York: Macmillan, 1984. The relationship between grandparents and grandchildren.

Spock, Benjamin and Michael B. Rothenberg. *Baby and Child Care.* New York: Pocket Books, 1992. Fully revised and updated for the '90s.

Wyse, Lois. *Funny, You Don't Look Like a Grandmother.* Avon Books, 1991. Entertaining look at the joys of grandparenting.

Zigelman, David. *The Pocket Pediatrician: An A to Z Guide to Your Child's Health.* New York: Doubleday, 1995. A handy, up-to-date medical reference.

Reading List for Children

Carlstrom, Nancy White. *Grandpappy.* Little Brown, 1992. The story of a boy whose greatest joy is visiting his grandfather, who lives alone on the coast of Maine. For all ages.

Fox, Mem. *Koala Lou.* New York: Harcourt, Brace, 1994. When Koala Lou was a baby, her mother told her "I love you" every day. After her many brothers and sisters are born, her mother does not have as much time to tell her anymore. Koala Lou is very sad and comes up with a great plan to get her mother's attention. Ages 6-8 years.

Falwell, Cathryn. *We Have A Baby.* New York: Clarion Books, 1993. Having a new baby is a happy event for new big sister or big brother. Ages 2-6 years.

Harris, Robie H. *Happy Birthday.* Cambridge, MA: Candlewick Press, 1996. Welcoming the new sibling. Ages 2-6 years.

Vulliamy, Clara. *Ellen and Penguin and the New Baby.* Cambridge, MA: Candlewick Press, 1996. Help adjusting to the new baby. Ellen and her stuffed toy, Penguin, have difficulty adjusting to a new baby brother. Ages 2-5 years.

3

Babies Are People, Too!

A journey of a thousand miles begins with a single step.
– Lao-Tsu

Carla was eager to be involved with her new grandbaby, and had kept up with all the latest recommendations in child care. So she was disturbed when her daughter Debbie decided to go back to work shortly after the birth.

"Sure, it's easier for them to get by on two incomes," Carla said. "But I don't think they have a financial problem. Debbie just thinks it's better to be absent while the baby is young and can be cared for by someone else. She says when he's a little older and more active, she'll stay home with him. But aren't the first few months the most important time in a child's life? All the books stress the importance of early bonding. I don't want to interfere, but I really feel Debbie is making a big mistake."

The Latest in Baby Research

I had the pleasure of visiting my grandson for a week after his birth. Even that early, he seemed remarkably alert and responsive. He would smile, look into my eyes, turn his head at the sound of his mother's voice, and even *hold* his pacifier with his arm. Looking back at my children and grandchildren, it occurred to me that this particular child appeared to be far more intelligent than the other babies were at the same age. But he wasn't *really* smarter – I simply interpreted his behavior from a new perspective. I had learned more about newborns, which enabled me to appreciate the full range of his newborn abilities as I never had before.

I was seeing my grandson differently because of the *baby watchers*. For the last 25 years, these child development specialists have studied infant behavior far more closely than ever before. They use stop-frame photography to film the baby's every movement, interaction and response, then carefully examine each frame of film. Specialists can detect and interpret very subtle movements which are *imperceptible* under normal research conditions. These baby watchers discovered a host of new behaviors and responses, and in the process reversed much of the previously established wisdom about babies. Although their findings have often been controversial, most of their results confirm the age-old intuitive knowledge of another set of experts – mothers and grandmothers.

Babies are perceptive and aware long before birth. If a pregnant woman repeatedly listens to a piece of music during her last trimester, after birth her baby will remember that music. Many expectant mothers have responded to this news by avidly introducing their unborn children to their favorite music.

It is less well-known that if a pregnant woman repeatedly reads the same Dr. Seuss book out loud during her last trimester, her baby will also remember those verses after birth. If you try these experiments with your own unborn grandchild, do not expect cries of joyful recognition from the newborn. Babies indicate recognition through very subtle head or eye movements, detectable only by careful analysis of research film.

By the time a baby is born, his perceptive abilities are highly developed. We once believed that newborns were unaware of their surroundings during the early weeks, and reacted largely based on need and satisfaction. *Wrong!* We now know that a newborn's senses are acute and well-developed from the moment of birth. A newborn can see, hear and respond to us.

If you pick up a crying baby and place her on your shoulder, she will often look around and stop crying. Why? She has looked for and found another person's face. Babies arrive programmed to seek out and respond to *faces*. One study tested minutes-old infants who had never seen a human face. They were shown three pictures: a human face, a scrambled-up face and a square. Every one of the newborns turned their heads around 180 degrees to keep the most human-looking image in view.

When my children were born, in the 1950s, baby experts claimed a newborn could see nothing except general outlines. Even Mother was a blurry head shape. I wondered back then why all the newborns I met appeared to focus intently on me, as if I appeared more interesting than the other blurry head shapes. We now know that babies not only have the ability to recognize faces, but are very responsive to color, especially strong colors such as black, red, yellow and blue. I suspect the special feature about me that likely attracted every infant's attention was my bright red hair.

Past generations were also told that newborns were incapable of social responses. Yet the *face study* indicates that babies instinctively seek out other people. I smile at my grandson, he responds with a smile, and both of us are thrilled. Yet his *smile* is the same grimace we once called *gas pain*.

This change of terminology has far-reaching consequences. If you believe your new granddaughter is only having indigestion, you are unlikely to respond to her attempts to communicate. When you realize that she is smiling back at you, you feel love and affection, and the emotional attachment between you grows. When my grandson and I exchange smiles, he learns that others respond when he expresses himself. As the child grows, that initial trust becomes the foundation for all future relationships.

Grandparents may wonder if the baby watchers' theories are nothing more than the latest fad. This is a valid question, but more research has been conducted on newborns in the last 25 years than in all prior human history. We simply know far more about babies than ever before, and this new knowledge is bound to illuminate our thinking.

Some of the new trends may seem silly to us, yet they often satisfy the mother's needs as much as the baby's. In some communities, mother-baby swimming classes have become so popular that infants often must be enrolled at birth for a class six months later. This trend began when some experts claimed that swimming greatly enhances a child's development. I do not believe that an infant really needs swimming lessons, but the activity may serve the mother's needs, and that can be equally important. Infant swimming class is a fun activity for mother and baby, and provides a further benefit of interaction with other mother-baby pairs. If you discover that your infant grandchild is taking swimming lessons, or some other sort of lesson, instead of questioning it, be supportive.

As a new grandparent, you may already keep up with child care news. You may actively seek out information, or perhaps you simply notice more stories on the subject in the media.

In a letter published in *The New York Times*, a distressed grandmother complained that she was banished from baby-sitting her 6-week-old grandson after the parents caught her putting the baby to sleep on his stomach.

"Don't you know about SIDS?" said the father, referring to the growing evidence that babies who sleep face down are at increased risk of Sudden Infant Death Syndrome (SIDS). The grandmother replied that she knew about SIDS and current advice to avoid face-down positions, but she could not get the baby to settle down on his back, and surely baby and babysitter needed some rest.

When doctors first started advising us to put babies to sleep on their backs, some grandparents resisted. They were taught to put babies to sleep on their stomachs, to prevent the baby from choking if he should spit up during sleep. That fear has since been disproved. By now, most grandparents are familiar with the latest findings about SIDS, or crib death. SIDS is the leading cause of infant mortality in the U.S., claiming about 7,000 babies a year, or one in every 1,000 live births. For some unknown reason, SIDS is more likely to occur in boys than girls. This syndrome strikes completely healthy babies, who stop breathing and die. Studies have shown that two simple recommendations can dramatically reduce crib deaths:

1. Always put babies to sleep on their backs (except for infants with certain rare medical conditions).
2. Put babies to sleep on a firm mattress with a tight-fitting sheet. Avoid placing soft bedding such as sheepskins, natural fiber mattresses, rugs or quilts beneath the baby. Do not leave pillows or soft toys in the crib.

The highest risk period is up to age 5 months, but the baby continues to be at risk until 1 year old. The American Academy of Pediatrics (AAP) formally began recommending the new sleeping position in 1992. (Not all crib deaths are related to these factors; other causes are still unknown.) For more information about SIDS call 1-800-505-CRIB.

Dr. Duane Alexander, director of the National Institute of Children's Health and Human Development, attributes the dramatic change in the SIDS rate to a campaign to bed babies on their backs, because nothing else has changed. According to a report issued in mid-1996, this has been one of the simplest and most effective public health interventions. Over 1500 babies have been saved in the U.S. over the past two years by a Back to Sleep campaign in which parents, caregivers and pediatricians were all educated about how best to put babies to bed. SIDS mortality rates fell by 30 percent, to about .75 live births per 1,000.

The Importance of Baby Bonding

Expectant parents feel a growing closeness to the baby even before birth. However, the physical contact that begins at birth is the first tangible act of bonding. The newborn is remarkably alert in the first minutes and hours after birth. By immediately arranging physical contact between mother and child, both begin to know each other. The baby gazes into mother's eyes, feels her touch and warmth, hears the sound of her voice, and identifies her scent.

The growing emotional bond between parents and child can be likened to falling in love. It does not happen all at once, but occurs over time; the parents *learn* to love the baby, and the baby *learns* to love the parents. This love affair between baby and parents forms the foundation for the child's future development. Recent understanding of its importance has led to dramatic changes in birthing procedures that enhance opportunities for parental bonding with the newborn.

Every birth is unique; sometimes the ideal bonding experience cannot occur at birth. Beth had a neurological reaction to her epidural and was *out of it* for three days after delivery; Mary Jo gave birth to a 1-pound baby boy that was placed in an incubator immediately; Stacie's marriage had broken up a week before delivery and she was in too much emotional pain to even look at her infant; Jamie's baby had a heart problem that required immediate surgery.

New parents can become unnecessarily distressed about this. Birth bonding is *not* a one-time opportunity, but simply the beginning of a life- long process. Bonding continues throughout the early years as the enduring dialogue of love, play and caring between parents and child grows. The importance of bonding extends beyond the mother to the whole family; father, siblings and grandparents can *all* be part of the baby's network of bonded relationships.

Among his many grandchildren, Granddad Roy is especially close to Bobby. The baby was born sickly, so Roy helped out for the first few weeks. Roy believes this extensive early contact is the reason why he still feels so deeply connected to Bobby years later.

Successful bonding helps the infant develop her capacity for self-soothing. From the moment of birth, tactile experiences such as holding, rocking and sucking teach the baby the soothing properties of touch. More sophisticated forms of self-soothing continue throughout childhood. As the infant develops, she may become extremely attached to a stuffed animal, a certain blanket or some other special soft something. The baby gradually transfers soothing attributes of mommy to her special something. As the baby continues to develop, the presence of this special item, known as a *transitional object*, enables her to comfort herself while waiting for mommy to appear. Grandparents, don't take it personally if your grandbaby's choice of her special something is not the wonderful stuffed animal you chose for her.

By transferring mother's nurturing power to a *transitional object*, the successfully bonded child is able to delay gratification for an ever-increasing amount of time as she grows. Not all children have visible *transitional objects*, and if your grandchild is not attached to his special blanket, do not despair. Sometimes the *transitional object* is not a thing; it may be the *memory* of mother's voice, the texture of the crib sheet, or even the musical sounds of a hanging mobile.

The type of bonding we are discussing here, including the use of *transitional objects* to delay gratification, are stepping stones to what Erik Erikson calls *basic trust* (the opposite being *basic mistrust*), which is the essential psychosocial task of the child from birth to 15 months. *Basic trust* is the building block of all future development. The child who cannot trust the special people in his environment during this infancy period is likely to be handicapped in his ongoing emotional development. These first 15 months lay the safety net for future emotional development!

Bonding Failure

If the mother is not especially nurturing, and father is un-available to compensate for mother's lack, the baby will still try to soothe itself, but his movements may become compulsive or obsessive. These babies, and later children, may exhibit compulsive rocking, rubbing or masturbation in their effort to fill the void left by their mother's lack of attention. The growth of the mother/baby bond is vulnerable and subject to the same stresses as other human relationships.

Some mothers have difficulty bonding. They hold their babies stiffly and at a distance, they feel anxious or depressed, or they lack maternal feelings. These situations are serious and require immediate intervention by a trained professional (who may be located through a pediatrician or an obstetrician's office, or mental health or child guidance centers).

Grandparents may also have difficulty bonding with their grandchildren. A few bonding suggestions for grandparents:

- Bonding with your grandchild takes a commitment on your part, and if that commitment is not present, bonding does not automatically occur.
- Bonding with your grandchild develops more easily if you live in close proximity and can enjoy frequent drop-by visits.
- It is much harder and takes much longer to establish the close connection you want and that benefits the baby when great distances separate you and the baby. I know from my own grandparenting experience that it takes longer, but gradually *falling in love* happens and thrives.

- Try to put aside the differences you may have with your grandchild's parents for the sake of bonding with your grandbaby.

Bonding Disruption – Postpartum Depression

Bonding may be delayed by postpartum depression – the *baby blues*. The combination of hormonal changes and the intensity of the birthing experience leaves some women feeling vulnerable. It is not unusual for a new mother to feel sad and depressed, or to cry for no apparent reason. This is nothing to be ashamed or concerned about, and it generally goes away within a few weeks. Plenty of emotional support and practical assistance are helpful. If the depression is severe and persists, threatening the baby's well-being, psychiatric intervention is necessary.

Postpartum depression may occur following one birth and not another birth. Like colic, there is no scientific data on predictability or ways to prevent it. Since in most cases the depression is very temporary, mother/infant bonding disruption is brief and resumes normalcy quickly.

Bonding Concerns – Full-Time Infant Care

We have seen that the baby's relationship with her primary caretaker impacts her ability to form relationships for the rest of her life. What happens if both parents must work? Research shows a strong potential for future difficulties if the mother (or other primary caretaker) works full time during the baby's first three years. Part-time work of 20 hours or less or full-time work after age 3 does not have such serious impact on most babies. If possible, one parent should stay home or work only part-time during the child's first three years, or at least for the first 15 months, which are the most critical. After that, both parents can work full time without seriously affecting the child's development, providing there is good quality substitute care.

It is not the *amount* of time the mother is absent, but the *quality* of the time she is present that is most important. How is that time spent? How emotionally available is she? How stressed or distracted is she? At the end of the work day, is she able to relax and enjoy the baby's company? Is she able to leave her work behind when she walks in the front door? Or does she run home to relieve the babysitter and then need the whole evening to unwind? If Mom is only physically present, but emotionally unavailable, the child's needs will suffer – even with the best child care plan in place. Grandparents are often in an ideal position to recognize problem situations and offer support.

Grandma Carla, mentioned at the beginning of this chapter, was upset because her daughter Debbie wanted to work soon after birth and planned to stay home with her child later. Debbie is making a mistake. There is much at stake here in the way of healthy child development, and professional support for Carla's position. This situation may be one of the few exceptions to the *no interference* rule.

Carla should speak up tactfully and diplomatically. She does not have to convince Debbie that she is wrong. It may be hard for Debbie to admit to her mother that she was mistaken. The best approach may be to show Debbie a few supporting articles or books, ask her to reconsider her decision, and then back off and let her decide for herself. No matter how Carla approaches the issue, Debbie may still get mad and say, "I don't want to do it that way," but at least Carla has spoken her mind and will not have a guilty conscience about it.

Bonding with Daddy

A new grandmother said, "My son tells me how closely he's bonding with his baby son. That's great, but I've always thought that a newborn bonds primarily with his mother. Is my son exaggerating?"

The idea that a baby's primary bond forms exclusively with his mother is outdated. The baby watchers tell us that the father can be as emotionally involved as the mother, and that the father contributes as much in his own way as the mother to the baby's development.

Although he has just spent nine months in his mother's womb, a newborn is strongly attached to both parents. It is quite amazing that a week-old baby can distinguish his father's voice from his mother's voice and will respond just as strongly (although differently). Even more surprising is the fact that babies sometimes *prefer* their fathers to their mothers for play and social activities (although when a baby feels stressed, he always reverts to the safety of his mother). This may happen because most fathers still see themselves primarily as a playmate rather than a caretaker to their babies. Since the father feels less anxious and responsible than the mother, he can be more playful with the baby right from birth.

This difference between the parents is especially obvious when the baby is premature or had a difficult birth and is developmentally immature. Such a baby often does not actively respond to playful interaction. The mother tries to play with the baby, but he does not acknowledge her. Her maternal need to bond with the baby makes this lack of response difficult to bear, and she tends to feel rejected and withdraws from the baby. But the father, who is less emotionally involved, does not get discouraged and continues to play with the baby as if everything is normal. In this case, the father's ability to behave normally compensates for the mother's tendency to become depressed and anxious.

Fathers play more vigorous, hands-on, physical games than mothers, but *both* kinds of attention are important to the baby. The mother's care helps the baby build a trusting foundation for relationships, and the father's care prepares the child for the physical challenges of crawling and walking.

Grandfather Bonding

In many books, research papers and articles related to grandparenting, the focus is on grandma, and grandpa's participation is barely mentioned. This is a significant oversight! Grandfathers are often as adept with new babies as grand–mothers, and may be every bit as capable at infant care from the start. It may be that grandpa has the right touch to pick up a restless or fussy baby in a firm embrace and walk her until she falls asleep.

(One note: throughout this section I have used the term *bonding,* which is the more popularly accepted word for the phenomenon I discuss. However, in professional writing the more appropriate word for describing this basic sense of human connectedness is *attachment,* drawing on attachment theory from John Bowlby's work, *Attachment and Loss*; 1980.)

Grandparents Are A Sounding Board

Parenting a new baby is not all love and play. We may not remember how difficult it is for inexperienced parents to struggle with doubts, anxieties and fatigue. T. Berry Brazelton writes, "Learning parenting by trial and error is a frightening process. Grandparents (can) give (the new parents) a sounding board, even if their advice is refused in the end." To be an effective sounding board, grandparents need to understand what new parents face.

A couple sought counseling about their infant grandchild's disturbing behavior. They wanted to help the parents, but they did not understand the situation or know what to do. Eleven-month-old Jeremy was miserable most of the time. He could not sleep or soothe himself, and his parents were unable to comfort him. The parents seldom had any relief, day or night, and were exhausted.

It turned out that Jeremy had a fever that required him to spend his first 10 days of life in the hospital, which must have been quite traumatic for his immature nervous system. The trauma itself could have caused his irritability, or the illness might have triggered neurological damage, or Jeremy could simply be a very high-strung child. In any of these cases, ongoing nurturing should eventually enable Jeremy to calm down. But under these circumstances, the parents needed some relief from child care. I offered the grandparents these suggestions:

- They can take care of Jeremy so the parents can have a break.
- They can help the parents relax, because as the parents relax, Jeremy may calm down, too. Help parents relax by:
    Encouraging them to return to a pre-baby exercise routine.
    Send in meals from time to time.
    Take them all on some pleasant outings.
  Reassure them by showing them this section of *Grandparenting: A Survival Guide.*
- Remind the parents not to become too overanxious, and reassure them that they will live through this and their baby *will* grow out of this stage.

Spoiling Children is Not What It Used to Be!

"My children never let the baby cry. Whenever he fusses, they pick him up. They're always carrying him or feeding him. I keep warning them, 'You're going to *spoil* that child.'" Perhaps the biggest change in parenting philosophy is the notion that spoiling isn't what it used to be.

In the past, the traditional wisdom advised parents not to pick up a baby every time it cried to avoid reinforcing such undesirable behavior. The fear was that the baby would become too accustomed to being soothed, and would become an out-of-control crybaby. Consequently, generations of mothers learned to resist their natural impulse to respond to a crying baby. Yet recent research has not only disproved this fear, but it has *reversed* it.

We now know that the first and most important task of a baby's primary caretaker – usually the mother – is to assure the baby that she is a dependable source of emotional support. She does this by responding promptly, consistently and appropriately to the baby's cries. When she does that, the baby learns that his needs for food, soothing or diaper change will be heard and met. Fortified by this confidence in mother's dependability and availability, the baby has a secure foundation from which to go forth and explore the world. Such a baby is developing a *basic trust*, the essential stepping stone to continued healthy development.

But if the mother fails to respond, or responds ambivalently by being inconsistent, controlling, neglectful or inappropriate, the baby will fail to develop maximum comfort with his environment. Instead, his insecurity will lead either to clinging, whiny behavior (the classic crybaby), or indifferent, sullen, aggressive and eventually bullying behavior, all characteristic of *basic mistrust* in his self and his environment. Loving, responsive care does not create dependency – it creates a firm foundation on which empathy and self-confidence can be built.

The first months of life hold the key to later development, and the results are clear. Mothers who withhold affection and nurturing, or offer it only with ambivalence, insensitivity or conditionally, may have children who eventually exhibit the demanding, fussy behavior of the stereotypical spoiled child. Young babies who are consistently shown responsive nurturing and physical affection – whose mothers truly respond to their every need – become confident, independent, affectionate and adventurous youngsters.

The baby experts who conducted this research concluded that it is impossible to *spoil* a young baby with too much attention. This explains why parents today appear to spend all their time carrying, holding or feeding their infants. Even if parents have never heard of this research, these ideas have permeated mainstream attitudes about baby care. This is also why babies are no longer left for hours to amuse themselves in cribs or playpens.

Remember, grandparents and parents: nobody can be the perfect mother. You need only be the *good enough mother* or *good enough grandparent.*

Babies Are People, Too

A child's basic temperament and personality is evident from birth. Researchers have found evidence of lifelong personality traits as early as the first week of life. Mothers know that babies are unique individuals from the moment of birth, if not before. A newborn's early temperament will not change significantly, nor will the baby *grow out of it* (although she can be influenced by external factors). The infant's personality type and the mother's personality type may be compatible or incompatible, and this often has a profound effect on mother/child bonding.

Many mothers tend to call an incompatible baby *difficult* and a compatible baby *easy.* But research on truly *difficult* and *easy* babies shows that categorizing infant behavior is not so simple:

- Ten percent of normal babies are classified *hyper*responsive, or *difficult* babies. These babies are very high-strung and sensitive to stress.
- Fifteen percent of normal babies are classified as *hypo*responsive, or babies who react slowly to stress. They usually appear sluggish. Their sluggishness can arouse fear in parents, who may wonder if something is wrong with their baby.
- Forty percent of normal babies are considered average. They are moderately responsive. Their personality falls in the middle ground between highly reactive and slow to respond. They have average reactions to stress.
- Thirty-five percent of normal babies show a mixture of both traits and cannot be classified into either category.

Yvette, age 32, came from a dysfunctional family with a history of mental illness. She was experiencing a tough emotional period and had been placed on psychiatric medication when she discovered that she was pregnant. Her doctor took her off the medication right away. Yvette subsequently gave birth to a *hypo*responsive baby. Since she had been on medication the first few weeks of pregnancy, the baby's slow responses frightened her. Yvette's baby Jake is now 1 year old and doing fine. Her fears seem to be unfounded because the baby's personality is simply very low-key.

*Hyper*responsive children are highly reactive to stimuli. They are constantly tense, temperamental, overexcitable, irritable and difficult to soothe. They cry more often and generally demand more attention than other babies. If your grandchild is such a personality type, the parents face a long-term challenge. The baby will probably always be active, but a few simple steps on your part may help the parents cope better.

Especially the mother may feel that no one understands the special problems she faces with this baby. Even if you suspect that she is feeling a bit sorry for herself, remember how much pressure she feels and do not minimize her difficulties. Avoid comments such as, "It's really not as bad as all that," or "She's such a cute baby, how hard can it be?" or, "*All* firstborn babies are difficult." Instead, affirm her feelings, empathize with her and try to soothe her anxiety:

- "I know how tough and frustrating this must be. Your baby is so different from you, and she really *is* more challenging than other babies."
- "Some babies are just born more excitable. It's not your fault, and I know you're doing the best you can."
- "I would be happy to go to the library for you and find some books discussing how to handle this type of child," or "Is there a support group or someone you could talk to?" Many pediatrician offices have nurse-practitioners

available to help parents understand their particular situation and to recommend helpful interventions.

Major developmental milestones such as teething, learning to crawl, using words, walking and toilet training can produce frustration even in the most placid child.

"Tommy is a year old and trying very hard to walk. He's cranky all the time, and so are his parents. What can I do to help?" asked a grandmother.

Since you have been through all this before, you can remind the parents that it is normal for children who are trying to master a new skill to become frustrated and irritable. With so much energy devoted to this task, the child often regresses in other areas. It is normal for eating and sleeping habits to suffer during a new learning phase.

Nursing and Feeding

Breast-feeding was not as commonplace a few decades ago as it is today. Today most mothers want to nurse their babies.

In addition, doctors believe nursing is best for both mother and baby. Nursing helps the mother's uterus to return to normal size. Breast milk is easy to digest, provides excellent, naturally balanced nutrition, and helps protect the baby from infection. Perhaps most importantly, there is nothing like breast-feeding to reinforce the growing bond between mother and child.

Mothers are advised to nurse on demand, whenever the baby is hungry. The primary reason for this advice is the bonding research (described earlier) that concludes, "You can't spoil a baby by being responsive to its needs." However, this recommendation is not always a child care issue.

With her first child, Audrey had trouble stimulating her milk. The old advice for this problem would have been to avoid feeding the baby too often, for fear she would run out of milk. But Audrey's pediatrician told her to stay in bed and take every opportunity to nurse the baby. Three or four days of rest and almost constant nursing stimulated Audrey's milk, and she never had the problem again.

Feeding and nursing can be a highly charged subject between parents and grandparents. Grandmothers, in particular, may question the new mother's choices and find themselves sorely tempted to become involved. The issue of how and how often to feed the baby has produced conflicts between the generations for ages. My mother advised me to nurse my babies on a fixed schedule, but that did not feel right to me. I nursed my babies on demand, against her advice.

A grandmother who did not nurse her own babies may feel envious of the maternal intimacy between her nursing daughter and her new baby. Some grandparents feel frustrated because the nursing baby spends so much time with the mother. They may want to be more involved.

One woman justified her interference in her daughter's nursing, saying, "He's a big baby, and her breasts are so small. She just can't be producing enough milk for him." The size of the mother's breasts has nothing to do with the quantity of milk she can produce. This grandmother finally admitted that she was feeling left out and wanted to make herself helpful.

Remember how it used to drive *you* up the wall when your mother asked you, "Are you *sure* he's getting enough to eat?" Resist the temptation to ask it now. Feeding is an intuitive learning process and the most personal of all interactions between mother and baby. By questioning or analyzing it repeatedly, you can profoundly undermine the mother's growing self-esteem and autonomy. Trust that she will find the best way to manage, just as you did.

If this is a difficult issue for you, reflect on your early nursing experiences and how you dealt with them. Did you have any problems feeding your babies? Was feeding your babies the focus of any conflicts with *your* mother? Perhaps nursing was wonderful for you and now you want to make sure that your daughter will have a positive experience. You may think that she wants or needs your advice, but if she has not specifically asked you, she is probably doing fine. Even if she is not, we have seen how sensitive new parents can be about uninvited advice.

Mothers today feel that breast-feeding is a natural function, and they are comfortable nursing openly, wherever they happen to be. Most women are discreet about it, but grandparents, especially grandfathers, may be uncomfortable when their daughter or daughter-in-law nurses the baby in public. If this conduct disturbs you, you may not be aware that social norms have changed. Breast-feeding in public is no longer considered inappropriate behavior.

Otherwise, what are your options? Do your discomfort issues interfere with going out together when the new mother might have to nurse the baby? If she nurses on demand, as most mothers do now, that might reduce your outings to short trips. Would you like to ask her to be more modest when she feeds the baby? She may be offended by your implication that her nursing could be considered indecent. If adaptation, compromise and negotiation do not solve the problem, try to understand the source of your discomfort. Does seeing a strange woman nursing in public disturb you? Why? Are you feeling more protective or modest because this is your daughter? How did you feel about this issue when your own children were babies? It is possible to find a resolution that fits your comfort level.

Colic: Still A Mystery

One evening when Kate's grandchild Mimi was a month old, she began crying hard and could not be comforted. Her face turned red and she drew her knees up as if in severe pain. Her parents took Mimi to the emergency room where the doctor on duty seemed uninterested.

"It's just colic," he said, and sent them home. The mother, still concerned, called her regular pediatrician the next morning.

That doctor said, "Colic isn't a real syndrome. It doesn't exist. So don't worry about it. It'll go away."

Despite the two medical diagnoses, Mimi's mother was beside herself with feelings of hostility and rage. She couldn't stand what was happening to her and her baby. In absolute frustration, she finally turned to her mother. "The baby was in so much pain, but neither doctor could help her. They didn't even seem to take it seriously. What do *you* know about colic?"

Doctors, parents and grandparents have been trying to understand colic for generations. The term *colic* seems to be a catch-all for a behavior that affects about one in five babies. It is not a specific illness, but rather a set of disturbing symptoms that disappear by the time the baby is 3 or 4 months old. If your grandchild is colicky, it will be apparent soon after birth. The only time you would normally call the baby's doctor about these symptoms is if the baby also shows signs of a fever – which is *not* a sign of colic.

There has been no thorough medical investigation to determine the cause of colic. Research efforts have been hampered because of the reluctance to subject basically healthy infants to potentially risky diagnostic procedures. So doctors continue to disagree among themselves.

Various theories advanced about colic include tension in the home, maternal anxiety, immaturity of the gastrointestinal tract, colon spasms, trapped intestinal gas, progesterone deficiency, allergies, faulty feeding techniques, and so on. There may well be many causes.

Colic causes great distress for parents. Feeding, changing, rocking and soothing the infant do not relieve the baby's discomfort. One young mother vividly described living with a colicky baby:

"Every day for three months I sat on the couch trying to block out the baby's screams," she recalled. "When my husband came home, I'd be in the same position and wearing the same old nightgown that I'd been wearing when he left in the morning. I just didn't care. I called my mother and said, 'You better come and rescue me, or your grandson is going to be thrown out the window. I can't take another minute of this.'"

No matter what the doctors call it, if your grandchild is going through this, the parents need all the support you can give. Support them in person if you can. If not, at least remind them their baby is basically healthy and will soon outgrow the symptoms.

Most grandparents do not panic over colic. It is tough, but most of us experienced it with one or more of our own children. We can usually be more calm about a colicky baby than the parents. We know the baby is not sick and that there is no need for medical intervention. For us, the hardest part may be the stress that it causes the new parents, our children.

Circumcision

The popularity of newborn circumcision (removal of the foreskin of the penis) has fluctuated sharply over the last generation. In the late 1970s, the U.S. circumcision rate was as high as 85 percent. It is now down to about 60 percent, but is rising again. Changing medical recommendations are chiefly responsible for these fluctuations.

Until 1975, newborn circumcision was considered standard medical practice. In that year, the American Academy of Pediatrics (AAP) declared there was no valid medical reason for the procedure, and within a few years circumcision rates began to decline substantially. However, in 1989 the AAP reversed its earlier position, having found that a compelling medical benefit had been discovered in new research which indicated that uncircumcised boys suffer 11 times more urinary tract infections than circumcised boys.

However, parents may still opt against circumcision because they do not want their newborn to experience the trauma of unanesthetized surgery. Local anesthesia is rarely used because it adds to the risk of the procedure. It was once believed that newborns could feel no pain, but that clearly is not the case. Babies circumcised without anesthesia show their suffering with crying, irritability and sleep difficulties. A hospital circumcision takes about 15 to 30 minutes. The surgeon straps the baby to a body board to hold him still, clamps the penis down, and makes several incisions.

Jewish families may choose a religious alternative, known as a *bris*, the Jewish circumcision ritual performed by a *mohel*. A *mohel* may perform a circumcision on any baby, regardless of religion. The British Royal Family has always called on the services of a *mohel* for their boy babies.

Larry and Barb's Protestant daughter, Elaine, married Joey, who was Jewish. When Joey and Elaine had a baby boy, they invited her parents to attend the *bris*. Like many young families, Joey and Elaine had originally planned the ritual because they thought it would please his parents. When his parents could not attend, they went ahead anyway. Larry and Barb, the Protestant grandparents, were eager to attend their first *bris*. Many friends of the parents attended the festive event.

Shortly before the ceremony, Elaine grew upset, telling her mother, "I can't bear to watch this," but her parents had no qualms about participating. In fact, since the paternal grandparents were absent, Larry accepted the honor of holding the baby during the ceremony. Safe in his grandfather's arms, the baby was given a suck of wine. Then the *mohel* made one quick incision; it took about 15 seconds. Afterward, the baby cried and wanted to nurse, but Elaine was still upset and could not nurse him. The *mohel* talked to her and helped her calm down. Eventually she relaxed and nursed the baby.

Stranger Anxiety

Your grandchild's personality will shift as he matures and faces new challenges. Around 8 months, the baby may suddenly seem less happy to see you. As one grandfather complained, "Abigail was such a sweet friendly baby. She always gave me a big smile.

But now she starts crying whenever I pick her up. And when I come to baby-sit she throws a tantrum."

Although Abigail's behavior upsets her grandfather and embarrasses her parents, the infant is going through a normal stage of development. She has become aware of the significance of her primary caretaker versus other adults, and shows this awareness with *stranger anxiety* and *separation anxiety.*

After her initial tantrum, Abigail usually calms down quickly and is fine. Her behavior is not a rejection of her grandfather, but a realization of her parents' importance.

Babies at this age are very sensitive about being with anyone other than their primary caretaker. They will cry whenever the primary care parent leaves, and it makes no difference who else is there. Mom may wonder, "Why does she cry so hard when I leave her with Daddy when I go to work?" Daddy may wonder, "What am I doing wrong?" When the nanny becomes the primary care person, the baby is likely to prefer her to his parents, much to their chagrin.

As a grandparent who has been through all this before, you are in a position to reassure them. You can remind them that this behavior is not a rejection of anyone, and that it *will* pass, although it may recur briefly again around the second year of life as the baby begins to explore her environment.

When Baby Comes to Visit

Unless you live quite far from your new grandchild, the baby is likely to visit you during his first 15 months. If you live nearby, you are likely to be asked to baby-sit. The first step in preparing for the child's visit is to *baby-proof* your home before you have a problem. Proper precautions can prevent 90 percent of all home accidents.

Take a look at your home from an infant's perspective. Remember how quickly a crawling and walking baby can get into trouble? They are great explorers and can move surprisingly fast. It is not possible to always hover over them. As soon as your attention wanders to pick up the phone, prepare a cup of tea, answer the front door, fix a bottle or glance at the newspaper, the baby will make a beeline for your electrical outlets, electrical appliances, under sink cleaning materials, kitchen knives, toxic liquids, fragile collectibles, lamps, nervous pets, sharp and pointed objects (scissors, pens and pencils), poisonous houseplants, prescription and over-the-counter medications. All these items must be secured before the baby enters your home.

One grandparent couple found out the hard way that even seemingly harmless vitamins can be dangerous to infants.

Mike and Helen were baby-sitting Jamie, their 11-month-old granddaughter. While exploring, the fast-moving youngster found Mike's vitamins and ingested an unknown quantity. They rushed Jamie to the hospital, where her stomach was pumped, saving her life.

Mike and Helen narrowly avoided a needless tragedy. This kind of accident is more common than you might believe. In 1993, there were 33 deaths nationwide among children under age 2 from ingesting high-potency vitamins.

Most of us agree that a house full of baby furniture is unnecessary. If you are tempted to pull out the baby walker you used with your children — forget it! The AAP issued a position paper declaring baby walkers unsafe in 1995. Apparently the high rate of tip-overs and falls down the stairs made the walkers unsafe. Old cribs with wide spaces between slats are equally unsafe. The baby may lodge his head between the slats with tragic results.

The only item you *definitely* need is a *car seat* – even for short trips and errands. You may share a car seat with the parents. Always resist the temptation for one grandparent to hold the baby while the other drives.

"Putting him in the car seat is such a struggle. We're just going down to the corner." *Always use a car seat.* There can be no exceptions to this rule. Car seats are required by law and for good reason. You cannot protect a baby by holding him closely in a car. If an accident occurs, even a minor one, the baby's light weight is likely to send him flying, with potentially tragic results.

It is important to use car seats correctly. As many as two out of three car seats are misused in some way, according to Dr. Heather Paul, executive director of the National SAFE KIDS Campaign.

Infant-only seats should always face rearward. Never place any car seat in a front passenger seat equipped with an air bag. Air bags provide protection for sturdy adults, but some infants have been killed when air bags open with extreme force during an accident. Safety experts say the safest place for the car seat is in the middle position in the car's backseat.

Once you have baby-proofed your home, unpacked a few old toys, and pulled out an unbreakable set of pots and spoons, you may feel ready for baby's visit. But those are only preliminaries. When the baby arrives and becomes your responsibility, your baby care expertise is really put to the test.

One common problem is *bottle feeding*. A very young breast-fed baby may be unwilling to take a bottle from you. Babies recognize the bottle nipple does not feel like mother's nipple. One helpful hint is to place something sweet on the tip of the nipple. The sweet taste helps the baby begin sucking, and once they taste the milk they will eagerly continue.

Grandparents Have Needs

A baby will quickly pick up her grandparents' fears and anxieties, just as she does with her parents. One spring day, Pat got a call from her daughter, Nina, who said, "Mom, I've been cooped up in the house for six weeks since Jason was born. Can I leave him with you for half an hour so I can go for a walk?" Pat was very busy, but she empathized with Nina, and it was only for half an hour, so she agreed. Nina said she was going bicycling and would be back in about an hour. Pat was annoyed, but before she could respond, Nina left.

Jason started crying right after his mother left and would not stop. Nina did not return for hours. Already stressed with her own busy schedule, Pat began to panic. "Maybe he's sick. What if it's colic? What should I do?" When she finally called me in desperation, I assured her, "That's not colic. You're irritated. Jason's hungry. And your nerves are affecting him. Take a deep breath and relax. You both need to settle down."

It is important not to forget your own needs in your eagerness to support the parents and spend time with the baby. Pat could have said to Nina, "This just isn't a good day for me to take Jason. How about tomorrow?"

Joan was worried about caring for her 10-month-old grandson, Coulter, while his parents were away for the weekend. He had started to walk, and she did not know if she could manage him. Joan was a vigorous young grandmother who had raised three active sons. In discussing her unusual anxiety over this visit, she finally admitted what was really bothering her.

Joan, a recent widow, lived alone and had recently bought a puppy for company, but the puppy was jealous of all the attention Joan gave Coulter. When her grandson came to visit, Joan had to keep the puppy in the basement for days, and she felt guilty about it. She was ashamed to admit it, but this was not a frivolous concern. The puppy filled an important need for love and companionship in her life.

Single grandparents need to develop new emotional outlets to cope with the loneliness of their empty nests, and these new involvements may conflict from time to time with grandparenting activities. There is no need to feel defensive about your social life, hobbies and relationships. Sometimes you may have to say no, or set limits when a child care request conflicts with your plans or is inconvenient. Family visits can also become *too much of a good thing*. If your home tends to be the extended vacation spot for your children's families, make sure your needs are considered in everyone's vacation plans.

Who Is the *Real* Baby Expert?

In our culture, we tend to look to our family doctor or pediatrician for advice and answers to baby care questions. Yet doctors often disagree. One might advise parents to boil bottles and nipples. Another says it is no longer necessary to boil bottles if you use a dishwasher. One doctor recommends 2 percent milk, while another says you should only feed a baby whole milk, and some suggest skim milk as the best choice. Different viewpoints such as these only reinforce what grandparents already know: there is more than one proper way to care for a baby.

In many parts of the world, grandmothers, not doctors, are the baby experts. When a new mother has a question, she would not think of turning to anyone but her mother. In our country, parents are encouraged to ask experts, read a book, join a support group — almost *anything* other than consult their parents.

You may feel hurt that your children automatically turn to their doctor for advice rather than consulting with you. Yes, it is a shame, but if your children do not ask for your advice, it is best not to interfere. Let them know you are available to answer any questions, but then wait until they request your advice. If you ever feel so strongly about a parenting issue that you feel you *must* interfere, your opinion will be more influential because you have not jumped in previously on every minor decision.

We can best enhance our relationship with the new family by being well-informed about contemporary ideas regarding child development. When I help my children with their babies, I like to skim through their baby care books (or the reading list at the end of this chapter). If they ask me for suggestions, I can communicate more effectively with them because I know what they are reading.

New parents need to be independent and blaze their own child rearing trails. Previous generations of parents may seem overly rigid to us now, but at the time they were advised to *shape* the baby to social norms. Even in my mother's day, *spoiling the baby* was still a big issue. My generation was more flexible, but we still confined our babies within cribs and playpens. We even tried to comfort a crying baby without taking her from the crib.

Today's parents take their child everywhere, respond to all his needs, and allow him to explore without restrictions. The experts now say it is impossible to spoil a baby with too much love and attention. Parents are no longer concerned with *shaping* their child. Instead, they respond to the baby's needs to create a firm foundation for the child's development.

Grandparents worry that new parents are unusually tense with the baby. We may not recall being as anxious with our own babies. This observation may be correct. Parents today *do* tend to be more worried and uncertain than we were, but they face more serious concerns and fewer social restrictions than we did. Their child-related anxieties have a real basis in the culture in which we live.

Kids are not doing too well. According to Daniel Goleman in his 1996 book, *Emotional Intelligence*, "Perhaps the most disturbing single piece of data in this book comes from a massive survey of parents and teachers and shows a worldwide trend for the present generation of children to be more troubled emotionally than the last: more lonely and depressed, more angry and unruly, more nervous and prone to worry, more impulsive and aggressive."

I agree with Goleman's answer to himself: "If there is a remedy, I feel it must lie in how we prepare our young for life." It is no wonder that parents of infants are tense. There is much we as grandparents can do to help.

(Note: The developmental psychologists and psychiatrists whose research and formulations are reflected in this chapter include: Mary Ainsworth, John Bowlby, T. Berry Brazelton, Beatrice Beebee, Virginia Demos, Robert Emde, Selma Fraiberg, Jerome Kagan, Joseph Lichtenberg, Daniel Stern and Burton White.)

Recommendations

- Accept current ideas regarding infant care and development.
- Avoid arguing about new research, even when you do not completely agree.
- Encourage grandfathers to play with the infant. Research confirms that infants benefit from male vigor.
- Do not be overly concerned about spoiling-the-baby issues.
- Be supportive of the new mother's commitment to breast-feeding.
- Read the same infant development and parenting books the new parents read to better understand their approach.
- Baby-proof your home before your infant grandchild visits you.
- Don't be afraid to share your thoughts with the parents when you feel *strongly* about an issue regarding baby care. They may not agree, but at least you have registered your concerns with them.

Reading List for Adults

Brazelton, T. Berry. *Infants and Mothers*. Revised edition. New York: Delta Books, 1983.

Brazelton, T. Berry, and B. Cramer. *Earliest Relationship: Parents, Infants, and the Drama of Early Attachment*. Addison-Wesley Publishing Co., 1991.

Caplan, Frank, editor. *The First Twelve Months of Life: Your Baby's Growth Month by Month*. New York: Perigee Books, 1993.

Dodson, Fitzhugh and A. Alexander. *Your Child: Birth to Age Six*. New York: Simon & Schuster, 1988.

Koop, Clair B. and Donne L. Bean. *Baby Steps: The Whys of Your Child's Behavior in the First Two Years*. New York: W. H. Freeman, 1994.

Leach, Penelope. *Your Baby and Child: From Birth to Age Five*. New York: Alfred A. Knopf, 1989.

Simkin, Penny, et al. *Pregnancy, Childbirth and the Newborn.* New York: Meadowbrook, 1991.

Spock, Benjamin and Michael B. Rothenberg. *Baby and Child Care.* New York: Pocket Books, 1992. Fully revised and updated for the 90's.

Stoppard, Miriam. *Baby and Child A to Z Medical Handbook.* Perigree, 1992.

Reading List for Children

Since babies up to age 15 months tend to taste and tear their books, the best choices are books made of cloth and vinyl. Reading to infants introduces them to words associated with familiar objects. They love to turn the pages and listen to you read. These first books you read to your grandchild should have single, easily-remembered images on each page. A few recommendations:

Dunn, Phoebe. *Baby Animal Friends.* Random House.

Ross, Dorothy. *Where is Your Nose?* Simon & Schuster.

Wik, Lars. *Baby's First Words.* Random House.

Audiotapes for Children

Listening to audiotapes can be very soothing to a young child. The ideal opportunity is during quiet time before bed, or when traveling in a car. A few recommendations:

Doucet, Michael, et al. *Daddies Sing Goodnight.* A collection of music sung by daddies who are also famous musicians.

McCormack, Mike and Carleen. *Beasties, Bumbershoots and Lullabies.* Alacazar. A lovely collection of classics.

Roger, Sally. *At Quiet O'Clock.* Alcazar/Round River. A collection of classic lullabies.

Resource Guide

Oppenheimer, Joanne and Stephanie Oppenheimer. *The Best Toys, Books, Videos & Software for Kids 1997: 1,000+ Kid-Tested Classic and New Products for Ages 0-10.* Prima Publishing, 1996.

4

Your Toddler Explores the World

*The capacity to care is the thing
which gives life its deepest meaning
and significance.*
– Pablo Casals

Yvette, her husband Ned and their son Jake were visiting nearby. The couple wanted to stop in and introduce their son to me. Jake, age 26 months, is the hyporesponsive baby we met in Chapter 3. I have known Yvette for quite some time. I was delighted to hear from her, and welcomed their visit. I looked forward to seeing her and having the chance to become better acquainted with Ned and to meet young Jake.

The beautiful blond, chubby, chatterbox toddler explored every corner of my child-proof family room. Conversation with his parents was almost impossible, as Jake took all of our attention. Finally Ned offered to take him outside so Yvette and I could catch up. Lest you think Jake was *spoiled, demanding, hyperactive and difficult,* let me assure you he was simply being a *toddler.*

There's A Toddler Around!

Every Christmas, our children and their families join my husband and me for a grand holiday visit. The 11 grandchildren range in age from 20 years to 6 months. After the holidays, when my house became my own again, and my friends asked me how everything went, I realized the visit was much easier this year. Why, I wondered. What had changed?

The answer was readily apparent: for the first time, we had *no* toddlers in the house. Six-month-old Graham was a delight, and Dylan, age 3, and Melissa, age 4, now preschoolers, were able to express themselves verbally and play alone for periods of time. It is toddlers who require the constant watchfulness and assistance that bring on early fatigue in adults, typically spiced with plenty of *Don'ts* in their vocabulary. Toddlers are wonderful, but they do keep everyone busy!

The docile, manageable baby has disappeared, replaced now by an explorer absorbed in every detail of the world around him. Grandparenting life with a toddler is a constant compromise between the child's fierce desire to manage everything, and the caregiver's good sense about what is harmful. Toddlers are delightful, particularly when grandparents can see and experience life from their point of view, which is fun but also challenging.

Grandparents, like parents, need to be reminded to love the toddler for what he *is*, not who he can *be*. Sometimes it can be difficult to consider the very active scamp lovable. It is easy to expect too much of him. As soon as the child begins to walk and talk, grandparents often tend to overlook how immature the toddler really is, how limited his patience and understanding is, and how negative and downright contrary he can be.

Have you taken your adorable little *imp* out to a restaurant – nothing fancy, just a neighborhood family establishment? While the three of you, Abbey, Grandma and Grandpa, wait for your table, other diners stop to smile and admire the beautiful 2-year-old on Grandpa's lap. Finally you are led to your table and the waitperson brings a highchair for Abbey. In typical toddler fashion, Abbey, with a mind of her own, refuses to sit in the highchair and threatens to begin a tantrum. Wishing to keep the peace at any price, Grandpa puts her on his lap and draws up to the table.

The hard-won peace lasts for all of 10 minutes, when Abbey decides she wants to get down from Grandpa's lap and explore the restaurant. By now the waitperson is ready to take the order, but Abbey's squirming and crying to climb down cause him to suggest he will come back in a bit – and on it goes. The point is that a toddler can be adorable one minute and then become a pain in the neck the next minute, without reason or warning, particularly when you want them to conform to *appropriate* behavior. This temperament comes with the age.

Let's consider another example of possible grandparent *over-expectation*. It is tempting to take your toddler grandchild to the supermarket with you, assuming he will sit calmly in the grocery cart child seat and munch on raisins. However, he may not be interested in raisins, and prefers instead to open the box of Fruit Loops cereal and produce a Hansel and Gretel trail as you wheel through the store. You may *hope* for appropriate behavior, but to *expect* it is an error. The world is his oyster, and everything lays before him for exploration. This is the toddler's charm, and the quality that most exhausts grandparents at the same time.

You are baby-sitting your lovable grandson Sam, age 2, for the weekend. All of you have enjoyed a fun day, but now bedtime has come, and Sam is having none of it. Sam is in his crib upstairs in the guest room, and you are relaxing before the TV. However, Sam is not ready to call it quits. He calls for you because he wants the light on. Grandma marches upstairs, switches on the hall light and returns to her chair. Sam calls again. This time he wants another story. Up you go to read yet another story, pat him on his back for a bit, and figure finally you can find some rest.

After a few minutes of quiet time, you hear a strange noise on the stairs. Grandpa jumps up this time, only to find Sam on the stairs. Nobody told you that the toddler was able to climb out of

his crib! Again, to expect that Sam will settle down like your 10-year-old grandchild when she visits is *over-expectation*.
   He is a toddler!

Safety: Toddlers Need Protection
   Making the house safe for visiting children is always a must, but with toddlers around it becomes more urgent. How easy it might have been for young Sam to get into something unsafe while you thought he was falling asleep in his crib. When you childproof your house, remember your grandchild is a great climber, so put worrisome items safely out of reach. Specifically:

- Be sure *all* your medicines are tightly capped and carefully stowed away.
- Avoid having items out and accessible that can cause choking: peanuts, hard candies, beads, marbles.
- Be careful about serving food that can cause choking, such as whole grapes; split them down the middle. Avoid popcorn; toddlers can easily choke on the hard kernels. Hot dogs head the list of foods kids most often choke on.
- Unload and lock up all guns.
- Never leave the toddler unattended in the bathtub. Children have been known to drown in the most minimal depths of bathwater.
- Lock away sharp objects such as razors, knives and scissors.
- Post emergency telephone numbers by the phone, including your local poison control center. Check the front page of your local telephone book for this toll-free Poison Control Center number.
- Make sure all cleaning, laundry and painting products are safely out of the toddler's reach.

Characteristics of the Toddler
   Toddlers age 15 months to 3 years become increasingly aware of the people around them. They become communicators,

learning words and using them to form more complex sentences. Language provides them with the ability to say what they like and do not like, what they want and do not want. In addition, they are learning independence, such as climbing, dressing, walking and eating by themselves.

In Chapter 3, we noted how important *basic trust* is for the infant's healthy development. According to Erik Erikson, the major psychosocial task for this toddler period is *autonomy*. The child who is denied the opportunity to struggle with autonomy experiences *shame* and *guilt*. Realizing how central *autonomy* is at this age helps us to accept or remain more tolerant of all the toddler's protests of "No!" and "I wanna do it myself." Expect toddlers to be:

- *Egocentric*: "The world revolves around me!" If mommy does not feel well, his sadness is not that mommy feels poorly, but rather, "How can she be so mean and not play with *me*?"
- *Independent*: "I want to do everything myself." She wants to dress herself, but heaven help you if you are in a hurry and she is not.
- *Confused*: Between what is reality and what is non-reality. What you recognize as a make-believe playmate is often a real playmate to him. When he tells you an untruth, it usually is not a lie, but rather confusion between reality and fantasy.
- *Curious*: "How does it work?" This curiosity can include everything from electrical sockets to your cherished antique clock.
- *Concrete Thinkers*: When Natasha was told they were flying to Grandpa's house, she thought she had to have wings.
- *No Concept of Time*: Time is moment to moment. What happens when you ask a toddler to wait a few minutes while you get ready to go on an outing? He is likely to be

out the door and lost in the few minutes it takes you to finish combing your hair.

- *Messy Eaters*: They do not want to be fed, but they are not well enough coordinated to get the spoon to their mouth without spilling. They will improve with practice.
- *Works at Play*: It is through play that the toddler learns about the world. The opportunity to work at play is essential to healthy child development.
- *Mistrusts Strangers*: This reappearance of *stranger anxiety* can extend to the infrequent visits of grandparents. This is particularly characteristic of the younger toddler. As the toddler grows older, he internalizes the memory of important people, even those he sees less frequently, such as out-of-town grandparents.
- *Temper Tantrums*: This is the height of the temper tantrum period. The tantrum is often related to the toddler's struggle for autonomy. The best way to handle a tantrum is to ignore it and wait until it abates.
- *"No!"*: This may be the most overused word of toddlerhood. Rather than confronting the *no*, it is better to distract the child and approach the issue from another way. Fortunately toddlers are very easy to distract.

Differing Generational Points of View

The mother of Rachel, age 2, told the child's grandmother that the child care teacher declared that Rachel demonstrated *leadership charisma*. Grandma answered, "In my day, it was called being *bossy*."

Another grandmother's son is a *house parent*. Tom's wife returned to her medical practice full-time when Brandon was 18 months old. Tom decided to give up his job in computer sales and service to take full-time care of his son. His mother was furious. "How can she go off to work and leave Brandon with Tom? Men are earners, not mothers!" It was extremely difficult for her to accept a situation so different from what she considered appropriate.

The most common complaint heard from grandparents is described in this grandfather's story. His daughter, son-in-law and granddaughter Terry, age 2, were visiting him. At breakfast, Terry's mother offered her a choice of Cheerios, Fruit Loops, Raisin Bran, bagels, or eggs. (You may ask, What kind of eggs?) Meal preparation halted while Terry considered her options. Two-year-olds are not quick decision makers. She finally chose waffles, which had not been offered.

While Grandpa wanted to say, "No, waffles were not one of the choices. Choose from what we offered," he held his tongue. In his opinion, there were too many choices already. Instead, the parents asked if waffles were available. Yes, there were some in the freezer. Finally breakfast was served. However, by now it was time for *Sesame Street* and Terry left her food on the table for the TV. Grandpa complained later that when he was raising children, food was set out and they ate it. He asked, "Why do little ones need to make these decisions? Who is in charge?"

Differing generational points of view demand considerable tact and understanding from grandparents. Parents today give their children choices at very young ages to develop their skill in decision-making. Parent goals have shifted from demanding obedience to encouraging autonomy. I agree with the principle, but in terms of child development, a toddler does better within the structure of an adult's decision, even if she revolts against it. Too many choices become overwhelming, because toddlers are simply too immature to handle this much responsibility. My recommendation regarding mealtimes is to learn in advance of the meal what the child likes and offer two (or possibly three) choices, without running to the freezer for a choice that was not offered. This presents a structure for the child, supports the parents' wish for decision-making, and protects the grandparents from running a *restaurant*.

Bedtime is another gripe of grandparents of toddlers. Bedtime is no longer sacrosanct as it was in my parenting days. Today, parents are quite casual about when they put their children to bed. I often hear grandparents complain about their tired grandchildren. "They don't get enough sleep, that's why they get sick so often" is a common refrain. I question this reasoning. Toddlers are quite adept at falling asleep anywhere, anyplace, when they are tired. What grandparents are *really* criticizing is a differing generational point of view that allows parents to be much more casual about sleep time. Accept your adult children's approach to sleep for their youngsters. It is doubtful that your toddler grandchild becomes sick from lack of sleep.

Here is another example of differing points of view that can make grandparenting stressful. A grandmother expressed concern that she and her husband had about their daughter Tania and Brian, age 15 months. Brian's father had left Tania before the boy's birth. After his birth, mother and child moved in with her parents, who then became very involved in Brian's care. Now the problem was that Tania and Brian had moved into very modest housing with Tania's new boyfriend. Brian's grandparents felt this was a bad environment for the child and wanted help in figuring out a way to persuade Tania and Brian to move back with them. I did not see it their way. This was Tania's choice. Since the grandparents did not describe any danger, neglect or abuse to Brian, Tania's parents needed to accept her decision. Most of my session with the grandmother was spent helping her adjust to the choice Tania had made.

A profound example of differing generational values arose when I lectured to a parent study group. A young mother raised her hand and related this episode to the group:

> "Bart, our 2- year-old son, was pulling a toy away from his cousin Heidi when my mother-in-law reached over and swatted him! Bart was startled and began to cry. We have never spanked Bart. I was shocked, but I didn't say anything

to my mother-in-law. Later my husband and I talked about it. He said he and his brother were always swatted when they were growing up if they misbehaved. I asked my sister-in-law, Heidi's mother, if she or her husband had said anything to our mother-in-law. No, they hadn't. What should I do?"

I told her I was sorry no one had talked to the grandmother. By not talking about an unpleasant event, animosity builds up. It is quite likely that Grandma, having used spanking as a way of controlling her children's behavior, never gave a thought to the possibility that her sons' families might use a different method.

Grandparents are usually happy to follow the *house rules* – but they do need to know what the rules are. Many child raising beliefs have changed generationally, particularly attitudes toward physical reprimands. My specific recommendation to this mother was that she and her husband discuss their feelings about spanking children directly with his mother.

Here are some general recommendations to help grandparents of toddlers cope with the myriad generational differences they will likely encounter:

- Remember that the parents are in charge! They are the teachers, while grandparents are the nurturers.
- Relinquish the rulemaker role to the grandchildren's parents.
- Your role is that of a delighted listener.
- Make an effort to understand the validity of the contemporary ideas your children endorse.

Fun with Our Imp

One morning grandfather Paul was helping dress his visiting grandson Jared. Jared gave out a holler, "Papa, help, I can't move my legs!"

Paul's wife laughed as she related the story. "Paul had both legs caught inside one pant leg. He's so inexperienced; he *never* did anything for his own children." For some grandfathers who feel shy with babies, and who were unavailable for their own little ones, caring for a toddler is a new experience for them – and a great one, despite episodes of clumsiness.

This is a wonderful age to develop closeness with the *imp,* your delightfully unpredictable toddler grandchild. When you live close to your grandchild, here are some suggestions to foster the best possible relationships:

- Stop-in visits are great. However, avoid unannounced visits. The last thing you want to be is intrusive.
- Offers of baby-sitting and outings with the child are wonderful, if they fit your lifestyle. Do not offer more than you can handle; grumpy grandparents are no fun.
- Birthdays and special events are super-important times to be with your grandchild.
- Grandmother Linda organized a cousins club. Every Saturday from 12 noon to 2 p.m. she offers lunch and child care for her three daughters, their husbands and their young children. The parents can stay for lunch if they like, but they usually use Grandma's child care time to go out on their own for two hours (which pleases Grandma Linda).

When you live out of town, here are some other suggestions (these may also apply to families that live close by):

- Ask to talk to your toddler grandchild after a telephone conversation with her parents. At this age, children cannot carry on a coherent conversation, but the telephone is an important part of their lives and they want to be part of it. Besides, they develop a greater recognition of your voice.
- Arrange extended family get-togethers during special events in their town, your town, or another sibling's town. It often

requires much effort and expense, but the great memories are worth it.

- Mail or fax cards, photos and letters to your toddler. They love the attention of receiving mail like their parents.
- Beginning with the toddler age period, and continuing forever, grandchildren love receiving gifts from you. Some may criticize this view and claim this establishes expectations. Still, I enjoy bringing modest gifts of toys, clothes or special food items when I visit my grandchildren. The only problem with a gift becoming an expectation is if you forget and arrive empty handed. (You can always substitute money for older grandchildren, but cash is inappropriate for toddlers, and *not* my gift choice in general. I prefer giving something more specific.)
- Prepare the children for goodbyes before the visit is over, so they are ready for leave-taking. Some children are more sensitive to transitions and separations than others, and may become sad and tearful when saying goodbye.

It is important for grandparents to be aware that sometimes your *fun with the imp* may not be good for the child, and other times it may not suit the child's parents' wishes.

As discussed in Chapter 2, with the birth of a sibling, grandparents may prefer to help out by caring for the toddler in their home in an effort to make the new baby's arrival easier for the parents. Besides, this is more fun for the grandparents. However, the potential fallout may not be so good. While you and your grandchild enjoy a wonderful visit during the birth and homecoming of the newborn, at some point your grandson returns home to the new baby. Every egocentric toddler feels displaced, loosing reign of his kingdom, when a new baby arrives. To be removed from the process of the baby's arrival and then to return to share his time with another is jolting. For the sake of the toddler's adjustment, it is much better for him to be around and experience the whole event. So grandparents, consider your assistance carefully, and if you are going to help with the toddler, do it in *his* home.

Regarding parent wishes, it is important to examine the sometimes ambivalent feelings on the part of parents toward grandparent involvement. Mike and Mary were a couple with young children who came to my office to discuss a marital issue. During one session, Mike and Mary began talking about the *Roman Rule*. What was that, I wondered? It turned out that they were talking about grandparent visits. When in Rome, do as the Romans do; and when the Romans come for a visit, do as the Romans do! For Mike and Mary, this approach resolved dilemmas related to grandparents. Other couples are perhaps less adaptable. When parents and grandparents disagree about general behavior and specific rules involving toddlers, disregarding the parents' wishes may anger the parents to the point that they limit grandparent involvement.

Another area in which grandparent behavior is hard on parents is when the grandparents continue to perceive and treat their offspring as children, long after their maturity and emancipation. This behavior seeks to deny adult parents their legitimate autonomy. When this occurs, parents rarely allow grandparents to become close pals with their kids.

Who is Raising the Toddler?

As we approach the 21st century, we see many of our grandchildren living in a variety of family arrangements. Your toddler may live in a single-parent (either mother or father) family, an unmarried mother and father family, divorced parents with a new spouse unrelated by blood, a two-female family, a two-male family, or a grandparent family. Of concern is whether the toddler, who is making great leaps in his awareness of the world around him, will experience gender confusion in his non-traditional family situation.

It is during this period of development (age 15 months to 3 years) that the adults composing his family become internalized as significant role models. Questions arise. How will the toddler develop his maleness when he is being raised by a single female, or a single male? What views will the child have of marriage if he is living with an unmarried couple? How confusing it must be for the toddler we are raising – we call ourselves Gramps and Nana, but he calls us Mom and Dad. These are realistic concerns. Of particular concern for grandparents is whether or not homosexual parents create homosexuality in children.

Same Sex Parents

Research reported in the January 1, 1996 edition of *The New York Times* described a study by two British researchers of 46 children over a 16-year period. The researchers found no significant difference in sexual orientation between children of lesbian mothers and those of heterosexual mothers. The commonly held assumption that children brought up by lesbian mothers will themselves grow up to be lesbians or gay is not supported by these well-documented findings.

Despite the research findings, it is important to comment on how difficult it is for the grandparent generation to have grandchildren growing up in a non-heterosexual home. A very close friend of mine, trained as I am in psychology, had a daughter in a homosexual marriage. Despite my friend's professional work and training, and her knowledge of how accepting her professional colleagues would be, it took her several years before she could tell us about the relationship. It was only when she found out that she was to become a grandmother that she revealed her daughter's lifestyle to us.

Rationally, she knew that her daughter was a mature, sensible woman, well-prepared to make her life decisions. Yet emotionally it pained our friend that her daughter's lifestyle was so different from most other women her age. Once our friend could talk about her feelings with us, she was on her way to dealing with her daughter's homosexuality. She now is a happy, busy grandmother of a toddler!

We often have a sense of failure as parents when we find our children in homosexual relationships. In the wake of increased openness about lesbians and gay adults, grandparents may begin to allow themselves to integrate the current research. In addition, we need to accept our adult children's decisions, as my friend finally did, be supportive of them and their lifestyle, and have confidence in their role as parents.

The following court case presents the opposite end of the spectrum. In 1993, the Virginia Supreme Court declared a lesbian fighting for custody of her 3-year-old son Tyler an unfit mother. According to the judge, her gay relationship would bring social condemnation on her child. The child was awarded to his maternal grandmother. The grandmother had argued that Tyler could grow up not knowing the difference between men and women if he was returned to his mother and her female lover.

This decision was made despite research to date which suggested that children of lesbian and gay parents have normal relationships with peers, and that their relationship with adults of both sexes is also satisfactory.

Grandparents Raising Grandchildren

You may be asked to raise your little tyke for a period of time. The social ills of our contemporary society can force unanticipated arrangements for grandparents of toddlers. Lauren and Alex, a terrific couple who are leaders in their community, are maternal grandparents of Emily, age 2. They have been asked by the court to care for Emily because Mom is in a drug rehabilitation program for six weeks, and Dad works out of town. Lauren and Alex are alternating weeks of care with the paternal grandparents. They hope that Mom will be able to resume her parenting role after rehab. If not, some serious decisions will need to be made with Emily's father and the grandparents.

The number of grandparents raising their grandchildren, taking over for parents who are sick, incarcerated, unemployed or otherwise unable to care for their children, is increasing. The

American Association of Retired Persons (AARP) has addressed this issue by establishing a *Grandparent's Information Center* to serve as a resource for grandparents. The information center provides grandparents with a listing of local support groups. (Contact AARP, Social Outreach and Support, 601 E. Street, NW, Washington, D.C. 20049; 202-434- 2296.)

Sylvie de Toledo, L.C.S.W., a grandparent advocate, in collaboration with journalist Deborah E. Brown, has produced an excellent book for grandparents raising children, entitled *Grandparents As Parents – A Survival Guide for Raising a Second Family* (Guilford Publications, 800-365-7006). De Toledo describes the book as "part map, part dictionary, and something of a group hug – a handbook for all grandparents who are raising grandchildren, to help them through the stressful times." I highly recommend de Toledo's book for grandparents facing this situation.

De Toledo is also founder of the national organization *Grandparents As Parents, Inc.* For more information on these issues, write the organization at: P.O. Box 964, Lakewood, CA 90714.

The Toddler at Play

Play is the work of toddlerhood. It is the way young children learn about the world. Toddlers do not divide their day into periods of learning time and playing time. Playing *is* learning. Sometimes play seems more important than eating or sleeping, which is quite normal.

In a span of ten minutes, a typical toddler ran around my office and then began jumping up and down with great excitement in the middle of the room. He spotted my wastebasket and became fascinated with the contents, emptying them piece by piece. Tired of that, he found the light switch and turned lights on and off seven times with squeals of delight.

His next move was for my desk drawer which, to my surprise, was no trouble for him to open. As he started to pull out my things, I grabbed hold of him and diverted him with some large building blocks on my shelf. Fortunately toddlers are very easy to divert! Their attention span is not very long, either, and soon I was following this one into another room.

It is tempting to say "No, no," but it is much better to hold our tongues and realize that by exploring and experimenting, the toddler is learning about the world around him. This play is not aimless. It has a purpose, although the purpose is not always clear to us. Actually, the toddler is learning how to handle his body – to shove and push, to lift and throw. He and all the toddlers like him are finding out how things work, where they go, and what fits where. As grandparents, we need to admire this play and allow plenty of time for it.

Not all toddler play is exploring the world or practicing new skills. Lots of time may be spent in imaginative and creative play. The toddler may become mommy, or daddy, or baby, or lion, or whatever creature they fancy themselves at the moment. Every night, Sean puts on his Batman pajamas and cape and flies off the sofa as Batman. If you pressed him, he knew he was Sean, but being Batman was more fun. Toddler Tiffany worked on pretend pregnancy, childbirth and nursing throughout the last trimester of her mother's pregnancy. Grandparents, enjoy this wonderful fantasy life of your chum because when she gets a bit older, she will become much more private.

Toddlers enjoy playing alone. If there are other children of the same age around, they tend to ignore them or just walk around them. So grandparents, there is no need to arrange play dates or companions for your grandchild yet. *You* are the best playmate for your pal.

Toys for Toddlers
Recommendations for grandparents:
- Grandparents need to have special toys at their home for the grandchildren.

- These toys should remain at your home (and not go home with the children) so your young visitor finds her special toy in the same place she found it the last time she visited. This offers consistency and security in the visit.
- If a toy is broken, throw it away. I do this with toys for my grandchildren, as well as with the toys I use for child therapy. Broken toys can make young children anxious and often fearful of becoming *broken* themselves.

Recommendations for types of toys for toddlers:
- Anything that stimulates big muscle movement, such as a wagon that carries items or a doll buggy that can be pushed around.
- Toys that represent life, such as baby dolls, pretend bottles, blankets, trucks, jets.
- Toys that simulate functions that adults perform, such as lawnmower, broom, kitchen equipment, dishes.
- Messiness that is acceptable to adults: sand, Play-doh, finger paints (try finger painting in the bathtub for easy cleanup afterward).

Tips for Buying Toys
    When I examine toys for my grandchildren at Toys 'R Us or Walmart – in contrast to an independent toy store where there is usually a clerk who has experience with children and can make helpful recommendations – and I have to choose myself, I look for the age range printed on the package and then buy something young for the child for whom I am shopping.
    What do I mean? If a toy, book or video is labeled 2-4 years, I will not buy that item for my grandchild who just turned age 2. Manufactures try to expand the age groups as far up and down as possible to enlarge their market. I want to select a gift that I know my grandchildren can use by themselves. If the item is too advanced, they will become frustrated unless they have

parental help. If parents want to *stretch* their children's minds, that is fine, but I want my gift to be fun for them to use themselves.

This holds true with older children as well as toddlers. I resent grandparents who think their grandchildren are so outstanding and can always perform well beyond their age level. Let babies be babies, let toddlers be toddlers, and let children be children!

I browsed through the toy section during a recent shopping trip to Walmart and observed a line of electronic toys which were marketed as *learning tools* ranging in price from $19.97 to $53.88. These items were advertised for children age 4-7 years, or pre-second grade. Grandparents – *wait*. I do not recommend buying such fancy, flashy tools for your toddler grandchildren. I am sure many of my friends will be tempted to choose such items, feeling that their grandchild is so especially bright that this expensive, attractive *toy* will be just right for him. Forget it. They do not need them.

The Best Toys, Books & Videos For Kids by Oppenheim and Oppenheim is a well-researched buying guide, and provides a great resource for grandparents. The book is updated annually. Page 28 of the 1995 edition recommends *avoiding* the following toys for toddlers:

- *No* toys with small parts, including small plastic fake food.
- *No* dolls and stuffed animals with fuzzy and/or long hair.
- *No* toys labeled for age 3 and up; there may be small parts in or on these toys.
- *No* latex balloons – the leading cause of suffocation death in toddlers.
- *No* electronic educational drill toys.
- *No* shape-sorters with more than three shapes.
- *No* battery-operated ride-ons.
- *No* pedal toys.

The Hurried Child

Just as grandparents may be tempted to buy toys that are too advanced for their toddler grandchildren, many parents are pushing their wonderful imps to give up their fantasy play and magical beliefs in an effort to train their minds. *Superbabies* miss the wonders of toddlerhood, and once gone, there is no going back.

Marcia, age 38, says, "There is so much pressure to get into college. You have to start them young and push them towards their goal. They have to be aware of everything – the alphabet, numbers, reading. I want to fill these little sponges as much as possible."

Some parents become so concerned that their kids are not left behind that, like Marcia, they frantically push infant academics. Most grandparents have better sense than Marcia, but with an explosion of information about young children's capabilities, it is tempting to focus on cognitive learning. The more appropriate thinking, backed by research, is that children can learn cognitive skills when they are older, but if play, the essential ingredient for emotional development during toddlerhood, is aborted, there will not be another chance.

Parenthood is a delightful early 1990's family film starring Steve Martin, about a family raising their children. The plot includes an incredibly bright little cousin who is constantly being cognitively drilled by her parents. One of the more humorous parts of the film occurs when this cousin visits the Buchman family. She displays her fancy vocabulary and ease with facts, and then reveals her complete inability to play or interact with her cousins. This *superbaby* has absolutely no people skills. It is amusing, but also quite sad. Her behavior is a painful example of the *hurried child*, a serious concern to many of us today. I hope you can guide your grandkids off the *superbaby* track.

Here are some suggestions:

- Find an occasion for parents and grandparents to watch a videotape of the film *Parenthood,* and discuss the hurried child issue afterward.
- Be proactive on this issue. There is too much risk of long-term developmental damage to your grandchild if the kind of play discussed here is thwarted and replaced by focused cognitive training.
- If you feel your advice will not be well received, intervene through actions when the grandchildren are with you. During the time you spend with your grandchildren, encourage learning by imaginative and problem-solving play.

Some experts warn that the current emphasis on infant academics may short-change physical, emotional and creative growth. David Elkind, a highly esteemed child development authority, warns in his book *The Hurried Child* that today's child has become the unwilling, unintended victim of overwhelming stress. Dr. Elkind's warning becomes even more pertinent in the next chapter of this book: *As Your Grandchild Grows Up.*

Recommendations

- Be as actively in contact with your grandchild as possible.
- With out-of-town families, frequent short visits (three or four days) are best.
- Make your house childproof for the visiting toddler.
- Watch what goes in their mouths and be alert for choking. Toddlers, ever curious, put everything in their mouths.
- Offer to baby-sit if it is convenient for you and the parents want you.
- Respect your children's efforts at discipline and follow their lead.

- Advise your adult children only when they ask for your advice.
- Be available for love, comfort, hugs and a sense of strength and stability.
- Accept and support your children's lifestyle.
- Let your children know when you think they are parenting well!
- Remember, you are not the parent. Be available, be good listeners, but in most situations hold back on the advice unless asked.
- Keep a collection of toys in your home.

Reading List for Adults

Brazelton, T. Berry. *Touchpoints: The Essential Reference.* A Merloyd Laurence Book, Addison-Wesley Publishing Co., 1992.

de Toledo, Sylvie J. and Deborah E. Brown. *Grandparents As Parents: A Survival Guide For Raising a Second Family.* Guilford Publications, 1995.

Elkind, David. *The Hurried Child: Growing Up Too Fast, Too Soon.* New York: Addison-Wesley Publishing Co., 1989.

Fraiberg, Selma. *The Magic Years.* Charles Scribner & Sons, 1959.

Greenspan, Stanley. *First Feelings: Milestones in the Emotional Development of Your Baby and Child.* Penguin USA, 1994.

Oppenheim, Joanne, and Stephanie Oppenheim. *The Best Toys, Books, Videos & Software for Kids 1997: 1,000+ Kid-Tested Classic and New Products for Ages 0-10.* Prima Publishing, 1996.

Reading List for Children

By the age of 2, the toddler understands a great deal. Toddlers can follow short, simple stories. They like rhymes and repetitive lines that they can join in with you. Choose books *you like* because they like them to be read over and over again. You can check with your local children's librarian or book store for current popular books for toddlers, or consult Oppenheim and Oppenheim's guide. Two of my favorites:

Brown, M.W. *Good Night Moon.* Harper Collins. This is my all-
time favorite storybook with all my grandchildren.
Scarry, Richard. *Cars and Trucks and Things That Go.* Golden
Press, 1974. Busy transportation scenes which older toddlers
love.

Audio
Music for moving, singing and dancing:

Dean, Karen. *Ants in My Pants.* BMI. Very child-friendly, and
comes with an action book.
Kimbo. *Car Song.* This makes a long drive fun.

Video
Many wonderful picture books have been brought to life on
video. Avoid Disney movie videos until the children are older –
they are too overstimulating at this age.

Johnson, Crockett. *Harold and the Purple Crayon and Other
Harold Stories.* Children's Circle. Another of my favorites.

Your Grandchild is Growing Up

Over the river and through the woods
To grandmother's house we go;
The horse knows the way
To carry the sleigh
As over the bridge we go ...
– Linda Child

"Grandma! Grandma! I've been waiting for you! I'm so glad you're here!"

What a treat – to arrive at my daughter's house with a warm, loving, genuine welcome from a beautiful 5-and-a-half-year-old granddaughter who can scarcely wait for the car door to open before giving me her biggest hug. Sarah's use of the word *grandma* and the loving inflection in her voice touch my heart every time. Her absolute acceptance and love are a wonderful emotional fix. How lucky I am!

As I leave the car and enter the house I receive a royal greeting from 3-year-old Dylan and their mom. However, the specialness of Sarah's greeting lingers most deeply for days after I return home. All my older grandchildren call me Margy, or Grandma Margy. That was my preference initially, because I felt too young to be called *grandma*, but as the years passed, I came to find something wonderful in Sarah calling me Grandma. I'll always be Margy – but I'm proud to be *Grandma,* too.

First Baby, Then Toddler, Now Big Kid

The grandparent/grandchild relationship changes as the children grow older, as does your relationship with your children, their parents. All family members gain more experience in their interrelationships, and certain patterns become set. One condition that remains fairly universal, as grandchildren grow and make more of their own choices, is that the early love affair with their grandparents continues.

Grandchildren realize their grandparents tend to be less critical, more permissive and usually more admiring of them than their own parents. Some may feel that their grandparents understand them better than anyone else. Being the apple of a grandparent's eye builds healthy self-esteem and helps the child feel more confident at home and at school. Contemporary family life tends to be more stressful for children than their parents may realize. Unconditional and unconflicted love and acceptance from grandparents can be a wonderful luxury for children – or even a desperate necessity and coping mechanism.

Grandparents can unwittingly treat one grandchild more special than another. One child may have more of one grandparent's unique traits, talents, looks and mannerisms than the others, thereby triggering special attraction unintentionally. On the other hand, some grandparents feel they can't identify with adopted or step-grandchildren, and bonding becomes difficult if not impossible. A grandchild with emotional or physical problems may receive less grandparent attention because their needs can be overwhelming.

Grandparents can help avoid this predicament in several ways:

- If you are aware of favoritism, try to find the specialness of *each* grandchild and make a connection – if we look closely, there is always some facet of each grandchild that resonates with us. Look to hobbies, talents and interests you can encourage, such as sports, computers, music, homework help, travel, drawing, and animals.

- If you are unaware of any favoritism on your part, check in with your children and ask their opinion. You may be surprised! If they help you realize you *are* playing favorites, you can take steps toward making a positive change.

As your grandchildren grow older, you find they are increasingly better able to participate in fun activities, both with you and on their own. However, grandparents, even with the best intentions, tend to misjudge their grandchildren's capabilities and capacities. Sometimes they push them too fast.

I live in a ski community, and I'm a consultant for the local young children's ski instruction program. I often observe grandparents trying to place their grandchild in more advanced classes than is appropriate for the child's age and skill level. This makes it harder for the kids to keep up, and they become discouraged and frustrated. It also puts the program directors and instructors in a difficult position.

Conversely, in one situation I worked with grandparents who had considerable responsibility for their grandchildren ages 5 and 7 because both parents worked out of town. The grandparents infantilized the children to such an extent that in one case they were afraid to let the children stay without one of them present at a friend's birthday party. Our work together enabled them to better understand appropriate vs. inappropriate supervision responsibility for these grandchildren.

It is essential for conscientious grandparents to do a little research among parents of children the same age as their grandchildren, or with professionals who work with children of the same age, to gain a more realistic appreciation of the grandchild's capabilities and limitations. Remember, other grandparents are often as unsure about what is *age appropriate* as you are. If you are very active in your grandchildren's lives, you may want to attend some grandparenting, or if unavailable, parenting discussion groups. Shared information can be most valuable. It does no helpful service to children to push them too hard, or baby them too much.

Another important caveat: don't offer something you can't follow through on. This applies to day outings, longer trips, and sport or recreational activities. For example, it may work better to plan weekend dates more informally a week or so in advance, rather than committing to a season-long schedule of Saturday or Sunday activities that may be difficult to meet. Also, don't neglect your *own* physical health and realistic capabilities by planning to share an activity beyond your stamina and endurance.

How Your Grandchild Thinks

A young child's thinking can be very entertaining, but be sure not to laugh! According to Jean Piaget, between the ages of approximately 2 to 7 years, the child is in the *preoperational* stage of thinking. Preoperational children cannot distinguish between internal mental states and external reality. They display an inability to take another's point of view, and they show rigidity of thought.

An example of the concreteness of *preoperational* thinking occurred when our granddaughter Heather, age 3, joined us at a family event. A friend of ours asked Heather how she enjoyed being with her grandma and grandpa.

She looked puzzled, then replied, "My grandma and grandpa are in Tacoma."

"Who are you with right now?" asked our friend.

"Oh, I'm with Margy and Pops," Heather answered.

A 4-year-old boy at the school where I consult scolded me when I commented on his being in Pre-Kindergarten. "I'm not in Pre-Kindergarten," he stated. "I'm in Pre-K. Next year I'll be in Kindergarten."

Matt, age 4, and I played a game of *Chutes and Ladders* as part of our play therapy. When his mother came for him, he told her that he *bowed* Margery. I realized he meant to say we had *tied.*

Most young children have favorite story books they want you to read over and over to them. Instead of finding this annoying, it helps to understand and accept that young children crave the repetition of a familiar story because it gives them a feeling of mastery and control over events they can anticipate.

From ages 5 to 8 years the brain goes through one of its most dynamic and fascinating states of change. This is a period of rapid learning. However, a huge variability can occur among children of the exact same age. A gap or difference of as much as two years between children in maturation is not uncommon. Each child has unique strengths and weaknesses among physical, emotional, intellectual and social characteristics.

Did you know most 7-year-olds think a tall thin cup holds more water than a wide flat saucer dish, even when they watch you pour the same amount of liquid into each container? This is an example of *preoperational* thinking.

What we think of as mature reasoning does not occur until sometime after age 11 or 12, which is when the brain's frontal lobes finally become the boss of the cerebral cortex. Until then, thinking has certain limits as shown in the above examples.

Another result of age appropriate thinking is that it often sounds as if the young child is lying, when in fact he or she is merely having difficulty distinguishing reality from fantasy.

What about Santa Claus and the Easter Bunny? Do you approve of the way your grandchild's parents handle the fantasy/reality issues here? Is it the same way you handled it with *your* children, or different? Have they asked your advice?

What may seem like silly, inconsequential decisions regarding such matters have a tendency to grow way out of proportion and cause hard feelings between parents and grandparents. Such disagreements arise when some grandparents feel too strongly that the way *they* did it was right, and they are critical when their children handle belief issues in a different way.

We often overlook that the grandchild is the offspring of two people who bring very different childhood experience to their parenting.

- Be less judgmental, be more accepting, and avoid situations where you or your parenting child has to be right or wrong about decisions.
- Realize that the opportunity to express your views and concerns openly is valuable in itself, regardless of whether or not your opinions are embraced. But do try to be non-threatening and supportive in your comments.

Staying in Touch

Maintaining contact with grandchildren is very different depending on whether you all live in the same community, or you live in different parts of the country.

First, let's talk about staying in touch when grandchildren live in the same town. This can be wonderful – or, sometimes, *not* so wonderful.

- Let your children know you are seldom available at the spur of the moment, without notice, but with some advanced warning you can usually help them out. This can help avoid resentments.
- Take the initiative and schedule events, outings, overnights and trips that fit in with your schedule.
- Consider being the regular chauffeur for some specific activity. This helps out busy parents. I also find car time with my grandchildren to be wonderful visit time.
- Beware of making a commitment and then failing to follow through – our young concrete thinkers have little tolerance for that kind of disappointment.

Telephone calls are important. Grandparents usually initiate calls. Make them at times when the grandchildren are most likely to be available. I say likely, because kids today have busy schedules, too, and not much free hanging around time. It can be tough to hook your grandchild's attention over the phone, particularly when you have dragged her away from her favorite TV show.

Avoid questions that can be answered by a simple *yes* or *no* in your phone conversations. Ask questions that require more explanation. Ask them to describe a specific activity or event in their day, or give an opinion about something important to them. Call to share a joke or funny story with them – maybe they have a joke for you in return. Tell them about something that happened to you that made you think of them. Children love to be reminded of how important they are to you, and that they are in your thoughts. If you can harness their attention, they can share some meaningful thoughts with you and you can all enjoy a great phone visit.

Why not fax grandchildren a fun note? Kids love to be part of the communication network, and fax machines are standard equipment in many homes. E-mail is also a great, inexpensive way to stay in touch for older grandchildren. Chances are they are probably already using e-mail themselves.

On a more traditional note, we send our grandchildren a little money for Valentine's Day, which we encourage them to spend on something fun or sweet, and then call us and tell us how they spent the money. It is also important to remember that young children may be reluctant to pick up the telephone to call you, or to ask mother to help them call you, even when you are in their thoughts.

Staying in Touch Out of Town

My friend Linda, who had weekly lunches with her grandchild (Chapter 4), moved away from the town where her children and grandchild lived. Her experience is illuminating.

"The change from living close to my grandchildren to living far away, interestingly enough, has changed our bond. I now work harder at staying connected, and I think our relationship is better," Linda said. During a recent visit back home, Linda and her 3-year-old grandchild Chris got into a discussion of how trees lose their leaves in autumn and the beauty of the fall colors. When Linda returned to her new home in Colorado, she took photographs of the fall colors and sent some exceptional leaves to Chris. Linda admits this certainly takes more effort on her part, but it's important – to her and to Chris. She makes a very conscious effort to stay connected. "I am always searching for ways to make a strong impression," she says.

An 8-year-old girl I know treasures a cassette tape her grandmother made for her filled with songs and stories of the South. Grandmother wanted to share her Southern heritage with her granddaughter. The child plays the tape at night to help her fall asleep. A lovely story. Other ways of staying in touch:

- Send your grandchild brief, interesting and entertaining cassette tapes you make for them about your life which your grandchildren can treasure as a personal remembrance now, and long after you are gone. Combine stories, songs, music, sounds. This also provides cherished family history and legacy that teach the child about where he comes from and where he belongs.
- Take photographs and assemble the best shots into photo albums. Our visiting grandchildren spend hours enjoying these pictures of themselves and other family members and friends at different ages and times.

Visits

Visits can be arranged in all sorts of ways and there are merits in all the variations – except when the visit is too short or lasts too long! Frequently, grandparents who live far away desire a long visit, especially if they seldom have the pleasure of *spoiling* their grandchildren, putting them to bed, fussing over a hairdo, or telling stories about the days when Mommy and Daddy were little.

Despite their wishes, shorter visits usually work better for all three generations. Small children traveling away from home become homesick, even though they are with loving grandparents. Parents may resent the difference in methods their parents use over a long visit, and grandparents, in spite of themselves, are apt to find the constant care of active children more time and energy consuming than they anticipated.

When children visit, we have no control over the fantasies that give rise to the feelings of homesickness they may experience. We once drove with our 8-year-old grandson from Illinois to Colorado. The first night out, he became very teary and needed to talk to his parents. Unfortunately, when we called home his parents were out for the evening. We left a message for them to call us when they returned home, regardless of the time. Our grandson was hard to comfort, but finally he fell asleep.

We were all sound asleep in our motel room when his parents called. We woke our grandson, and after only a word or two, he fell into a relaxed sleep. A day later, as we pointed out wonderful wildlife along our drive, his tears again erupted unexpectedly. This necessitated another phone call home – and again the sound of his parents' voice soothed and calmed him.

In retrospect, a portable tape player with a cassette tape of his parents' voices which he could listen to whenever he wanted or needed might have eased the separation. I usually recommend that parents send their children with a number of family pictures when they take trips away from home. I now suggest an audiotape of their family's familiar voices. This is not only for the grandparents' convenience – it also puts parents' minds at ease knowing their children are less likely to experience some of the anxiety of homesickness. A videotape of a family holiday or birthday can similarly provide show-and-tell during an extended visit away from home, and an accessible reminder of familiar faces.

A few thoughts about homesickness:

- You are fortunate when your grandchild can confess to feeling homesick and you can intervene.
- Homesickness is normal, and you should not feel like *bad* grandparents because the child is having a hard time separating from home and parents.
- Avoid the temptation to distract the child rather than to help him work through his feelings. Try talking about what might be happening at home at this particular hour and what he misses most. Find out when he started worrying about this trip. Discuss what stories he can tell everyone when he returns home. Assure him he can call home whenever he wants. Make sure the child has the parents' phone number written down.
- When a child knows you understand how he feels and that you accept his feelings, and when you give him permission to call home whenever he likes, he usually feels comforted to the point that a call is less necessary, and you can all move on and enjoy the rest of your visit together.

Consider the special benefits of having a single grandchild visit at a time. One child often acts entirely different alone with his grandparents. The presence of siblings may simply extend their normal quarreling to their grandparents' home. You can share more quality time on interests and activities in which the single grandchild is the focus and sole beneficiary of all your attention. This makes the visit extra-special for them. A visit of cousins of similar age who are otherwise usually unable to spend time together can also be wonderful – for you as well as for them.

No matter how delightful the visit, I unabashedly endorse my friend's limerick:

"I've seen the lights of Paris,
I've seen the lights of Rome;
But nothing is more beautiful
Than the lights of the car
That takes my grandkids home."

This same friend and his wife take their children and grandchildren on many trips as their guests, but they refuse to pay for their meals because they object to "the waste of food by their grandchildren." Concerns about food waste at restaurants are valid, but there are more constructive solutions. Dine at less expensive family restaurants, insist that young children order only from the children's menu, and avoid between-meal snacks. Uneaten restaurant leftovers can be taken home to replace snack foods.

In a larger sense, my friend is also saying something very significant and noteworthy about avoiding conflicts that can spoil the trip for everyone. This approach is important for all grandparents. Protect yourself from controversial issues whenever possible so you do not become *the ogre.* The most important ingredient of generational get-togethers is compatibility. Identify those trivial matters that can spoil your good time together, and find ways to handle or resolve them in advance.

The length of visits is useful to consider, too. The trend in vacation travel has shifted from one long vacation each year to travelers choosing more frequent trips of shorter duration. When financially possible, this option works well for families, too. Keeping trips shorter but more often usually insures that everyone gets along well for the length of the visit and makes the most of the time together.

Families also tend to fall into visitation patterns: "We always visit our out-of-state grandchildren for a week every summer." You can vary visits throughout the year to take advantage of seasonal activities and climate, other school holidays, and alternate visits between the grandparents' home, the parents' home, and a *neutral* third location. But be aware that behavioral and authority roles may change markedly depending on where the visit takes place.

Taking Trips Together

The options for extended family travel together are practically limitless. An entire segment of the travel industry has developed around family travel. Your travel agent can offer you a variety of resources.

Since retiring, John and Carolyn enjoy frequent travel in their motor home. They recently rented a second motor home for their son and his family, and they all toured the Northwest together with great success, mixing family members among the two vehicles.

In our family, we have successfully arranged a special trip with each of our four children and their families. We took care to plan each trip around that particular family's special interests and the ages of their children. As grandparents, Bob and I have found this a very rewarding way for all of us to have fun together, to interact and to really get to know and enjoy each other, and to accept and appreciate the differences between each of our four families. Here are some ideas:

- Plan far enough into the future so that all family members can attend without serious schedule conflicts.
- Make sure the trip does not put undue strain on any family's budget – there are a wide range of travel options available to different budget travelers.
- Extended family travel should take every family member's age, stamina, physical condition, recreational and cultural interests into consideration.
- Allow time and space for all family members to spend time together – and time apart resting, relaxing and enjoying personal interests.

- Extended family travel may be as exotic as viewing wildlife in Costa Rican rainforests – or as simple as a city visit to zoos, parks, museums and movie theaters.

The Essence of Grandparenting

In many respects, we all wish we could be the grandparents Margaret, a mother of three children, describes in this vignette about the essence of grandparenting.

Every Thanksgiving, the eight adult children of John and Jane Johnson, their spouses and children are invited to join the Johnsons for the holiday weekend at their retirement community in Arizona. John and Jane have been married 52 years, and Margaret describes them as wonderful people – low-key, undemanding and accepting.

The visiting families either stay with the Johnsons at their home, or at a hotel nearby. The Johnsons help individual families with the expense of the trip in a very private way if the cost is too great a stretch for their finances. When the trip is in the early planning stage, one of the daughters will call around the country to make sure *all* families will attend. There are other visits between grandparents and various families throughout the year, but this is *the* all-important annual get- together when the Oregon, California and Colorado families all travel to Arizona. This holiday has become a tradition, and it keeps the family together and intact. No one would dream of missing it.

The excitement of the visit increases for the kids as they grow older and can stay together as a *cousins* group. Because of the easy-going, undemanding behavior of the grandparents, the four-day visit is a treat for all 16 adults and 20 children ranging in age from 2 to 26 years.

Margaret knows all grandparents are different. Many of her friends don't think much of their in-laws, but she thinks hers are great, and she loves talking about them. One of the special qualities about these grandparents is how attentive they are to every family. As an example, Margaret told about a serious medical problem that arose in her family. The grandparents not only came out to help, but they also researched the medical interventions and procedures to become more knowledgeable and to offer valuable added input and support. Since then, John has died and Jane is now on her own. She remains a wonderful woman that Margaret really admires and hopes to emulate as a mother and grandmother.

Another story of caring and commitment, told to me this time by a grandmother, helps describe what I call *the essence of grandparenting.*

Martha is a spry 75-year-old widow. Her son, daughter-in-law and 8-year-old Jesse live in the same community. For a number of family reasons, Martha and her husband (until his death when Jesse was age 5) have cared for Jesse for extended periods since Jesse's birth. Being a nurturer comes naturally to Martha. Whenever she is asked and is available, she continues to take Jesse into her home. She sees her home as an additional home for Jesse, one that he has come to rely and depend upon. It's as simple as that.

Martha's advice to other grandparents is, "Too much love never hurts." She tries her best to adopt Jesse's parents' values, and have his life in her home be as similar as possible to his parents' home. Now that he is older, she finds the major problem with his staying with her is that none of his playmates live nearby, and he misses that.

While teenagers and grandparents are somewhat beyond the range of this survival guide, they need to be mentioned when we talk about *the essence of grandparenting.* As I work with adolescents in a therapeutic situation, and as they share details of their lives, it is not uncommon to hear about their fondness for their grandparents. While critical of parents, teachers and authority figures, grandparents are usually described as their advocates, as comfortable, caring sources of support. The unconditional love they feel from their grandparents may be what sustains them when they are rebelling against the world around them. Grandparents, your grandchildren may never tell you this, but take it from me: there really is something special about your relationship with your adolescent grandchildren. Don't give up on them, and don't let them down!

Grandparents Dying

Life is not forever, and despite increased longevity and medical advances, children are likely to experience the failing and death of one or more of their grandparents during their childhood. The mourning and grieving process is discussed further in Chapter 7.

What is most important here is that a grandparent's death is frequently a child's first experience with the mysteries of life and death. Often the child is not told that a sick grandparent is dying in the mistaken belief that "they are too young to understand." No child should be shielded from the knowledge that a beloved grandparent is dying. Doing so can make it much more difficult and traumatic for a child to deal with their loss. Here are some suggestions:

- If for some reason the parents are not handling this situation well, the healthy grandparent should take responsibility for explaining their spouse's condition to the grandchildren.
- These facts can be explained in simple terms – and repeated as needed. The unpleasant facts that children first ignore or deny are often absorbed if repeated in different ways at appropriate times.
- If the impending death and the cause is not made clear to children, they are left with their own very active imaginations to conjure up all sorts of reasons for their grandparent's sudden departure. We know that children under the age of 10 view the world as revolving around them. So if a grandparent leaves, particularly without saying goodbye, the child may feel he has done something very bad to precipitate their departure.

- The often common practice of excluding the child from the dying process may add to their feelings of guilt. In the child's mind, exclusion can be punishment for somehow *killing* grandma or grandpa.
- Such guilt can be a very destructive force in the child's life. As with most other matters discussed in this book, openness, honesty and frankness are always the best policy.
- Encourage children to ask the questions weighing most on their minds, and answer as honestly as possible. They will often indicate very clearly their comfort level with the subject, and you can proceed from there.

I treated Gail, a 9-year-old girl who had been appropriately potty trained, but had somehow regressed to involuntarily defecating in her pants. The parents were naturally beside themselves with shame and anger. They had tried everything – medical interventions, scolding, tolerating, punishing. Nothing worked.

My first step in a child's psychological evaluation is always to obtain a complete developmental history from the parents. In this case, I learned from the parents that Gail had been a healthy, happy baby. When she was age 4, her mother went back to work full time and Gail's maternal grandmother moved into the house. Grandmother became an integral part of her life, playing a significant role in child care while mother worked, and even when Mom and Dad were home. Gail described how close she was with her grandmother and how much she missed her even now, years later.

The parents explained that Grandmother had suddenly become sick, went to the hospital, and unexpectedly died a few days later. When I asked about Gail's involvement at that time, her parents said everything happened so fast Gail never saw her grandmother at the hospital, and she stayed with neighbors during the funeral.

The parents never realized that Gail's involuntary defecation problem started shortly after her grandmother's death until we explored this part of her history. Gail's case is a perfect example of unhealthy signs of coping with loss. As we worked together in therapy, talking, drawing and playing, it became clear that Gail never really understood what had happened to her beloved grandmother and had not been given a safe, approved outlet for her sadness and grief about her grandmother's death.

We worked through her feelings about this in our treatment sessions. Gail became less regressed, used the toilet properly and was shortly able to get back on the age appropriate developmental track.

When you are concerned about how your grandchild is handling her loss, if you observe some of these behaviors it is likely the child is having trouble coping with the loss:

- Looks sad all the time.
- Keeps up a hectic pace and cannot relax.
- Takes little interest in clothing or appearance.
- Seems tired and unable to sleep normally.
- Has trouble falling asleep.
- Has bad dreams.
- Avoids social activities and prefers to be alone.
- Appears indifferent to school and hobbies previously enjoyed.
- Eating habits change.

If these behaviors persist for many months following the death, the family should consider seeking professional counseling for their child.

Funeral attendance is another troubling issue for families. I believe children should be told what is happening and have the details of a funeral explained to them, and then the family should accept their preference of whether or not they want to attend without exerting undue influence one way or the other. The most important point is that they should not be excluded if they want to participate or attend.

Parents and surviving grandparents can help grieving grandchildren cope with their loss in many ways.

- Don't avoid talking about the deceased because it is too painful. Encourage talk and telling stories, recounting wonderful memories. This helps keep the departed grandparent alive in the child's memory.
- Suggest or encourage a healthy outlet for the child to help process and express feelings – perhaps a journal, photo collage or scrapbook about their grandparent, including episodes up to and including their death.
- Engage in some productive activity the grandchild and grandparent enjoyed together – finish an unfinished project, assemble a photo album, help organize belongings.
- Give the child an appropriate keepsake they can hold and carry, but one that will not cause upset, anger or resentment if it is lost. This could be a familiar article of clothing, jewelry, a pocket knife, hat, belt or photo. Let the child choose the appropriate item.
- Help the child understand that their feelings are OK – anger, fear, sadness, even what may appear to be inappropriate levity, hysteria or withdrawal. Help them experience these feelings and work through them to a renewed place of normalcy.

Alzheimer's Disease

Alzheimer's Disease (AD) will be one of the most painful, frustrating and costly health problems of the next century. AD is a progressive, irreversible brain disorder that strikes more frequently with advancing age. Symptoms include memory loss, confusion, impaired judgment, personality changes and loss of language skills. In later stages of the illness, patients no longer recognize friends and relatives and become increasingly dependent on others for care and assistance in performing the most routine tasks. Brain activity diminishes until the patient lapses into a coma and dies. The course of the disease typically averages seven or eight years from the time symptoms first appear.

Over four million American adults have AD, presently af–fecting one in ten families in the U.S. If this trend continues, 13 million Americans will be over age 85 in the year 2040, and nearly half of them, as well as younger people, will be suffering from this disorder.

It is really hard for kids to experience this gradual deterioration of a grandparent from AD. Their wonderful friend and confidant gradually regresses and becomes increasingly childlike and undependable. This illness and its terrible process must be explained. Children can handle reality articulated to them much better than avoidance, vagueness or denial. The truth, told in age appropriate ways, is always best for a child's mental health.

Most states have regional and local chapters of the Alzheimer's Association which can provide excellent resource material and information for families coping with Alzheimer's. Children may react with emotions ranging from fear and anger to shame and disgust. Educational materials can help them develop more healthy coping mechanisms to make the best of a difficult situation for everyone involved.

A woman came to see me with deep concerns about what her husband's Alzheimer's illness was doing to her and to her relationship with her children and grandchildren. Burt lived at home with her. She could not leave him alone because he might light the stove and forget to turn it off, or wander outside the house and become lost. She had become his constant watchdog, and she seldom experienced any relief from this 24-hour responsibility.

Because Burt did not yet act noticeably *out of touch* during brief contacts, she felt she was not receiving the support from her children she needed. In addition, she had given up all her activities to care for Burt. Her grandchildren missed her and didn't understand. They were losing both grandfather *and* grandmother. This woman's issues were very real. I referred her to a newly-formed support group in our area for people dealing with Alzheimer's. There she was able to meet and talk with knowledgeable people experiencing similar issues who could share strategies and methods for coping with this debilitating illness of a family member.

Involvement vs. Intrusion

There is a fine line between being *involved* in your children and grandchildren's behavior, and *intruding*. When Betsy, a grandmother, shared her experience with me, I found her behavior intrusive. In the midst of an argument with her daughter during a family visit at Christmas, she snapped at her granddaughter to sit up straight at the table.

Useful boundaries help define the difference. As grandparents, it should *not* be our role to criticize the children regarding behavior that does not affect us, but if behavior *does* affect us we should feel free to say something about it. One year when my extended family came to visit, I found myself disappointed when the older grandchildren didn't spontaneously pitch in to help with kitchen chores. Yet when I spoke up and requested their help, the response was immediate and enthusiastic. I involve myself in their behavior because it affects me. Of course, all interventions should be kind and appropriate. My reaction must have impressed them, because they have been extremely helpful during subsequent visits.

Another interesting vignette illustrates this point. Michael, now an adult, shared this significant childhood memory with me. His family enjoyed a wonderful tradition of weekly dinners at his grandparents' home. At one meal, Michael, then about age 8, accidentally knocked over a glass of water at the dinner table. His father reached over and smacked Michael's hand for behavior that upset the family dinner. Without missing a beat, Michael's grandfather reached over and smacked his *son's* hand – Michael's father. No words were exchanged, but everyone understood the message: "This is my house, my table, my rules. That was an accident, and you overreacted." Michael recalls his father never smacked his hand again – and he was more careful with the water glass in the future. The grandfather's admirable response was involved but unintrusive.

These examples all relate to discipline episodes. How do we determine when to intervene and not to? When the behavior does not directly affect us, such as how the child sits at the table, it is best to leave the discipline to the parents and not intrude.

This raises the issue of how much to interfere when you see *the children* bringing up the grandchildren in ways you disapprove. There are no easy answers, but some solutions may be found through your relationship with your adult children. It is always best to address parenting criticism to your blood relative rather than your in-law.

The following misunderstanding occurred because there had not been enough communication prior to the family visit. Consider how you might have dealt with this situation. Carol and Bob arrived for a summer visit with their son, daughter-in-law and their three children. Apparently the daughter-in-law assumed the grandparents wanted to be with the children all day, so she kept them home from day camp. The parents went off to work, and Carol and Bob were left in charge of the children. Carol and Bob had expected their trip to be both a vacation for themselves and a visit with family. They complained about the child care role they found themselves thrust into.

My recommendation here: accept the situation that developed this time, but next time remember to make your wishes clearer before the visit begins. Attempting to change the routine during a visit may lead to hard feelings. Plan ahead by inquiring about the family routine *before* your visit, and express your intentions in advance.

Despite the trouble it takes or the tension it causes, getting together and staying involved with the grandchild is more than worth it; it is *urgent* these days, according to T. Berry Brazelton, world-renowned pediatrician, neonatal researcher, best-selling author and champion of the family.

In his 1989 book, *Families: Crisis and Caring*, Brazelton says, "As a grandparent, you may serve many purposes for a child which no parent can fulfill. You can offer comfort, family love, experience, hugs, and a sense of strength and stability for each member of the family." Brazelton adds that the nuclear family of the '90s is a lonely one. When grandparents are available to pass on the family's history and beliefs, the child learns there is more to family life than surviving day to day.

From my own practice as a child psychotherapist, I would add that kids today are so often on their own from such an early age that being *the apple of their grandparents' eye* is a much-needed self-esteem boost. Sometimes the most significant feature of my therapeutic work with children is the importance they attach to their weekly hour with me during which they are my prime focus and enjoy my complete attention and acceptance of whatever they have to show me or tell me.

Special Grandparent Events

In recent years, my husband and I receive invitations to Grandparents Day at the various schools, pre-schools and religious institutions our grandchildren attend. The first invitation we received was to visit our grandson's Sunday School class. He lived in the same community as we did, so it was easy to participate.

My husband and I mistakenly thought this event was unimportant, but we reluctantly attended. The children were studying their heritage, so we as grandparents fit right into their studies. Being there turned out to be a wonderful experience for us. It was obviously very meaningful for the fourth grade kids as well to have their grandparents participate in their class routine and in some special activities that involved us. The teacher sensitively arranged alternatives for children who did not have available grandparents; they were encouraged to bring a special adult friend. Attendance at these events sends an important message to children: *My grandparents are really interested in what I do.*

Arthur Kornhaber, a child psychiatrist, grandparent and founder of the Foundation for Grandparenting, launched a special camp for grandparents and grandchildren in 1985. They spend a week together at the camp site, the Sagamore Institute in the Andirondack Mountains of New York State. A grandfather who attended the camp with his 7-year-old grandson said, "This is a place where I can hang out with Josh. I keep this for myself and my grandson." Kornhaber says, "Grandparents can be the home plate, the safe, constant place for the child."

While camp may not be the answer for all grandparent/ grandchild groups, the idea of establishing special activities together is valuable. Other suggestions:

- Find a special skill or hobby to share with your grandchild, whether you live close by or during long distance visits, or by phone, fax, e-mail or ordinary mail.
- Become a helper at school, whether it is your grandchild's school or another school nearby. Your efforts will be greatly appreciated – and you will discover unexpected rewards, too. The principal of our local elementary school recently posted a notice in the Senior Services Monthly Bulletin: "Seniors to be 'adopted' by the school for interaction of all kinds."
- Arrange your *own* Grandparent/Grandchild party or Grand Persons Day.
- The Kohl Children's Museum in Wilmette, Illinois offers a special Monday Afternoon Club for grandparents and their grandchildren. Are there similar opportunities in your community?

- Be creative and innovative in planning your special activities.

Remember: the individual, undivided attention you give as a grandparent is very valuable and cannot be substituted or replaced easily.

Grandparents or *grand people* of grandparent age who want to do more can fill a much-needed spot in a Foster Grandparent Program. This national program is available in many communities in the United States where it is locally funded and administered.

I am most familiar with the program in Grand Junction, Colorado. Men and women must be over 60 years of age, in good health, and love to share time and activities with children. They must be able to serve 10 to 20 hours a week. Lower income participants are paid a stipend; otherwise the program is voluntary.

Foster Grandparent volunteers share their lifetime of experience and their boundless warmth and patience with physically, mentally and emotionally disabled children, abused and neglected children, and troubled youth. Program directors claim the grandparent volunteers truly change these lives forever with a touch of love.

Older Americans and youngsters are two groups in need; the Foster Grandparent Program brings them together. According to Rachel Hilliard, "Being a foster grandparent is the most rewarding thing I have ever done." Art Bungart says, "Being a foster grandparent keeps you mentally alert. It's fun to go fishing by yourself, but that gets stale."

Play and Toys

Giving gifts is an important part of being a grandparent. It can be overwhelming to choose the right gift. A gift of clothing is not too hard. Mom is usually available to help out with size and style. Or you may enjoy taking the grandchildren shopping with you.

When the gift is toys, the choice becomes more difficult. Today, simply walking into a toy store can be intimidating. Dolls do everything from tan in the sun to simulate pregnancy. Armies of action figures brandish ferocious names and weapons. A whole new world of electronic games and computers has appeared overnight.

As mentioned in Chapter 4, it may be easier to avoid the mega-stores and find a local toy store with a knowledgeable, enthusiastic salesperson who is willing to answer questions. Ask to see the toy out of its box and have it demonstrated. Often there is a special department with a trained sales staff to help grandparents select that special gift. Promises Kept, a mail-order company in Minneapolis, devotes a section of its catalog exclusively to quality toys for grandchildren. According to a study by the Data Group of Plymouth Meeting, PA, the average set of grandparents spends a whopping *$819 per year* buying toys and gifts for their grandkids.

From my own experience, you can seldom go wrong with Fisher Price and Tonka toys for children up to 6 years of age. These toys are safe and durable. It is always a good idea to read the directions and labels carefully.

Gift-giving time can create stressful dilemnas for grandparents. Do we give gifts we think will develop our grandchildren's physical, intellectual and social skills? Do we follow our children's wishes and buy them items on their wish list – sometimes good choices, sometimes not! How do we handle those heavily advertised and promoted TV toys they want and we dislike?

There are no easy answers, but parents can help involve grandparents in gift-giving by offering them suggestions, making specific requests, or simply hoping they make appropriate choices. These issues concern most families and become a commonly discussed topic at holiday and birthday time between parents and grandparents.

The best approach is a combination of discussion and persuasion. Children need to feel their wishes are being heard and responded to, but often parents can help their children adapt their wishes in a direction parents think is more appropriate.

The toys our grandchildren use play a significant role in their physical, emotional and intellectual development, as we discussed in the previous chapter. In contemporary society, as children grow older so much of their non-school time is spent in structured activities that they have too little time left to play. Yet they continue to need the opportunity to express their ideas and emotions through play.

Through play, the 5 to 10-year-old child experiences the following:

- Learns about the external world.
- Figures out how things work.
- Establishes individual patterns of approaching experiences and problem- solving.
- Builds strength and control of their bodies.
- Practices skills.
- Learns to talk and share ideas.
- Develops and expresses imagination and creativity.
- Increases the ability to concentrate.
- Gains the opportunity to play out feelings and master emotions which would otherwise overwhelm them.

For more specific suggestions, please refer to the chart *What are some good toys and play materials for young children?*

Grandparents can be an important advocate for this kind of play experience in the toys and games they select for their grandchildren.

What are some good toys and play materials for young children?

All ages are approximate. Most suggestions for younger children are also appropriate for older children.

	2-year-olds and young 3's	Older 3's and 4-year-olds	5- and 6-year-olds
Sensory materials	Water and sand toys: cups, shovels Modeling dough Sound-matching games Bells, wood block, triangle, drum Texture matching games, feel box	Water toys: measuring cups, egg beaters Sand toys: muffin tins, vehicles Xylophone, maracas, tambourine Potter's clay	Water toys: food coloring, pumps, funnels Sand toys: containers, utensils Harmonica, kazoo, guitar, recorder Tools for working with clay
Active play equipment	Low climber Canvas swing Wagon, cart, or wheelbarrow Large rubber balls Low 3-wheeled, steerable vehicle with pedals	Larger 3-wheeled riding vehicle, roller skates Climbing structure, rope or tire swing, plastic bats and balls, various sized rubber balls Balance board, planks, boxes, old tires, bowling pins, ring toss, bean bags and target	Bicycle Outdoor games: bocce, tetherball, shuffleboard, jump rope, Frisbee
Construction materials	Unit blocks and accessories: animals, people, simple wood cars and trucks Interlocking construction set with large pieces. Wood train and track set. Hammer (13 oz. steel shanked), soft wood, roofing nails, nailing block	More unit blocks, shapes, and accessories Table blocks Realistic model vehicles Construction set with smaller pieces Woodworking bench, saw, sandpaper, nails	More unit blocks,s shape, and accessories Props for roads, towns Hollow blocks Brace and bits, screwdrivers, screws, metric measure, accessories
Manipulative toys	Wooden puzzles with 4-20 large pieces Pegboards Big beads or spools to string Sewing cards Stacking toys Picture lotto, picture dominoes	Puzzles, pegboard, small beads to string, parquetry blocks Small objects to sort, marbles Magnifying glass Simple card or board games Flannel board with pictures, letters, sturdy letters and numbers	More complex puzzles Dominoes More difficult board and card games Yarn, big needles, mesh fabric, weaving materials Magnets, balances Attribute blocks
Dolls and dramatic play	Washable dolls with a few clothes, doll bed Child-sized table and chairs Dishes, pots and pans Dress-up clothes: hats, shoes, shirts Hand puppets Shopping cart	Dolls and accessories Doll carriage Child-sized stove or sink More dress-up clothes Play food, cardboard cartons Airport, doll house, or other settings with accessories Finger or stick puppets	Cash register, play money, accessories, or props for other dramatic play settings: gas station, construction, office Typewriter
Books and recordings	Clear picture books, stories, and poems about things children know Records or tapes of classical music, folk music or children's songs	Simple science books More detailed picture and story books Sturdy record or tape player Recordings of wider variety of music Book and recording sets	Books on cultures Stories with chapters Favorite stories children can read Children's recipe books
Art materials	Wide-tip watercolor markers Large sheets of paper, easel Finger or tempura paint, 1/2" brushes Blunt-nose scissors White glue	Easel, narrower brushes Thick crayons, chalk Paste, tape with dispenser Collage materials	Watercolors, smaller paper, stapler, hole puncher Chalkboard Oil crayons, paint crayons, charcoal Simple camera, film

(Reprinted with permission from *Young Children*, November 1984, published by the National Association for the Education of Young Children.)

There is nothing wrong with giving a girl a truck or a boy a doll. In a 1992 revised edition of Dr. Benjamin Spock's landmark text, *Baby & Child Care*, the doctor retracted his 27-year-old advice about sex appropriate toys and wrote, "I think it is normal for little boys to want to play with dolls and for little girls to want to play with toy cars, and it is quite all right to let them have them. A boy's desire to play with dolls is parental rather than effeminate, and should help him be a good father."

Play is important, and a red flag goes up in my mind when a child referred to me for psychological evaluation ignores all the toys in my office. If the child sees me for subsequent appointments and continues to ignore my toys, I become concerned about what is going on with that child psychologically. Each child is different and I hesitate to generalize, but *play avoidance* is often a sign of pathology.

If the child does not play with toys in my office, it is likely he does not play outside my office. I ask myself, "What is inhibiting him from play? Is he afraid of something? Has a traumatic experience halted his development?" For children who don't seem to know how to interact in my playroom, I use a tape recorder as a communication device. I am intrigued by how much more willing many children are to talk about what is really bothering them when they are play-acting at being interviewed or being a guest on a talk show.

Donning my grandparent hat now, I wish to share some specific toys and play opportunities that have proved successful with our family:

- Cardboard boxes from large appliances can become wonderful creative outlets for a young child's imagination. We save all large cardboard containers for the kids.
- For girls and sometimes boys, ages 3 to 10, visit a fabric store and select a number of two-yard cuttings of chiffon fabric in wild colors. The imagination potential is unlimited from dress-ups to animal leashes.

- Playing with cards intrigues kids of all ages – from sorting by number, color, and building card houses to actually playing card games.
- My grandchildren from age 5 years up loved to play with the *Scrabble* game, adapting the play with letters to their particular cognitive development.
- Another useful resource in being prepared for visiting grandchildren is to have spare batteries or a battery recharger available.
- Children always want to play with the computer and watch videotapes, but I prefer to encourage more active, imaginative and cognitive play.
- I keep the same grandchildren toys available year after year. Recently Bob suggested getting rid of a few toys that we have had a long time. My answer was no, the visiting grandchildren expect certain toys to be here and I believe the continuity is important. But that doesn't mean we can't add to the supply.
- Never keep broken toys around. If they break, get rid of them. Broken toys can make some children quite anxious in identifying the broken toy with themselves.
- Choose toys *you* will enjoy playing with the grandkids.

As grandparents, we have more free time to play with kids than do most adults in their homes. Remember, play is their most important work. Play is also a significant way for the child to learn about his or her world.

Are You Good Grandparents? How *Good* is Good?

- Your son-in-law calls and wants to take your daughter with him on a business trip next week. Can you sit with the grandkids? Your choices are to: (a) drop everything and help out; (b) offer to pay for a babysitter; or (c) say no, that if you sit for them you will have to sit for all the kids, and you don't want to do that.

- Your 8-year-old grandson Willie calls. He wants to spend the night – can he come? Willy is a hellion, and his endless energy exhausts you. What do you say? Yes or no?
- Your son Frank calls. Tonight he came home to a wife in tears because you told her that their daughter Erin was spoiled. Why did you do that? What right do you have to interfere with his family? Do you: (a) tell him Erin *is* spoiled and her parents better do something about it; (b) apologize and admit you may have spoken out of turn; or (c) offer to pay for counseling for the whole family?
- It's the weekend and no one calls you. Do you scold them? Are you becoming too self-centered to remember how busy they are? Or maybe you need to develop more interests of your own.
- Margo, your daughter-in-law, calls. "Your son Henry is a lousy father," she says. He never helps with the kids, and with her job she can't do it all herself. She's thinking about asking for a divorce. Do you: (a) tell her how wonderful your son is and all the things he does do for the family; (b) tell her you will talk with Henry; or (c) explain that it sounds like a matter between the two of them and you prefer not to get involved?

Each reader may have an entirely different approach to these five dilemmas. That's OK. We can't be the perfect grandparents – but we can be *good enough*.

Recommendations

- Enjoy your 3 to 10-year-olds now, because when your grandchildren enter early adolescence and on through the adolescent years, they become so busy with their own lives that it is likely they will be much less involved with you.

- Try not to show favoritism among your grandchildren. Children are highly attuned to the adults they are close to and are very sensitive to unspoken attitudes and behavior.
- Try to keep up with what life is like for your grandchildren today – very different, for better and for worse, from how things were when you raised your children. To keep current, you may want to attend some family movies, read popular culture magazines like *TV Guide* and *Entertainment Weekly*, help at school, eat at McDonald's, visit the local mall or playground.
- Avoid telling your adult children *how to do it;* instead listen and be available when they ask your advice.
- If you are asked to help out, baby-sit, whatever, do it if it works for you, but don't be a martyr and don't do what is uncomfortable for you because then no one will be happy.
- Try not to be overprotective or over-permissive when the children are in your care – try to support the lifestyle and values their parents have established.
- Don't compare one child's family with another because each family does things differently, and you need to be the one that adapts.
- It is likely that you will enjoy your grandchildren at one age better than another age.
- Each of us gets along better with a certain age group of children – so don't be too hard on yourself if the endearing grandchild of last year is less endearing this year. It will probably be different again next year.
- *Enjoy* your grandchildren!

Reading List for Adults
Ames, Louise Bates, and Ilg. *Your Three Year Old.* Delacorte Press, 1993.
Ames, Louise Bates, and Ilg. *Your Four Year Old.* Delacorte Press, 1994.

Ames, Louise Bates, and Ilg. *Your Five Year Old*. Delacorte Press, 1995.

Ames, Louise Bates, and Ilg. *Your Six Year Old*. Delacorte Press, 1994.

Ames, Louise Bates, and Haber. *Your Seven Year Old*. Delta, 1993.

Ames, Louise Bates, and Ilg. *Your Eight Year Old*. Delacorte Press, 1994.

Ames, Louise Bates, and Ilg. *Your Nine Year Old* Delta, 1994.

Brazelton, T. Berry. *Touchpoints: Your Child's Emotional and Behavioral Development*. Addison-Wesley, 1992.

Doka, Kenneth J., editor. *Children Mourning, Mourning Children*. Hemisphere Pub., 1995.

Gardner, Howard. *Frames of Mind – The Theory of Multiple Intelligences*. New York: Basic Books, 1993.

Hallowell, Edward M., and John J. Ratey. *Driven to Distraction: Recognizing and Coping with Attention Deficit Disorder from Childhood through Adulthood*. Simon and Schuster, 1995.

Healy, Jane M. *Endangered Mind – Why Children Don't Think and What We Can Do About It*. Touchstone Books, 1991.

Healy, Jane M. *Your Child's Growing Mind – A Parents Guide to Learning From Birth to Adolescence*. New York: Doubleday and Co., 1987.

Oppenheim, Joanne, and Stephanie Oppenheim. *The Best Toys, Books, Videos & Software for Kids 1997: 1000+ Kid-Tested Classic and New Products for Ages 0-10*. Prima Publishing, 1996.

Spock, Benjamin, and Michael B. Rothenberg. *Baby and Child Care*. New York: Pocket Books, 1992. Fully revised and updated for the '90s.

Wyse, Lois. *Funny, You Don't Look Like A Grandmother*. Avon Books, 1991.

Reading List For Children

Buckley, Helen. *Grandmother and I*. Lothrop, Lee & Shepard, 1994.

Buckley, Helen. *Grandfather and I*. Lothrop, Lee & Shepard, 1994.

Fassler, Joan. *My Grandpa Died Today.* New York: Human Science Press, 1983.

Hazen, Barbara. *Why Did Grandpa Die? A Book About Death.* New York: Goldencraft, 1985.

Saint-Exupery, Antoine. *The Little Prince.* GK Hall & Co., 1995.

Sendak, Maurice. *Pierre – A Cautionary Tale.* Trophy Press, 1991. Lovely book with charming illustrations. Ages 3 to 6 years.

Shaw, Eve. *Grandmother's Alphabet.* Pfeifer-Hamilton, 1996. A picture book featuring young, energetic career grandmothers. Ages 5 and under.

SECTION TWO

Grandparenting in Today's Families

6

Working Mothers and Child Care

There was a child went forth every day
And the first object he looked upon,
That object he became.
– Walt Whitman

While most of us believe in the ideal of full-time mothering, working mothers and child care are a necessity in many families today. The archetypal nuclear family of the '50s (working husband and stay-at-home wife) has given way to a host of customized child-care arrangements – many of which affect grandparents in startling new ways.

Maddy and Joe are grandparents of a recent college graduate. Now, after all these years, they are expecting their second grandchild. Their friends are so excited for them that they threw a baby shower for Grandma Maddy.

Maddy was reluctant to talk about this thirty-something couple's child-care arrangements. After six weeks, mom plans on returning to her job and dad will be the *home parent*. Maddy always worked with Joe, so the idea of a working mom is not foreign to her – but it is more difficult for her to accept her son-in-law staying home and serving as the primary parent. The couple's rationale for their decision is that the wife has the higher paying job, and the husband is unhappy with his work.

This situation is not unusual. According to a 1992 Population Reference Bureau report (the latest available), one in five preschoolers (20 percent) now have their father as primary caregiver, up from the 15 percent figure that remained constant from 1965 until the late 1980s. One reason is that more fathers are working part-time.

Options and Choices
The most popular arrangements for preschool child care today are:

- Full-time mom or full-time dad – or split time between mom and dad.
- Friend or neighbor care.
- A child-care person hired to come into the home.
- Children taken to home daycare.
- Enrollment in a daycare center.
- Grandparent child care.

As with Maddy and Joe, some baby-care arrangements seem strange to grandparents. Unfortunately, no expert can recommend which arrangement works best. That depends entirely on each specific family's situation, and in particular on what option they prefer, as well as which options are available to them, and cost considerations. However, one important qualification remains constant across the board: whoever the primary daycare provider or caregiver is, make sure the individual is physically and emotionally healthy and has an innate love of children.

Criteria for choosing child care will be found in the section on *the Child Care Decision.*

Ideally, it is in the child's best interest for mother (or father) to stay home or work part-time until the child is at least 3 years of age. Most child development experts agree that young children receive a much better start in life when they spend the majority of their waking hours cared for by their own parents and other family members rather than substitute care. Parental love and attention are the most important ingredients in building basic trust in young children. Without trust as the first building block of a child's development, he is likely to see the world as dangerous, hostile, and threatening (Erik Erikson, 1968). Consequently, as the child grows he may shun close personal relationships and even avoid casual social interactions. While we can never predict the stresses and traumas youngsters face as they grow, basic trust provides a safety net throughout development. No members outside the family can take the place of parent/child attunement (or if necessary, grandparent/child attunement) to foster this kind of trust.

Added to this is the important security young children gain by remaining in their own home. The first three years of a child's life is a vital period in their emotional development. While nurturing child-care professionals will often applaud and reinforce a child's achievements, they simply cannot match the excitement and enthusiasm expressed by most parents. The dilemma, of course, is whether a mother or father should stay home and provide the values, discipline and security their children need and let his or her hard-earned job skills and ambitions go unfulfilled, or take a chance that their kids will be fine without them and pursue a life that brings them more personal satisfaction and economic advantages.

It can be argued that career satisfaction and economic advantages can enhance mom's self-esteem and enable her to be a better mother. There is a lot of truth in this statement. The real challenge is the delicate balance between career and nurturing parenting. Some moms, with lots of help from dads, can do a great job at this and then everyone benefits. Other career moms choose to move from the *career track* to the *mommy track* hoping to resume their career when the children are older. Some moms fool themselves into believing that they are super women and then everyone suffers.

T. Berry Brazelton suggests that the early days of the baby's life are a critical time to establish a secure and warm parent/infant relationship. He urges that working mothers take at least the first four months of their babies' life as a time for baby and parents to feel comfortable with each other. He feels that when your baby can communicate well with you and can also relate well with others, you may feel more confident that your baby is ready for the experience of substitute care.

In my professional experience, I have encountered too many overworked and stressed out parents and small children to support the argument for heavy-duty, full-time work for both parents of infants and toddlers. The following vignette is fairly typical.

The director of the daycare center where 2-and-a-half-year-old Hayden was enrolled referred the boy and his family to me for an evaluation. Hayden's behavior of hitting, biting and screaming had become so impossibly aggressive that his teachers did not know how to handle him any longer, and they were prepared to expel him from their program. When mother, father, Hayden and 4-month-old Samantha arrived at my office, I quickly saw how beyond control their lives had become.

Hectic mornings were spent getting everyone up and out. Samantha was dropped off at a different center than Hayden. Evening daycare pick up and dinner were even more frantic. Mom had an important job and had returned to work after six weeks of maternity leave with Samantha. Dad worked long hours, and although he tried to help out, he was not home much. In talking with me, it became clear that the family could manage on the father's earnings, but Mom was reluctant to cut back on her job.

Before Samantha was born, Mom and Dad had been able to balance working outside the home, supporting the growth and development of Hayden, keeping up the home and still having some time together. Now with the addition of Samantha, the work load seemed to have quadrupled. Mom hoped that when her hormones became balanced again, she would be better able to manage. Dad, perhaps more realistically, wasn't too sure and was urging his wife to cut back on her work hours. Mom felt a huge responsibility to the company she worked for and didn't want to let anyone down.

We diagnosed Hayden's trouble in daycare as an appropriate reaction to his new sibling, but highly exacerbated by the stress and tension he experienced from his parents.

After seeing them as a family, I suggested the parents make a second appointment to see me without the children. Just the process of finding a sitter and the time to meet with me was a challenge. However it was a very productive session, as it gave the frantic parents a quiet hour together to sort out their priorities. The session ended with them agreeing that Mom would take a six-month leave of absence.

They returned once during her leave period, and the change in her demeanor was remarkable. She had calmed considerably and Hayden no longer had problems in school. While she missed her work and the people in her office, she realized that she was not indispensable. She decided to return to work when her leave was up. During her leave, she prioritized her life and felt she would be much more able to handle work and family. Additionally, her husband reduced some of his overtime and found that he was enjoying his family much more.

Now let us examine the role of grandparents in daycare and working mother situations. Your role is usually reactive, and seldom active. My purpose here is to educate and inform grandparents about the very real stresses in your children's lives today, and to enable you to be more comfortable with the decisions they make. When your children discuss daycare options, you will be knowledgeable, and if they ask your opinion, you will be informed. There is really only *one* decision you have to make regarding child care: *Do you want to help?*

If so, the next issue becomes *how much* help you are willing to give – and how *capable* you are of giving.

- Does your daily work or retirement schedule realistically allow you the time necessary to help with child care?
- Are you physically capable of providing child-care assistance for your grandchildren? Do you or your spouse have any health or medical conditions that should be considered?
- Are you willing and able to make a time commitment and keep to it consistently, knowing that this will restrict your own personal time and flexibility?
- Can you offer certain days or blocks of time on a consistent basis?
- Will the grandchild child care take place in your home, or in your children's home? (Have you considered various factors for each choice?)
- What are your options if, for a variety of reasons, the parents cannot take care of their children?

The Child Care Decision

One-third of our nation's 14.8 million families with preschool children are composed of homemaker mothers married to breadwinner fathers. The other two-thirds are dual-income families and single-parent families that face a real struggle arranging child care. The following list offers an overview of the alternatives:

1. *Shared Mother and Father Care:* When mother and father can arrange their time and work schedule to accommodate each other, this is usually the best situation for young children. However, it may be harder on the marriage and this stressor should not be overlooked. This arrangement becomes a stressor when, unfortunately, some moms feel their husband is not as good at parenting as she is. Whether this thought is overt or covert, she is constantly telling him what to do – interfering and undermining his self-esteem.

Of course, this is a myth. Fathers can be excellent caregivers and nurturers. In the past, our society has not encouraged men to put fathering at the top of their list. However, high schools are currently including young men in parenting classes and classes for fathers are available in many communities. The claim that *he doesn't know how* is just not accurate.

2. *Child Care with a Friend:* This option can be accomplished by barter if two families are willing to share daycare. If not, having a friend provide child care may be easier on the pocketbook than other providers operating a daycare business. One advantage is that you have much less risk with friends; you know them. The drawback is that if the friend's life situation changes with little notice, she (or he) may no longer be available. Consistency of care is essential. Young children need the opportunity to attach and learn from one person, and it is wise for parents to try to make sure the situation they establish is stable.

3. *Hired Child-Care Person in the Home:* This is probably the best option for parents who can afford the cost. This person may come into the home when mother leaves, and depart when mother returns, or the in-home provider may be a live-in nanny, an au pair, or a housekeeper. The family must always give up some degree of privacy with a live-in provider. If this person lives in the guest or *grandparent room*, the arrangement may necessitate the out-of-town grandparents staying elsewhere during visits, and possibly enjoying less time with grandchildren. The caveat here is to take all the time necessary to find the right person. The *friend network* is usually the best resource to direct the search. Also, if the situation does not work out as well as you anticipate, trust your judgment and make a change. Remember, the children's best interest is the prime criteria.

4. *Home or Family Daycare:* This option is especially popular for infants and children under 3 years of age. Often a mother will *set up shop* in her own home and take care of one or two more children in addition to her own. This works best when all the children are within a few years of each other in age. Each state has licensing requirements for home daycare. Usually licensing requirements are minimal, but I recommend that families only consider licensed home care. In most situations, licensing indicates the caretaker has had some child development training, and the daycare environment passes minimal health and safety regulations. I have conducted child development training for home daycare providers in Illinois and Colorado, and I generally have a high regard for the qualities of the women who perform this work.

5. *Daycare Center:* This is more of a school-like setting in which all daycare is provided by trained, licensed teachers. Parents often prefer daycare centers because they allow children valuable early learning and socialization experiences. These centers tend to have inflexible arrival and departure times, and most will not accept children when they are ill (which may require parents to find substitute care on very short notice, or miss work to stay home and look after a sick child.)

Studies have concluded that no single type of child care is better than another for *all* children. Here are some important considerations to bear in mind when contemplating *other* care options:

- The structure of individual programs can vary enormously. Parents need to take time and care to find the right situation for their children.

- Parents should plan carefully *when* they put their infant in child care. During certain growth stages, an infant is acutely sensitive to any loss or replacement of his primary caretaker. Making any change at those points can be extremely difficult for everyone involved. The most sensitive period is about age 6 to 9 months, and again around age 14-18 months (See Chapter 3: *Separation Anxiety*). At those times, parents should avoid any change in primary care, such as returning to work, or replacing the daycare or babysitter already in place.
- Child care during the first 15 months should be as stable and personalized as possible. Since the baby will form a deep bond with the child care provider, it is essential for parents to be confident that he or she is as responsive and caring as they are.

There may be an organization within your community that provides something called R&R – Child Care Resource and Referral. These groups offer in-person or over-the-telephone information about available local child care. After hearing your specific needs, such as cost requirements, hours of coverage, age of child, and preferred location, an R&R staff will provide a list of referrals and related information. Then they will follow up later to see if you found a satisfactory arrangement. The main benefit of such an organization is that they are in touch with many parents and receive constant feedback from them as well as from licensing authorities. Consequently, they are able to refer people to high quality programs and providers. (More details on this organization may be found in the section on *Community Resources for Parents and Grandparents.*)

Must My Daughter (or Daughter-in-law) Work?

Some mothers of babies and toddlers work because their salary is essential to put food on the table. Some work because the extras they are used to are irresistible. They may be unwilling to give up the luxuries their second income provides. Some women love their jobs and do not want to give them up. Others find staying at home so lonely that they prefer to go back to work. The American Association of Pediatricians (AAP) points out that a woman who is satisfied because of her job may be better in her parenting role than if she were at home but dissatisfied.

When a new mother is in her third or possibly fourth decade and has worked for all or most of her adult life, she may not possess the flexibility, energy and resiliency it takes to be a full-time mother. Some new moms do better when they are able to find some occasional or consistent relief from child care.

Other mothers feel guilty for *not* working. I recall speaking as an expert on child-care concerns at a daytime parenting program. As I described the benefits of full-time mothering for infants and toddlers age 0 to 3 years old, expressions of relief came over the audience's faces. I could almost hear their sentiment: "If the expert says it's good for my children for me to stay home, I'll continue staying home – and I won't feel guilty about it!"

Grandparents may disapprove of the two-income working family. When they visit, they may notice fast food meals, a messy house and piles of dirty laundry. Lois Wyse, in her perceptive book, *Funny, You Don't Look like a Grandmother,* advises, "Grandmotherhood does not give us the right to speak without thinking, but only the right to think without speaking." However, whether we speak out or not, our children usually know what we are thinking. Full-time working mothers often feel unsupported or unadmired by their mothers or mothers-in-law. Are their feelings justified? Comments such as these are not uncommon:

- "The weekly phone call from my mother always includes the question: 'And when are you going to quit working and take proper care of your children?'"
- "My mother keeps telling me, 'You're letting the daycare center bring up your child.'"

- "I'll bet Allen's mother is feeling sorry for him. She is concerned that by my working, I am neglecting him and the children."

Surprisingly, one of the less obvious but still quite serious concerns about full-time child care is the impact on the *mother* who completely relinquishes care of her child to another. When mom is absent, she loses the opportunity to grow as a mother. By denying herself a chance to tune into her child, the two become emotional strangers. This is a major loss for both mother and child.

Additionally, we need to be concerned about how these unmothered children will nurture their future children. We become good parents when we were parented with loving care by our parents. As an example, the most nurturing fathers are those men who were well nurtured as children. Moms who are not around to nurture their children are not preparing their children for parenthood.

Grandparent Care

Sometimes grandparents have a choice in the matter, and sometimes they have little or no choice. Following are several examples of grandparents choosing to be *child caretakers.*

Marcia, mentioned earlier in Chapter 2, has been the prime babysitter for her infant grandchildren, as each of her three daughters returned to their careers after their children's birth. She loves it! When Marcia and Jim became parents, they had a falling out with her parents which lasted many years. Marcia wants the close relationship with her grandchildren that her parents never had with her three daughters. Marcia has a vested interest in grandma care. Offering this assistance to her children is her way of making up for past disappointments.

Another example of grandparent care: following college graduation, Mia, Frank and baby Noelle returned to her parent's home temporarily while they looked for work. After several months, Frank, unable to find work, left his family and never returned to the marriage. Mia's parents, Laurel and Lou, were concerned about how Mia and Noelle would manage. They realized that if they offered Mia and Noelle a home with them, it would alter their lives forever. Their second daughter was now away at college and Laurel and Lou had looked forward to the year alone with their youngest child, a son in high school. But there were really no options – they invited Mia and her baby to live with them in their large roomy house.

The grandparents posed three conditions on the offer: Mia had to get a job to help support herself and her child; they would help with child care but Mia needed to know she was the number one caregiver for Noelle and was expected to be the sole caregiver on the weekends; and Mia would need to make a commitment to get professional help in putting her life back on track. In sharing this story with me, Laurel feels that she and her husband had to make a number of adjustments, but it has been worth it because they feel their grandchild, now 6 years old, enjoys a quality of life that many children of single working moms miss.

Recently, Noelle told her grandmother, "I'm such a lucky girl. There are many people that love me." Laurel and Lou are happy to be providing a safe, caring, and loving environment for Noelle.

Tom McMorrow, age 68, writes in *Modern Maturity* (December 1990-January 1991) of his experience taking care of 3-month-old Alexandra when the baby's mother wanted to return to work and his wife was also working and therefore unavailable. Friends were astonished. "Take care of a *baby*?" gasped another grandfather. Tom is especially grateful for this opportunity because of his own guilt pangs over not having spent more time with his children.

"When they were little, I worked six days a week to make ends meet. I missed out on a lot of great moments: first steps, first words, first temper tantrums. A generation later, I have the opportunity to make that up to Alexandra," he recounted.

More and more grandparents are becoming surrogate parents out of necessity, and assuming responsibility they never sought or anticipated. Between three to four million grandchildren live with grandparents who care for them on a full-time or part-time basis. Social conditions ranging from drug abuse and divorce to financial hardship and teen pregnancy have turned carefree grand–parenting into full-time parenting.

While multi-generational households have long been commonplace in working-class neighborhoods and in many African-American and Hispanic communities at any income level, this phenomenon now cuts across race and class lines. Currently among white middle-class grandparents, a demo–graphic group that has traditionally treasured its independence, an ever-increasing number are providing substantial care for their grandchildren.

Hands-on grandparenting is hard work. By hands-on, I mean custodial grandparent, either by official or more informal designation. Roles and labels can often present problems. Who does the child call mommy and daddy? Who is in charge? Who disciplines, and how? At a time when grandparents might savor more personal time, they may find themselves sitting up late with sick grandchildren, or filling in at the last minute for harried parents or a single parent with an emergency at home or at work.

Taking care of children can wear out anyone, grandparents included. Many grandparents feel isolated and ashamed that their children have shirked their parental responsibilities for whatever reason. The grandparents must then deal with a whole range of concerns, from financial and legal issues to medical and emotional problems. Two valuable advantages grandparents have in the parenting game is their wisdom and experience. We have been through it all before, we are more mellow this time around, and we understand much more.

Grandparent caregivers can find help:

- *AARP Grandparent Information Center* provides infor–mation and resources to help people who have become primary caretakers for their grandchildren. Write AARP Grandparent Information Center, Box MM, 601 E. St. NW, Washington, DC 20049, or call 202-434-2296.
- *Grandparents As Parents, Inc.* (GAP): Links grandparents up with support groups across the country or helps grandparents start their own support group. Write P.O. Box 964, Lakewood, CA 90714; tel. 310-924-3996 or fax 714-828-1375.
- *Grandparents Raising Grandchildren:* write P.O. Box 104, Colleyville, TX 76034; tel. 817-577-0435.
- *Grandparents United for Children's Rights;* tel. 608-238-8751 to find a chapter near you.

A 1994 study by the American Association of Retired Persons (AARP) pointed out that grandparents are continually at war with unfriendly laws and officials in their search for the most basic entitlements for their grandchildren. If financially needy grandparents qualify, they will receive some government funding for child care and medical care for their grandchildren. However, payments to grandparents are less than payments to foster parents.

The 723,000 mid-life and older adults in full charge of their grandchildren, with no parent present, deserve better than this. As parents increasingly are unable to care for their children due to serious drug and alcohol abuse, or health problems, they are turning to their parents as the caregiver of choice. It is essential that grandparents begin receiving the financial support necessary for the new role many find assigned to them. The book *Grandparents As Parents: A Survival Guide for Raising A Second Family* by Sylvie de Toledo and Deborah Brown includes an excellent chapter on "Grandparenting and the Law" (See Reading List for Adults, Chapter 4).

Community Resources for Parents and Grandparents

In one way or another, communities are mobilizing to help identify resources for child care. As described earlier, many areas have a *Resource and Referral* agency funded by local, state or federal funds. In 1990, my community established an R&R agency, Kids First, to help both providers and kids. Providers learn of resources to upgrade their skills to qualify for licensing, and parents can obtain listings and details of approved child care options. Kids First offers tuition assistance for families that need help. While each community handles R&R services differently, sometimes the county social service agency is the resource. All produce newsletters that serve as a network of shared knowledge about what they are doing. In the small community of Aspen, the agency director receives three to four calls a day from parents or grandparents searching for child care.

Although my community has a reputation for glitz and glamour, Aspen has a permanent population of typical small town working families struggling to make a living and raise their children – no different from other American small towns. From my professional experience, I can see what a help Kids First is for parents and grandparents.

Long-Term *Other* Care is Not Ideal

Let me conclude by emphasizing that leaving a very young child for long periods of time in someone else's care is not ideal for the child's social and emotional development, even if that caretaker is a highly qualified nurturer. As discussed earlier, the baby's relationship with her primary caretaker imprints her with the underpinnings she needs to form relationships for the rest of her life.

The recommendations of Burton L. White, Ph.D., the highly regarded author of *The First Three Years Of Life* and a specialist in the study of child development for more than 25 years, offer a very realistic assessment of mother care versus *other* care.

White believes that most children get off to a better start in life when they spend the majority of their waking hours cared for by their parents and other family members rather than *any* form of substitute care. The quality of substitute care babies receive varies greatly. High quality programs may not harm infants in any way, but White questions what *good* they do.

White considers *part-time* substitute care more favorably. He supports part- time substitute child care for all families that want and need it. Parents working part-time 20 hours per week or less, or working full-time once their children have passed the age of 3 years, do not seem to have a negative impact on the child. White further suggests that fathers and grandparents are not encouraged to assist with care often enough.

According to White, "Unless you have a good reason, I also urge you not to delegate the primary child rearing task to anyone else during your child's first years of life. Nothing a young mother or father does out of the house is more important or rewarding than raising a baby. Furthermore, it is a one-time opportunity. Babies form their first human contact only once. Babies begin to know the world only once. The outcome of these processes plays a major role in shaping the future of each new child."

Some grandmothers reading this book were stay-at-home moms. Others of you worked when your children were in school, while some of you worked when the children were very young. Grandfathers may have been the primary care-giving dads. Your parenting experiences when your children were young, both good and bad, should be shared with your parent children. Perhaps honest retrospective insights from you will be helpful to them.

Recommendations

- Grandparents should continually remind themselves that, as we approach the 21st century, there is no best way to raise children. Each young family makes their own choices from a variety of options about how best to care for their needs and their young children's needs.

- When child care requests are made to grandparents, they should realistically evaluate their lives and time commitments and offer to do only what they can live with comfortably. Children are more in tune with our feelings than we recognize, and grandparents who feel disgruntled and imposed upon project these feelings and are not good caregivers.
- Conversely, sometimes grandparents are more available to help than the young family is aware. Both grandmother and grandfather should be sure to communicate their availability.
- Be concerned citizens and take an active role in encouraging businesses and government to be more responsive to current child-care needs and standards.
- Be proactive in helping grandparents who are raising grandchildren receive government benefits equivalent to those offered parents.

Reading List for Adults
Berzin, Judith. *The Complete Guide to Choosing Child Care.* New York: Random House, 1990.
Clark-Stewart, Alison. *Daycare.* Revised edition. Cambridge, MA.: Harvard University Press, 1993.
White, Burton, Ph.D. *The First Three Years of Life.* Revised edition. Fireside, 1995.

Books For Children of Mothers Who Work
Bauer, Caroline Feller. *My Mom Travels A Lot.* Viking Press, 1985. Ages 5- 8 years.
Berenstain, Stan and Jan. *The Berenstain Bears and Mama's New Job.* Random House, 1984). Ages 5-8 years.
Hazen, Barbara Shook. *Why Can't You Stay Home with Me? A Book About Working Mothers.* Goldencraft, 1986. Ages 5-8 years.
Leiner, Katherine. *Both My Parents Work.* Watts, 1986. Nonfiction, ages 5-10 years.

7

Divorce, Death and Mourning

All creatures to survive adapt themselves
to the changing conditions under which they live ...
– Edna St. Vincent Millay, Conversations at Night

There has never been a divorce in the Thompson family. When their daughter married Arnie, Sylvia and Jeff Thompson were delighted and threw the happy couple a wonderful wedding party. Mary was their youngest child and only daughter. After a few years Mary and Arnie were the parents of two boys.

When the second baby was 18 months old, Mary and Arnie mutually agreed to end their marriage, much to Sylvia and Jeff's surprise and dismay. It was a friendly divorce, as divorces go; joint custody with the children living with Mary.

Mary and Arnie each established new relationships soon after the divorce and from all outward appearances, parents and children seemed calmer, happier and better adjusted than during the marriage. It was Sylvia and Jeff that were experiencing the most pain in mourning the loss of the marriage. They were ashamed, hurt and embarrassed that the daughter they so admired, their pride and joy, chose to get a divorce. As time passed, the Thompsons remained close with their ex-son-in-law but had a hard time liking their daughter's new husband. How would this situation change the grandparents' role and relationship with their young grandchildren?

Facts About Divorce

Divorce in the '90s is a fact of life. One in every two marriages ends in divorce and multiple divorces are not unusual. Half of all children under age 18 spend some time in a single-parent home. Many adults, like Mary and Arnie, say they are happier after they terminate their marriage. The dichotomy is that what makes the parents happier, makes the children unhappier. Divorce usually brings a decline in the standard of living for the mother and children. According to one study, in the year following the separation, a single mother's income declines on the average of 30 percent, while the father's income increases 10 percent to 15 percent. On average, divorced parents remain single six years before remarriage.

When the divorce rate began skyrocketing in the 1970s, it was thought to be a temporary crisis. Twenty-five years later we know differently. In 1985 the annual divorce rate peaked at 23 divorces per 1,000 people. Since then it has ceased the rapid climb and has more or less leveled off at 21 divorces per 1,000. Currently 9 percent of our population is divorced.

Grandparents are Victims

As grandparents, we wish we could say that divorce is their problem, not ours! The truth is that, like our grandchildren, *we* become victims, too. In the same way that we have no choice in becoming grandparents, we also have no say in becoming the ex-laws. Suddenly everything is different – the weekly Sunday morning phone call, the family celebrations. Are we still *Mom* and *Dad* to our child's ex-spouse? If not, who *do* we become?

Grandparenting should be fun; all pleasure and no responsibility. But now a new dimension has been added to the family relationship. Our child's family is falling apart. Our daughter is depressed, our son is angry – and sometimes the reverse is true. Our adult kids are in trouble, and often they want and need our help.

- They need help with their children.
- They need assistance in managing money.
- They seek our advice.
- They may become much more dependent on us.
- They may need to live with us for a period of time.

The following case is one example of how divorce impacts our lives.

Jon is a 21-year-old father. He and Suzanne were living together in college when Suzanne become pregnant. They decided to have the baby and went to a judge to get married. Shortly after their daughter Emily was born, they divorced. Jon graduated and went home to his parents. Every other week he drives three hours to pick up Emily for the weekend. And Jon's mother spends all weekend caring for 6-month-old Emily.

This is certainly not what Jon's 45-year-old mother expected grandparenting to be like. She doesn't know what to do. She was not consulted about the marriage or the divorce and now, all of a sudden, she is deeply involved. Jon's father is having a difficult time, too, but he handles it differently. He continues to treat Jon as a single son, and when Emily is there, he ignores her. Just when they were in a position to begin to enjoy life and *play,* Jon's unanticipated marriage, a grandbaby, a divorce, and now child care all in one year, threatened their happiness and security.

Jon's mom and dad sought counseling. There were no easy solutions to their predicament. However, in counseling they were able to express their feelings toward Jon and his baby, as well as their feelings about themselves in this new situation. In talking together with me, we could see how much their son needed them to help him become a man and a father. They would *play* a little later.

Eventually they were able to feel less victimized and became more emotionally supportive for Jon and Emily.

They worked on specific issues:

- Help Jon develop in his role as a father.
- Explore ways for the grandfather to accept his son as a father and himself as a granddad.
- Relieve grandma of full-time child care on weekends.

While some grandparents feel imposed upon by their divorcing kids, others feel unwanted.

To his parent's incredible shame, Craig deserted his wife and three children after 12 years of marriage. Grandparents Paula and Shel had been close to the children during the marriage and helpful in time, money and love. When Craig left, his wife became so angry that she refused to let Craig's parents have any contact with the children. The grandparents loved the grandchildren, but there was nothing they could do to convince their daughter-in-law that they, too, disapproved of their son's behavior and wanted to continue to have a relationship with the kids. Their relationship with their daughter-in-law changed dramatically as a result of their son's choice.

Paula and Shel could have gone to court to request visitation privileges. In all 50 states, grandparents can petition the court for visitation, and if the court deems this in the child's best interest, visitation is ordered. However, going to court does not automatically grant access to your grandchildren. It is up to grandparents to show the judge that time spent with the grandchildren is in their best interest. If you are awarded visitation, there may be specific limitations: seeing the children at a specific time at a specific location, a court-appointed legal guardian or overseer present at visits, and so on. Often the thought of becoming involved in the legal system is so uncomfortable for grandparents that they sadly accept the rejection and hope time will improve things. It is tough being the enemy!

Suggestions for Paula and Shel and other rejected grandparents:

- Explore creative ways of staying in touch that will not anger the custodial parent: phone calls, fax, e-mail, letters, tapes or gifts.
- Continue trying to repair the damage between you and the custodial parent – above all, *don't give up.*
- Consider contacting the other grandparents for help.
- Work on improving your relationship with the children's other parent.
- Join a grandparent support group or start one in your town.
- Contact AARP Grandparent Information Center, 202-434-2296.

Understanding Divorce

Divorce is not a simple one-time event. It is an ongoing process that manifests itself in many ways over an extended period of time. The process begins with marital conflict and proceeds to separation. There can be a number of separations and reunions before a formal separation is agreed upon. Eventually the marriage is ended legally and divorce occurs. During this period, studies indicate that grandparents are encouraged by their children to become more involved in their lives. While the nuclear family is the preferred dynamic for most American families, when our adult children experience stress in the divorce process they are likely to regress to a more dependent state and feel more need to include us in their family life.

Being a grandparent is often radically different after the divorce. Many grandparents feel like yo-yos, trapped in a quandary between "If I do too much, I will have to do it all," or "If I do too little, I might lose them."

It takes two to three years for the divorced adults to reorganize themselves and develop a new family system. When they reorganize, the relationship with the grandparents changes once again. The grandparents who filled the void as comforters and supporters are gradually eased out of that role.

I observe over and over again from children I treat in psychotherapy that the divorce belongs to the whole family. Children talk about "our divorce," "when we got divorced," or "*The Divorce.*" I have never heard a child say, "When mom and dad got divorced."

Divorce is a loss. For the divorcing couple it is the loss of a marriage and a relationship, regardless of how bad that relationship might have been. For grandparents the greatest loss is likely to be the fantasy that their child would live happily ever after. (The process of mastering this loss is discussed later in this chapter in the section *Grief and Mourning.*)

Dorothy W. Gottlieb, Inez Gottlieb and Marjorie A. Slavin, in their excellent book, *What To Do When Your Son or Daughter Divorces* (Bantam Books, 1988), offer this advice:

> *"Divorce does not end with the tolling of the first bell, but goes on for a while. Being aware of this should help you keep your perspective, even your sense of humor. As one (grand) parent said, showing us her album of family pictures, 'My family is never boring. Every Thanksgiving I go through the most unbelievable suspense, wondering who's coming, who isn't. I take pictures partly just to keep track of who's together, who's not from year to year. Sometimes I'm disappointed, sometimes I'm pleasantly surprised'."*

Most disheartening is what we learn from Judith Wallerstein's research, the longest study to date of divorced families. Wallerstein found that 10 to 15 years after a divorce, it continues to be a wrenching long-lasting experience for at least one of the former partners. The divorce also exerts powerful and wholly unexpected effects on virtually all the children involved. To the surprise of the Wallerstein researchers, the children who were the best adjusted 10 years later were those who showed the most distress at the time of the divorce – the youngest.

In general, preschoolers are the most frightened and show the most dramatic symptoms of discomfort when the marriage breaks up. Many are afraid that they will be abandoned by both parents and consequently have trouble sleeping or separating from their parent. It is therefore surprising to find that 10 years later, these same children seem better adjusted than their older siblings. The researchers are unsure why they recovered so well. I would suggest that the younger children are less defensive than older children, more comfortable showing their feelings, and thus better able to work through their unhappy, sad and angry emotions.

Divorce is particularly hard on adolescents. They feel a tremendous sense of loss which, with typical adolescent bravado, they refuse to talk about and instead act out their feelings in potentially dangerous ways.

At a difficult time when teenagers need their parents to supervise them, help them stay organized, take an interest in their interests, and support them when they are down or confused, parents are so involved in their own problems that they have little energy left for their kids. Grandparents who have had a good relationship with their grandkids in earlier years can provide important support during this time.

In the '70s and '80s, many professionals were optimistic about divorce. We expected children to benefit from a calmer, unconflicted home. This did not happen!

Today I feel differently. Other than supporting ending a marriage because of abuse and violence, I have become convinced that parents should put aside their wishes for instant gratification and concentrate on repairing a struggling marriage. Children need two parents in their home much more than most parents need to move on and "find happiness."

Mary Pipher, psychologist and author of *Reviving Ophelia - Saving the Selves of Adolescent Girls* (Ballantine Books, 1994), writes:

> *"My own thinking about divorce has changed in the 20 years I've been a therapist. In the late 1970s, I believed that children were better off with happy single parents rather than unhappy married parents. I thought divorce was a better option than struggling with a bad marriage. Now I realize that, in many families, children may not notice if their parents are happy or unhappy. On the other hand, divorce shatters many children. As one girl said when I asked her how she felt living with her dad and seeing her mother once a month, 'I try not to think about it –it hurts too much. I try not to feel anything.'"*

Today I work very hard with families to help them find ways to resolve their differences and stay together in the best interest of their children.

In the Best Interest of the Child

Grandparents ask, "How will the divorce affect my grandchildren?" My answer: The process is stressful and dislocating for *all* children.

- Most children feel that in some way their behavior triggered the separation. This is seldom true, but it is almost impossible to convince kids otherwise. They need help and reassurance to avoid feeling responsible and guilty.
- Custody, domicile and visitation are all wrenching decisions.
- Attorneys who are hired to help often become a source of anger for all involved.
- Property and money distribution can seriously impact the lives of the children.

- If the children have to move as a result of the divorce, this adjustment that might otherwise be fairly easy with both parents around becomes an additional trauma in light of the situation.
- Birthdays, holidays and family events are all different now!
- Continuity, which is supportive to a child's emotional development, is gone.

A nurturing, caring and empathic environment is essential for the healthy development of children. Can the mom and dad who are going through this stressful period of disorganization nurture their children? Most moms and dads are so self-absorbed during the marital disruption that they have little energy left over for anything but providing the basic essentials for their children. Grandparents can be sensitive to this neglect and find ways to fill the void.

In the best interest of the child, it is important to let the child know what is happening as much as possible – that is, as much as they can handle. It is disturbing that parents of young children often don't tell them what is going on, rationalizing that they won't understand, or assuming that if matters are handled quietly the children won't notice or be as upset. Children can usually handle difficult situations better if they are clearly and compassionately informed.

I was told that Josie, age 2-and-a-half, "won't know the difference because Daddy is so seldom home anyway." *Wrong!* Another client said, "I told Zack. He went right on playing. It didn't make any difference to him." *Wrong!* Grandparents, don't believe your kids. This is a very disruptive period in your grandchild's life. It is essential that parents and children talk about it.

Grandparents who may have experienced divorce in their own lives need only reflect back to how their own children were affected. Some families think talking about divorce means both parents sitting down with the children and having a talk about daddy (or mommy) moving out because mommy and daddy aren't getting along anymore, and that's the end of it. *Wrong again!* Divorce and the changes it will bring need to be discussed again and again in a language kids can understand.

Reading books about divorcing families is another way of helping children understand what is going on and what to expect. (See *Reading List* at the end of this chapter.)

Observe your grandchild's drawings and make-believe play for clues to how they are feeling about what is happening at home. Often through drawing and play a child will show feelings that no words can express.

During a consulting session at a preschool, I observed 4-year-old Mark painting at an easel. I quietly watched and listened as he talked to himself. Making long, gentle, light red brush strokes, he spoke in a sing-song voice, "Mommy loves Mark, Mommy loves Mark." Then he took another brush load of red paint and repeated his brush lines farther across the paper, saying, "Daddy loves Mark, Daddy loves Mark." With great deliberation, he then dipped his brush into the black paint and assertively scribbled over his light red lines, repeating, "Mommy doesn't love Daddy, Mommy doesn't love Daddy."

The staff had not been told of any marital difficulties in Mark's home, but they noticed how unusually whiny and cranky he had been all week. When I shared my observations, his teacher realized why Mark was having such a hard time.

Subsequently, the preschool staff spoke with Mark's mom and when she confirmed the marital problems, his teacher was able to talk to Mark about his feelings about what was happening at home.

Children don't understand their feelings the same way adults do. Grandparents can help. When you say to your grandson, "I wonder if you're feeling sad because Mommy's not here," it can lead him to discover that he indeed feels sad, and that his feelings of sadness are perfectly valid. Instead of feeling bad and not knowing what is wrong, he now has some acceptance of his inner turmoil and validation that it is okay to feel that way.

Grandparents Experience Divorce

It can be quite difficult when your divorcing daughter tells you that you are not allowed to see your ex-son-in-law anymore. You may like him – after all, he is the father of your grandchildren! Do you continue to maintain contact, or do you follow your daughter's request?

Perhaps you are the father's parents, and your son no longer lives at home with the children. Do you still call the house every Sunday to talk to Mom and Jennifer? Must you wait until Jennifer visits your son to make contact with her? Do you remain friends with Jennifer's mom?

Each situation is different and each one seems to have its own share of unhappiness. Sometimes grandparents have a harder time coping with the divorce than the divorcing parents. My advice is to put your pride in your pocket and make every effort to maintain, continue and even increase your connection with both parents of your grandchildren. They need you now more than ever! Your initial efforts may be rebuffed, but persevere with patience and sensitivity.

Limited research on grandparents and divorce indicates that maternal grandparents generally maintain more long-term contact with the divorced family. Immediately after the divorce the paternal grandparents seem able to keep up contact with the children, but it becomes increasingly more difficult over time. While the ex-daughter-in-law may no longer be your son's wife, she remains the mother of your grandchildren, and you need to work hard at staying in touch.

The following clinical vignette presents a different scenario which is sad, but unfortunately not unusual.

Ginger found her marriage untenable. As a very committed and caring mother of Ellen, age 10 months, and Tyler, age 2-and-a-half, she knew how hard a divorce would be on her children. She tried everything to improve the marriage – marital counseling, individual counseling for each of them – all to no avail. They both loved the children and were good parents, but their own relationship was fraught with open anger, verbal abuse and intense unhappiness.

As described earlier in Chapter 2, Ginger's only family member is her mother, who lives in another town, while husband Paul's family lives nearby. Over the course of their marriage, and even more so since they became parents, Ginger had developed a warm relationship with Paul's parents, as well as with his sister and brother and their respective families.

Despite her closeness to his family, Ginger felt she could no longer remain married to Paul and initiated a separation. Paul was angry. He did not want the marriage to end. His family continued their close relationship with Ginger, encouraging her to reconcile. When this was no longer a viable option and she filed for divorce, the grandparents and the rest of the extended family dropped her completely. She was *bad*. She had done something terrible to their son and brother.

Today Paul spends a lot of time with his family when he has the children. The children are fortunate to continue their loving relationship with their grandparents. It is mom who is left out in the cold. The other family members may not appreciate what the sad loss of these relationships means to her. How do family members determine their loyalties in such a situation? Is the family instructed by Paul, who in anger insists that they sever all relationships with his children's mother? Is Ginger really the *villain*? As she struggles with all the vicissitudes of being the single custodial parent, is the family of her ex-husband behaving in the best interest of the children by acting as though she doesn't exist? Are they aware of how their behavior affects Ginger and the children?

Some of these issues that appear hopeless at the moment may work themselves out over time. Other times the end result is a permanent fracture in which each individual must cope and accept the situation.

Grandparents do not have the power to hold bad marriages together, try as they may sometimes. Even if they had the power, it would be an inappropriate solution. Following are a few recommendations to parents of divorcing children:

- If you have experienced divorce yourself, review in your mind how *your* parents helped you or didn't help you during that event, and apply that wisdom on behalf of your adult children.
- Be aware that children of divorce, as adults, are more vulnerable to marital breakup, and try to be supportive of them in every way possible.
- Your grief over the divorce may last from six months to two years, but time will help you make peace with your child's divorce.
- Be careful that your individual reactions to your child's divorce do not stress your own marriage beyond repair. Divorce can be contagious.
- At the time of divorce your adult child may regress. Be prepared and realize it is only temporary.
- You may be caught in the middle between your needy divorced child and your needy aged parent. There is only so much financial, emotional and physical support you are capable of giving. Try to ration your involvement in a sensible way, as a couple or as individuals, so as not to harm yourselves.
- Your other children may resent the time and energy you are giving to the divorcing family. Discuss your plans to help the family in trouble with your other children to gain their approval of what you see as your role.
- Being a grandparent is different after the divorce. The shift in family relationships now requires premeditation and

planning for events that were spontaneous before – birthday parties, holidays and family events.

Death in the Family

Death is a much more painful loss than divorce to all those involved. As disappointed as you may be in your child's disrupted marriage and possible neglect of the children, at least everyone is alive. With life there is always hope! Death ends all this. The deceased family member is beyond anger, beyond help, beyond comfort.

For children, the death of a parent is their life's most painful experience. The same is true for parents who lose a child. I have heard grandparents bargain with God to take them rather than their dying adult child. When it is the death of your grandchild, you have to deal with your grief and your adult child's grief. This is a very heavy load. Although the pain is shared, you may be the ones who have to pull together to help your child, the parent.

A divorce is a death, the death of a marriage. It becomes very complicated to be angry, hurt, enraged at one's spouse and mourn the loss of the marriage all at the same time. But that's what happens. Many of us in the mental health field have witnessed through years of intensive work with death and divorce that, surprising as it may sound, the recovery from a death is often easier on the survivors than the recovery from a divorce. Divorce is a *process*. Death, in contrast, is an *event*.

For example, children of widows do better than children of divorced mothers. Widows with children living at home differ from divorced mothers in three major respects:

- Widows are economically more secure – through inheritance, private insurance or Survivors Insurance and Social Security.

- Widows are less likely to disrupt their children by moving from the neighborhood in search of cheaper housing or in search of a job to sustain them.
- The authority structure of the family is less radically disrupted. When a father dies, while no longer physically present, he is not dethroned as an authority figure in the child's life. (A common expression is "Your father would have wanted it this way.")

When the mother dies, the father faces the same child care and management problems as fathers with sole custody. The difference again is that mom's absence is less conflictual. As painful as it is, there is a finality to mother's absence.

Death is never easy, never without the pain of loss to those who survive. I don't mean to minimize or diminish the trauma a family suffers. Grandparents can provide a tremendous help, but acknowledge that it is stressful and tough on you to give to the family when you feel so devastated and needy yourself. For many, providing comfort and relief to others helps alleviate your own sense of loss.

Michael, a very gifted young man, was diagnosed with an inoperable brain tumor when Karen was pregnant with their first child. Michael's last hospital stay took place at the same time Karen gave birth to Joshua. Michael saw the baby's birth and came home to spend the first four months of Joshua's life with him before he died.

The family's grief was inconsolable. The grieving paternal grandparents obtained a wonderful child care person to help care for baby Joshua during this acute grief period. With time, as the grieving lessened, Karen took charge of her baby and resumed her life. While she had a number of male companions who were very caring toward Joshua, she never remarried.

The paternal grandparents took much longer than Karen to get their lives back on track, which is not unusual, but eventually they did. Living close to Karen and Joshua, they were always available to them, during their grief and later on when they were better. People never completely *recover* from such a loss, but they do develop ways to come to terms with the loss in order to continue living.

As Joshua grew, Grandpa in particular became an essential person in his life, exposing him to a host of *male* experiences that he might have missed altogether without a father – from camping trips to sporting events, from attending important school activities to teaching him to drive. At one point the grandparents considered moving away, but they postponed their move until Joshua graduated from high school and went off to college. Now Joshua no longer needed their close proximity, so they made the move they had long contemplated. Today Joshua is a wonderful young man, and his grandparents deserve credit for the pivotal role they played in his development.

Grandparents not only make a difference – sometimes they can make *all* the difference!

The Death of a Grandparent

The primary purpose of this guide is to offer grandparents a better understanding of their many roles – and how to survive them – as we approach the 21st century. However, it would be remiss of me not to mention divorce and death of grandparents because these unpleasant events have such an impact on children and grandchildren. How do we prepare the children for the unexpected grandparent divorce? They say, "They're too old to divorce," or for death: "They're not old enough to die!" Both can happen. If caring grandparents divorce it is unlikely that the children will feel too abandoned. Usually grandparents can continue their grandparenting role whether they remain single or remarry. They are unlikely to change this role much unless the divorce or a remarriage involves moving to another location.

I strongly encourage separated and divorced grandparents to attend their grandchildren's special events. Hopefully you can both be there and be mature enough not to make the family feel uncomfortable. Kids like having their grandparents at special events and they are not much interested in your marital status. If a new spouse wants to be part of the group, they should come, too.

The death of a grandparent is often the child's first experience with death. (This is discussed in more detail in Chapter 5.) When someone a child loves dies, the adults in his life need to help him understand what has happened. Attending the funeral, if the child wants to, helps him come to grips with the reality of the loss. This may be followed up by parents encouraging the child to remember this loss in healthy ways: "We cannot forget that Grandpa died, but we can always remember how he lived." This is much preferable to an atmosphere in which the child is discouraged from discussing the loss of a grandparent because it is too painful for the parents. It may fall to the surviving grandparent to play a key role in helping grandchildren cope with this loss by sharing the joy and sadness of loving memories.

Grieving and Mourning the Loss

Ending a marriage, no matter how bad the marriage may be, is an emotional trauma to both partners, their children and their parents. A divorce, or a death, disrupts the accustomed routine of life and causes a painful separation. It is so important for everyone involved to be able to share how they feel. Being able to *talk* about your feelings of pain, sadness, anger, rejection, anxiety, loneliness, relief and finally optimism about the future is the cornerstone of *recovery* from the loss. Grandparents, you may be needed to simply listen to other family members describe their feelings.

Quite often you can accomplish the grieving and mourning process on your own, with close friends or family members, but if not, many highly competent therapists trained in helping people with grief and loss issues are available. If you need help, get help. If someone close to you needs help, you can help them find help.

As psychological consultant to our community Hospice, I often speak at monthly Grief and Loss Support Group meetings. The saddened people that attend our group are enlightened enough to know how helpful it is for their recovery to share their sadness and to learn from the experiences of others. Working with this group of people is one of my most difficult and rewarding professional commitments.

Some of the topics I have spoken on include *A Death in the Family – Memorials and Anniversaries; Intervention with Grieving Children; Unexpected Death; Grief and the Holidays;* and *Moving On ...* The discussion that follows my presentation generally covers the important tasks of mourning:

- Accept the reality of the loss.
- Experience the pain of grief.
- Adjust to an environment in which the deceased is absent.
- Withdraw emotional energy and reinvest in other experiences and relationships.

These grief and loss issues are more commonly associated with divorce and death, but they also apply to subjects discussed elsewhere in this book in chapters on remarriage, infertility, and the *nonperfect* child. I find Dr. Elisabeth Kubler-Ross's work on the mourning process in her book, *On Death and Dying,* particularly helpful for understanding the ways with which we can finally come to terms with unanticipated life crises, no matter what they may be. What follows is my adaptation of her landmark work.

- *Denial*: The first stage of dealing with loss is to deny the impact it has on you. In a divorce, kids and grandparents try so hard to deny what is really happening: "If I don't think about it, it won't happen," or, as Scarlet O'Hara said in *Gone With The Wind:* "I'll think about it tomorrow!"

- *Anger:* This second stage is most frequently a response to the helplessness and powerlessness people feel as they lose control over events happening around them. In the earlier example of the young man dying of a brain tumor, the family was tremendously angry that this tragedy should happen to them.

- *Depression:* Periods of anger and periods of depression may alternate for a long time during the grieving period. When depressed, the griever may have little energy to do anything. Eating and sleeping habits may change – too much or too little. Bouts of depression can often cause grandparents to withdraw from their children and grandchildren just when they are needed most.

    Children show depression in different ways from adults. They may *act out their depression* by getting into trouble – fights, drugs, delinquency. They may become suicidal. They may be unable to function well in school or, quite the opposite, they may use school as a safe haven and show no pain at school.

    When there is no relief from depression, it may be helpful to talk with your physician about antidepressant medication. With the lifting of depression, anger may reappear. While anger isn't easy or pleasant to deal with, at least it does not immobilize us the same way depression can.

- *Acceptance:* There comes a time when you can accept the loss and continue your life. Acceptance comes to different family members at different times. Acceptance does not mean the absence of pain, but rather the ability to adapt to it. It is unlikely that you will be able to fully work through these stages and arrive at an acceptance until after the first anniversary of the loss. For some, the period of mourning goes on much longer. These four stages do not represent a clear progression. It is not unusual to go back and forth between stages. Be patient with yourself and give yourself – and others – the time your psyche needs to heal.

Some people remain in denial and refuse to allow themselves to continue the process of working through their loss. They tell everyone how fine they are! While they appear strong following their loss, psychologically what they are doing is denying their feelings. At some later time in their life, these unresolved feelings will affect them in unanticipated ways. Often people who enter therapy with generalized complaints learn that the underlying cause of their unhappiness is an unmourned loss! When they can finally talk about these long-denied feelings, they begin to feel better. (See the case study of Gail in Chapter 5.)

A father who suffered the terrible tragedy of losing his adult son to AIDS could not talk about his loss. He went about his business in his usual cheerful manner, until he suffered a stroke six months later. While no one can prove the stroke was caused by his bottled-up grief, I believe the two events were related.

Children mourn differently, and at a different pace, than adults. Here are some suggestions to help children mourn in a healthy manner:

- Children need to have the event explained repeatedly. Children can be so distracted by emotional turmoil that they don't really comprehend what is being said until they have heard it many times in many ways.
- A child's capacity to understand the finality of death or divorce continues to expand with each stage of their development.
- Each child in a household will interpret the death or divorce in a different way, and as they grow older each child will need to revisit the topic periodically to continue to make sense of it.

- Many conversations will be needed over the years to fully integrate the loss.

As a grandparent, it is important to support your grandchild's mourning process in any way you can. To reiterate, children don't express their feelings the same way adults do. Some children will break into tears, but others may show no immediate response to the news. Then days, weeks or even months later, a child's moods or behavior may begin to change. He may start fighting on the playground, have difficulty in school, regress to earlier behavior, all without showing any obvious emotional pain.

Children tend to regress when they feel emotionally overwhelmed. Your grandchild might begin to exhibit less mature behavior, and may not be able to tell you what is wrong. Even when you are trying to be very supportive emotionally, encouraging her to share her feelings about Daddy and Mommy's separation, you may get no response. That doesn't mean that you should stop trying. Although she may have turned down your overtures many times before, some day she may suddenly start crying and talking to you about her feelings. You never know when a child is ready to open up.

You can also try a more active approach. Take the child for a walk. Even if she doesn't express any feelings, spending quality time together will help her feel comforted and supported. Remind her frequently that you are available whenever she feels like talking, or you can share an activity together that may elicit a reaction.

It can be quite restorative for kids to talk to their grandparents about their parent's death – how it happened as well as their ideas about dying. Listen quietly and give them plenty of time to talk. You may be the only people the kids can talk to. They may have lots of distorted ideas about what happened and what it means to die. That's OK. There is plenty of time to teach them about the reality, but give them a chance to express their ideas.

And don't change the subject because you think the conversation is making all of you feel too sad. If they can share their feelings with you, you are playing an important role in helping them work through their grief and mourning.

Don't have this time together only once. If an opportunity presents itself for an ongoing dialogue, continue to offer them this important therapeutic experience – it will benefit you, too. This sort of ongoing interaction with the kids can be helpful for them in working through their feelings about their divorcing parents as well.

To conclude, each person experiences loss differently and mourns in their own way. The grief experience will always be affected by the nature and the quality of the relationship, the availability of support, the circumstances of the loss and the psychological resilience and coping skills of the individual. Grief and mourning know no boundaries of age, gender or circumstances.

Recommendations
Divorce:
- Grandparents are most helpful to the divorcing family when they can remain neutral and not become embroiled in the emotions of the divorcing parents.
- Be supportive to your adult child as the stress of the divorce unfolds. Your goal should be to help your child pull together and resume a healthy adult life. It is non-growth promoting to allow your adult child to remain regressed and wallow in self-pity.
- When possible, grandparents should be available for crisis intervention, child care, emotional support and financial support.
- In a divorce the marital relationship ends, but the parenting relationship continues. The children that do best years after the divorce are those who have satisfying contact with two caring parents. If grandparents are convinced of how important

this is, they can often help promote co-parenting on the part of their children.

- Several children in the Wallerstein research study (five years after the divorce), told interviewers that what helped them the most was having loving, devoted grandparents who kept them in mind and provided summer vacations for them, made telephone calls at frequent intervals, and provided an ongoing relationship attentive to their needs.
- When divorcing parents are unable to help children understand the divorce, it often becomes the grandparents' task to help the grandchildren understand.
- Parents of the non-custodial parent should make every effort possible to remain on good terms with the custodial parent.

Death:
- Children are never too young to learn about death. Explanations can be tailored to the child's age. Tell a child as much as you think they can understand and handle. As they grow, discuss death so they continue to learn as their level of understanding increases.
- Treat the death of a pet as seriously as the loss of a person to a child.
- Never lie about death to a child.

Grieving and Mourning the Loss:
- Any significant loss leads to a grief response.
- Do not protect children from experiencing loss. It is important for adults to share the facts and their own emotions with children. Lacking this opportunity, children are more likely to find loss confusing and may act out instead of expressing their feelings.
- Recovery from loss cannot be rushed.

Reading List for Adults
Divorce:

Baris, Michael A., and Carla B. Garrity. *Children of Divorce.* Psytec, 1988.

Gottlieb, Dorothy W., Inez B. Gottlieb and Marjorie A. Slavin, *What to do When Your Son or Daughter Divorces.* New York: Bantam Books, 1988.

Ricci, Isolina. *Mom's House, Dad's House – Making Shared Custody Work.* Macmillan, 1982.

Truly, Traci. *Grandparents' Rights: Take the Law In Your Own Hands.* Clearwater, FL: Sphinx Publishing, 1995.

Wallerstein, Judith, and Sandra Blakeslee. *Second Chance: Men, Women, and Children a Decade After Divorce.* Houghton Mifflin, 1996.

Wallerstein, Judith, and Joan Kelly. *Surviving the Breakup: How Children and Parents Cope With Divorce.* New York: Basic Books, 1996.

Death:

Grollman, Earl A. *Living When a Loved One Has Died.* Boston: Beacon Press, 1995.

Kubler-Ross, Elisabeth. *On Death and Dying.* Collier Books, 1993.

Meyers, E. *When Parents Die: A Guide For Adults.* New York: Viking Press, 1986.

Grieving and Mourning the Loss:

Viorst, Judith. *Necessary Losses.* New York: Simon & Schuster, 1986.

Reading List for Children
Divorce:

Bloom, Judy. *It's Not the End of the World.* Macmillan, 1972. Ages 10-12 years.

Brown, Lauren and Marc Brown. *Dinosaurs Divorce: A Guide for Changing Families*. New York: Little Brown, 1986. Ages 4-8 years.

Hazen, Barbara. *Two Homes to Live In, A Child's Eye View of Divorce*. New York: Human Science Press, 1983. Ages 5-10 years.

Krementz, Jill. *How It Feels When Parents Divorce*. New York: Knopf, 1988. Ages 10 13 years.

Mayle, Peter. *Why Are We Getting a Divorce?* New York: Crown, 1990. Ages 5-8 years.

Vigna, Judith. *Grandma Without Me*. Whitman, 1984. Miles won't be going to Grandma's for Thanksgiving because his parents are divorced. Miles misses Grandma terribly and they keep in touch with a scrapbook. Ages 5-8 years.

Death:

Grollman, Earl. *Talking About Death: A Dialogue Between Parents and Child*. Boston: Beacon, 1991. Ages 5-10 years.

Krementz, Jill. *How It Feels When A Parent Dies*. New York: Knopf, 1988. Ages 10-13 years.

Viorst, Judith. *Ten Good Things About Barney*. New York: Antheneum, 1971. Ages 3- 8 years.

8

Remarriage and Your Grandchildren

This time, like all other times, is a very good one,
if we but know what to do with it.
– Emerson

Gordy was divorced from Helen two years ago. The divorce involved a bitter custody battle, in which Helen prevailed. Shortly afterward, she took the children across the country to live. Gordy's parents have found it difficult to stay in touch, and haven't seen their grandchildren in over a year. Suddenly they hear through a mutual friend that Helen has remarried. They are stunned, and wonder what to do now that their grandchildren are being raised far away by two *strangers*. How can they stay in touch? Should they accelerate the frequency of their calls and letters? Will Helen resent this as an intrusion into her new life?

Ann was divorced four years ago. She and her two children have struggled to get by since then, and during this time her parents have been supportive in every way. They have become especially close to the grandchildren, spending a lot of time with them so that Ann can work. Unexpectedly Ann announces that she will be marrying her boyfriend of six months – a widower with three children. Her children like him but are worried about having three new siblings. Her parents are happy that Ann has found love and that the grandchildren will have two parents again, but are uncertain and wary about the dramatic change in the family. They also wonder how this complex family will function with both parents working full time.

Then there's Barry, who longs to have a special relationship with his only grandchild. This very normal desire is complicated by the fact that Barry's grandson has *six* grandfathers.

Stepfamilies are so commonplace today that there is a tendency to underestimate the many difficulties they may encounter. Are grandparents behaving in an old-fashioned manner when they feel concerned? *No!* Remarriages fail at an even higher rate than first marriages – more than half end in divorce. Whatever we call this new family – blended, reconstituted, merged, combined or remarried – it remains complicated and confusing for everyone involved, especially the children. There are no familiar rules or guidelines to follow, least of all from previous generations.

Remarriage: A Confusing Time

Thirteen hundred new stepfamilies are formed each day, with one in five U.S. children having a stepparent. Stepfamilies vary in complexity, from the widow with one child who marries a bachelor, to a household formed by two new parents, each with joint custody of children from more than one previous marriage. In addition, the number of grandparents who are themselves remarried is rapidly growing.

Although remarriage is perhaps the most complex and difficult issue today's family may have to deal with, it has received surprisingly little public attention, and the issues that you face as grandparents have received almost no acknowledgment. Like so many other situations you will face as a grandparent, remarriage is a scenario beyond your own choosing, over which you have no control, and one that deeply affects those closest to you. Even when you have warm, positive feelings about a new spousal addition to the family, remarriage shifts previously familiar relationships into confusion and complexity. Suddenly a new person has joined the family with different needs, preferences, and relatives.

You may experience a range of fears and concerns:

- What can I do if I just don't like the new family situation?
- How will my grandchildren's home environment change?
- Will I have less time with my grandchildren?
- How should I behave toward my stepgrandchildren?
- How will my grandchildren get along with their stepparent and stepsiblings?
- With whom will the new family spend the holidays?
- To which members of the family should I give gifts?
- How long will it take for everyone to adjust to the new situation?
- How can we get along when the new partner comes from a different culture, religion, race, or economic status?
- How can I help the new couple maximize their chances for a successful marriage for the sake of the grandchildren?

Accepting and resolving the complicated issues raised by a remarriage can be a long, painful process, requiring a profound readjustment of your values and expectations, but it's both possible and worthwhile – if only for the sake of the grandchildren. *Creativity* and *flexibility* are the key words when dealing with issues this complex. There is no room for rigidity in a blended family. In fact, remarriage probably requires more willingness to be flexible than any other situation that grandparents may face.

Fears, Myths and Expectations

Family members rarely anticipate the complexities of remarriage. All the actors in this drama are likely to find that they are playing unfamiliar roles. Relationships, responsibilities and expectations are conflicting and confusing. Remarried couples and their children face challenges that first marriages do not, which may be one reason why they fail at a higher rate. Grandparents who have difficulty accepting or understanding the thorny issues raised by remarriage can inadvertently create even more stress for the new family. If you haven't been through a remarriage with children yourself, you may find it helpful to learn more about the added stress that stepfamilies face.

Remarriage is surrounded by fantasies. Family members usually start out believing, or at least wishing for, three major myths:

1. Forming the new family will fix all the pain and problems of the past.
2. Everyone in the new family will love each other just as much as the new couple does (or, "love me, love my children").
3. Prior history and connections will fade away and the new family will feel and act just like a biological family.

It takes time for a stepfamily to become a nurturing, effective family unit, and unrealistic expectations increase everyone's stress level. The first three to four years are the most difficult. During the first year, the *outsider* is integrated into the family, becoming an insider. This becomes complicated when two families merge and everyone in the family feels like both *insider* and *outsider* for a while. Throughout the first years, memories of prior partners and parents frequently arise, complicating the new family. So temper your expectations of *normalcy* and don't be disappointed, disillusioned or critical when the going is slow and difficult.

As a somewhat uninvolved observer, you may notice glitches in their family life. I suggest you think long and hard before pointing out these problems to your child. You could be a great help to the new family, or an interference. This is a call only *you* can make.

Although death and divorce involve a mourning process (as noted in Chapter 7), their effect on children is profoundly different. In the case of death, the mourning period may be more intense, but the child's adaptation to a new parent is less conflicted. A child who has lost a parent to death is generally receptive to a new parent, and may reach that point quite rapidly – perhaps well before their remaining parent feels ready for a new spouse. In contrast, the divorced child *always* retains the fantasy that the biological parents will get together again. Remarriage puts a painful end to that fantasy, complicating the child's acceptance of the new stepparent.

As grandparents, you may also feel some ambivalence about the new marriage. The new spouse may not meet your hopes and preferences, yet you must somehow find common ground with this person who will have a profound impact on your grandchildren. During the divorce or bereavement preceding the remarriage, you may have grown quite close to your grandchildren and the custodial parent by baby-sitting, offering advice, and providing emotional and financial support. Suddenly somebody else is taking over your role, relieving you of an extra burden, or pushing you away. Even if you like the new spouse and believe that it's great for your grandchildren to have a new parent, you may think, "That isn't how *I* would handle things."

Avoid complaining to your adult child about their new mate. It will either sow seeds of mistrust between them (which is in *nobody's* best interest), or draw them closer together against your meddling. If you are concerned about your relationship with the couple, for the sake of your grandchildren, voice your worries to someone else, such as a good friend or family member who has faced similar issues, or perhaps a sympathetic sibling of your adult child. With their help, you'll probably discover that there *is* a way to establish better communication with the new couple and build a stronger bond with them. You may also discover that discussing your concerns about the new spouse may alleviate those concerns. You need to talk about your feelings and not repress them – but you *do not* need to talk about them with your adult child right now.

I find that my friends often share more intimate family concerns with me because of my professional work than they do with their other friends. It is not unusual for me to hear about family concerns while hiking, or riding up the ski lift. These people are not looking for answers, but rather for a friendly ear with whom they can share their concerns – and that is good.

A particularly challenging situation arises when your son does not have custody of his children and his ex-wife remarries. She may or may not be on good terms with your son, and you may feel awkward pursuing your prior grandparent relationship. You may fear that the new marriage will weaken your already fragile bond with your grandchildren. That is a valid fear. Noncustodial grandparents *can* be left out of the new family's circle, intentionally or unintentionally. If you feel you could lose contact with your grandchildren, look for diplomatic ways to stay in touch such as:

- Pursue all options for contact that don't alienate the parents. Diplomatically ask the parents when and how they would prefer for you to stay in touch with your grandchildren.
- Fax or e-mail communications can be a fun way of keeping in touch.
- Send special cards, homemade or store-bought, for events and non-events.
- When you write, be sure to ask questions that stimulate answers. To help, enclose a self-addressed, stamped envelope.
- You might want to consider modest gifts recognizing your grandchildren's success in athletics, school achievements, civic endeavors and religious activities.
- Offer to baby-sit.
- Invite the new family over for a occasional meal or out to a restaurant.

- Attend your grandchildren's school plays and sport games.
- Invite the new family to visit you. To ease the new family into a visit, you can offer to help them find special accommodations if they prefer, such as an historic hotel or a charming bed and breakfast. You can also offer to have the grandkids stay with you, which gives you a *grandchild fix*, and allows the new couple valuable time alone, too.
- Send them audio and videotapes of your activities, especially if they include an angle that will interest or appeal to your grandchildren.

You may be no longer welcome when your grandchildren are being raised by adults who aren't related to you. If this happens, it is not helpful to withdraw into resentment or self-pity. Your only recourse may be to go to court for grandparent visitation rights. You will need to convince the court that such contact is in your grandchildren's best interest.

This is such a stressful procedure that many grandparents avoid court. If you decide not to go to court, or if you fail to persuade the court to grant you visitation, and the new couple persists in excluding you, you will have to explore even more creative approaches. Don't give up hope, because there are always ways to stay in touch.

Time can heal and improve estranged relations. You may need to give the situation a rest and try again in three months, six months or even a year. Following remarriage, the new family may need time to bond, and your care and concern may be misinterpreted as interference and distraction. Holiday time and birthdays provide an excellent opportunity to remind everyone that you are still there, and you still care.

Regardless of who raises your biological grandchildren, it is important for you to reach out to them in every way possible. Don't feel too hurt or slighted if the remarried couple do not encourage your efforts. Often they are working so hard to consolidate the new family that they have little energy left over to worry about your feelings. But to your grandchildren, your love is irreplaceable. That's what matters most.

How Can We Help?

Usually your fears of rejection will turn out to be unfounded. You'll discover that the custodial parents are glad to hear from you, even if they haven't encouraged you to stay in touch.

Karen had custody of her children after the divorce, and remained very close to her ex-husband's parents. When she remarried and moved a short distance away, they backed off, thinking that she wouldn't want them in her new life. After a while they called her again, very tentatively, and were surprised to find that she had really missed their support. She had been afraid that "they won't want to have anything to do with me or the kids anymore." Karen was delighted when the grandparents offered to care for the kids occasionally. It gave her more time to solidify her new marriage.

Phil was and had always been an unavailable father. However, he was happy that his parents were back in touch with his children. In a sense, I think he felt that his parents were doing what he was not able to do.

In most first marriages, the couple has time to explore and develop their own relationship before they have children and need to take on parental responsibilities. In a remarriage, the marital and parental relationships arrive simultaneously in the same package. The parents have no initial bonding or preparation time. It's very stressful to take on these two roles at once under the best circumstances. The transition can be quite difficult. Most stepfamilies start out believing the myth that the new stepparent will immediately love the stepchildren, but they soon confront the reality that the children interfere with the time the couple needs for their own relationship.

As grandparents, if you are able to help the new couple find more time together, the whole family will benefit. It doesn't matter if you are related to either of the new parents, or to their children.

A friend once mentioned that she was taking care of her two preadolescent grandchildren and, intrigued that a woman of her young age already had grandchildren that old, I inquired further. One child was actually her husband's grandchild. The other youngster was the child of her son's wife from an earlier marriage. My friend had no blood ties with either of the children, yet she treated them as *her* grandchildren. She had them for a month every summer. This arrangement worked out great for everyone involved.

In earlier generations, kinship followed bloodlines down the generations. Families today can form and reform themselves repeatedly within one generation. It is increasingly common to have a variety of *family* relationships that have no biological link. What used to be considered unconventional is now quite acceptable, and can enrich the lives of all involved. It can be especially beneficial for children to have a close, loving relationship with non-biological grandparents. It's much better for a child to have a loving stepgrandmother than no grandmother at all.

Children don't care if you are their blood kin. They just want to be loved. The more caring, supportive, involved adults there are in a child's life, the more they will feel secure and confident in their ability to form healthy, loving relationships. The somewhat overused African proverb says, "It takes a whole village to raise a child." We may be returning to a more tribal approach to child raising, and this aspect of modern life is beneficial from the child's point of view.

Despite all the talk about *family values,* few writers mention the vital role that grandparents can play. This is a significant oversight because grandparents can be an essential support system and sounding board. With all the stress on the family, it can be so helpful to know that a friendly ear is available. Much counseling today is essentially listening. Other people are often too busy with their own problems to nurture someone who needs a helping hand. This is where grandparents can take up the slack.

We can listen, share our own parenting experiences, but mostly, just *be* there. You don't have to meddle in your child's home life to be a good listener, and unless you suspect abuse or neglect (see Chapter 10), meddling is unnecessary.

Coping with the Stresses of Remarriage

The new stepfamily is formed by the parental couple. Yet even when their relationship is strong, other relationships within the family may be difficult and painful. One couple complained to me, "We love each other, but his children are driving us apart." This is a serious and common problem in stepfamilies, although it is not usually expressed so openly.

When a parent remarries, the bond between parent and child is always of longer duration than the bond with his or her new partner. Unfortunately, our society is very insensitive to the stress involved in parenting someone else's children. Raising someone else's child is quite a challenge, as is allowing a new partner to help raise *your* child.

Frequently, grandchildren turn to their grandparents to complain about their changed life. It is important that you listen and be supportive for them. Sometimes you may have a suggestion to help them cope, but also be aware that just having you as a listener to their woes is a great comfort and relief. Available grandparents can really make a difference. Here are some of the more common complaints:

- They complain about their new stepsiblings.
- They are angry and resentful of their new stepparent.
- They don't like their living situation.
- They may take major exception to minor situations. (One small child told his new stepmother that her pancakes weren't as good as those his dead mother used to make.)
- They miss having their one parent to themselves and resent sharing their parent with their new mate.

Despite shared parenting, the primary responsibility for child care still falls disproportionately on the wife. A new wife who has never had children before may be ashamed to admit that her husband's kids are a handful, that she doesn't know how to handle them, or that she doesn't like being a stepmother. She is probably working and trying to learn how to care for the children at the same time. She has little time for herself or to nurture her marriage. Even Mary Poppins had her day off!

So how can you help? If you're in a position to relieve her of child care now and then, she will be most appreciative. You can let her know that you realize how difficult things are, and that if she wants to talk, you're available to listen. However, just as with any new parent, *do not* offer unsolicited advice. She may easily interpret it as implied criticism of her parenting skills. You can be encouraging, supportive and reassuring by acknowledging or complimenting her parenting ability when she handles a tough situation well in your presence.

When both new parents have custody of children from previous marriages, sooner or later conflicts will arise in merging the two sets of kids. Even the visit of noncustodial children can cause serious complications in a stepfamily. In some households, a wholesale shift of personnel occurs every weekend. *His* noncustodial children may come to visit, while *her* custodial children visit their father. This kind of constant shifting causes stress and disruption in even the most stable family. Be patient, aware and forgiving. Signs of stress may be expressed in your direction that have little or nothing to do with you.

The tension that often exists with newly merged families seldom carries over to grandparents and stepgrandkids. As grandparents who love their grandchildren, it is likely you will welcome the addition of more kids to love, and your step-grandkids who are giving your adult child a hard time are likely to relish all the grandparenting they get from you. Being a generation removed makes these new relationships much easier for the kids and for you.

Counseling May Be Helpful

Most new stepfamilies have already been through a lot of stress due to divorce or bereavement. Counseling can be a helpful resource for grandparents, the new couple, and their children, when the strains of readjustment become overwhelming.

A grandmother expressed concern about her son's children, who were in the custody of his ex-wife. The couple had reconciled, lived together for a while, and then separated again. The grandmother wondered how to talk to her grandchildren about this second loss. She also asked me if her daughter-in-law should consider therapy. I felt that it would be appropriate for both her and her daughter-in-law to have their own counselors. (You may ask, "What about her son?" Unfortunately, he was unwilling to acknowledge that his behavior might be causing the problem.)

Divorce and remarriage are difficult transitions for any family. Seeking professional help is perfectly justified, and it can be a real benefit. There is no need to *tough it out* alone. In fact, doing so may only serve to prolong hard times and delay healing.

Another woman described a situation troubling her. She and her husband strongly disapproved of the woman with whom her divorced son was living. She wanted to know how she could convince her son to leave the relationship. I tried to help her see that while this partner might not be *their* choice, she could not judge her son's relationships based on *their* preferences. She and her husband really needed help in learning how to distance themselves from their son's life choices. We talked about trusting their son's judgment and showing their love by respecting his choice, regardless of the eventual outcome, *for better or for worse.*

We grandparents are often too emotionally involved to have a realistic assessment of our children's choices. Every relationship is different, but as a rule, as long as there is no abuse or neglect, it is best not to intervene. *If it ain't broke, don't fix it* operates as a wise maxim in this respect.

Another common counseling issue occurs when grandparents have been very involved during divorce or bereavement, but now need to back away and allow the new family to become more independent. Even if both you and your spouse want to take a less active role, you may not agree about how or when to do this. Suppose you say, "Well, they seem to still need a lot of support," while your spouse may say, "Look, we're retired, let's enjoy ourselves!" Sometimes the grandmother, especially, has been very attached to her adult child and needs to let go and be a partner for her husband. When either the young family or the grandparents cannot make this transition to greater independence, counseling can be an option to move the process forward.

Let's Keep Communicating

As the family situation becomes more complicated, the more important it is to strive to improve communication among all family members. Grandparents today can be just as busy as parents. We do not always have the time to keep in touch, sort things through, and figure out the best way to handle tough situations. Yet it is worth it to spend the extra time. Strong, loving family relationships are no accident or *good luck*. They come to those who are willing to put in the effort, to share feelings and problems, lend an ear, or simply say "I love you" for no particular reason. Children especially will respond eagerly to a little extra attention at this vulnerable time.

Communication is the glue that holds healthy families together. When people feel particularly hurt, sad or angry, they may talk about other things, but hold back when it comes to the *really* painful or troubling subject. Communication is more than a means to convey information and make decisions. It is also about being willing to talk honestly, openly and nonjudgmentally about even the most difficult feelings and issues.

If you sense a deeper issue is being avoided in your communication with another family member, you can try probing gently by asking, "Is that the real issue? Is there something else going on you want to talk about?" Sometimes that gentle nudge is all that is required to open the door. If necessary, seek a counselor to facilitate the process, but above all, do not shove the painful subject under the rug indefinitely. Healing, acceptance and reconciliation can only begin after an issue is brought out into the open.

Mourning the Loss of the Family

Remarriage is the result of a loss. Both death and divorce entail a process of mourning the hopes and dreams of the original family on the part of all family members, including the grandparents. As described in Chapter 7, the mourning process generally requires one to three years, and involves feelings of denial, anger, depression, and finally, acceptance. During this process, it is quite normal to move back and forth within these stages, as opposed to a straight progression from one to the next. A wide range of other feelings may also arise: grief, guilt, sadness and anxiety. We have seen that stepfamilies tend to be founded on the myth that the new union will erase all unpleasant feelings and old attachments. So after remarriage, there is a strong tendency to repress the remaining unresolved feelings.

Grandparents, parents and children must finish mourning before they can truly be available for new relationships. Remarriage is complicated by the fact that we all mourn loss at different rates and different levels of awareness. Each family member's ability to accept the new arrangement depends on the stage of the mourning process that they have completed, or where they are stuck. You may find yourself still mourning, while your son is quite ready to move on to a new partner. Your daughter may be deeply mourning, long after you feel she should begin to explore new relationships. In another situation, your granddaughter's unresolved grief may complicate her adjustment to her mom's new marriage, which was readily accepted by both you and your daughter.

When a person has been through a marital breakup, they must resolve old issues from the first marriage before they can successfully remarry. Although the completion of the mourning process can take years, most people are ready to move on after the first anniversary of the loss. So I recommend a minimum one-year waiting period before remarriage, even if the new partner has been waiting in the wings. There is still a tremendous difference between a relationship and a marriage!

Unresolved mourning can lead to a hasty second marriage, or *marrying on the rebound.* You may sense that the new marriage is not founded on a healthy basis, and that it will simply create further family complications. What can you do if this is the case? Express your care and concern for your grandchildren's welfare as well as your adult child's, without telling them what to do. This is no easy task!

Jim had custody of his son, and his first wife had custody of their other two children. When Jim met Brenda right after the divorce, she made it clear that she did not like living with his son or having the other children come to visit. Yet Jim was so emotionally dependent on Brenda because of the unresolved loss of his first marriage that he ignored those issues and soon married Brenda. After the wedding, their arguments about the children only worsened. Jim could not bring himself to leave. Brenda finally broke up with him a year later. If Jim had waited a bit longer to marry, he might have realized that the relationship was stalled on an important issue and was destined to fail.

Complications are likely to arise whenever any member of the family is unable to complete the mourning process. A younger child may have less difficulty with memories of an earlier family than an older child, but we have seen (in Chapter 3) how deeply young children are affected by the emotions of their caregivers. Even when the new family is far more nurturing than the old one, unresolved grief for a lost parent can cause deep-seated problems.

Carly was in the second grade when her mother, Lois, first sought counseling. "Her teachers can't handle her," Lois explained. "She throws tantrums and disrupts the entire class. She hasn't responded to our attempts to change her behavior. She just seems to be getting worse." I asked Lois about Carly's past. She described Carly's biological father as an abusive and negligent spouse, but a loving father, who she left when Carly was 18 months old. After that, Lois and Carly led a difficult, unstable life until Lois met and married Rick. Rick was a caring husband and father, and so devoted to Carly that he wanted to adopt her. Since Lois had cut off contact with Carly's father and his family, she thought it would be great for Carly to have a *new* father who would really love her.

Carly finally seemed to have a nurturing home life, and yet she still could not control her toddler-like outbursts. What was wrong? I suspected that, although she hadn't expressed it, Carly deeply missed her real father. It took some time before Lois agreed to let me contact Carly's father and his parents.

I discovered that both he and his parents missed Carly and were eager to play a role in her life. Once contact was reestablished with her father and his parents, Carly's behavior problems began to improve. Rick eventually dropped the idea of adopting Carly as he realized that she already had a loving father.

Although she was very young when her parents separated, Carly's loss of contact with her biological father created emotional difficulties which took years to resolve. It is very important for children to stay in touch with their noncustodial parent and his or her extended family. They should know how and when they can contact the *other* parent and grandparents, and the terms of the visitation agreement. Young children are very concrete, and knowing this information gives them a sense of security.

When Active Intervention is Helpful

Don't hesitate to interpret your grandchild's feelings. You may consider this a task for a psychotherapist. Not true! If something is bothering your grandson and you ask, "What's bothering you?" or, "Why are you so upset?" most of the time he won't be able to tell you. It's not that he doesn't want talk about it. He really doesn't know. But if he seems upset and you know that he has not seen his mother in a long time, you could say, "I wonder if you're sad because you haven't seen Mom in a while."

You may be concerned about suggesting a *wrong* inter–pretation, but it's okay to be wrong. What he hears is, "Grandma (or Grandpa) are really interested in what I'm going through." He hears that you care about him enough to want to understand his feelings. It is much more helpful to offer an interpretation than to ask, "Why?" He *does not know* why, and even if he did, he probably could not express it.

Here is an example of making an interpretation.

You may know that your granddaughter's mother always fixed pancakes on Sunday morning, and now her mom is dead. When your granddaughter visits you and acts fussy at breakfast, instead of asking her, "*Why* don't you want pancakes this morning?" (expecting her to tell you), it's better to say, "You know, I wonder if the reason you don't want pancakes is because it reminds you of Mom and you miss her a lot." That's a very loving thing to say. She may respond, "No, no, that's not why," but don't be discouraged. After that her mood might change and she will be carefree for the rest of the day. She may not be able to acknowledge that you were right, but deep inside it makes a big difference to her that you cared enough to notice her feelings.

You may consider other types of subtle, unobtrusive interventions. The books you read to your grandchildren can also be helpful. Look especially for stories dealing with divorce, remarriage, stepsiblings, and a new mate for their parent. Many young children also like to make up stories. Encourage them to make up their own stories, including stories about the losses in their family. The story does not have to be about Joey himself, but it can be about his pet cat, his toy car, or his favorite dinosaur – whatever he is interested in.

Creative activities such as drawing pictures, play-acting, and making up stories and songs can be both fun and therapeutic. Another idea is to help the child put together a scrapbook that depicts the old family and the new family. The idea is to bring her feelings out into the open, rather than keeping the loss a secret. We grandparents today are much more comfortable dealing with feelings than *our* grandparents were. We may not be able to change the loss itself, but we *can* give the child the priceless opportunity to mourn that loss. Feelings talked about and expressed in stories, pictures and scrapbooks are never as painful and destructive as feelings hidden in secret, and are far less likely to lead to emotional problems down the road.

Nontraditional Remarriages

Even if you accept the concept of marriages that blend racial, religious, gender or cultural differences, it can still be a shock when your own child announces such a decision. If you strongly believe that these unions are wrong, never assume they cannot happen in your own family. In any case, your attitude (and that of the other grandparents) may well be the primary factors that determine whether this marriage will tear your family apart, or enrich it beyond measure.

Religious differences are perhaps the most common (and age-old) issue in blended families. In general, people today are more accepting and tolerant of religious differences than they used to be. A woman from a Catholic family married a man who had been raised in a Jewish family. At first the couple didn't give much thought to their children's religious education. When the children visited the Catholic grandparents, they went to Sunday mass, and sometimes to daily mass as well. Eventually the parents decided that they wanted religion to play a greater role in their children's lives, and chose to enroll them in a Jewish religious school. The Catholic grandparents didn't object; they were simply pleased that their grandchildren were finally receiving a religious education. Perhaps the most important factor in this situation is exposing the children to their religious heritage, values and traditions, so they have a foundation from which to make an informed choice about their religious beliefs when they are older.

When there is resistance to a religiously mixed couple in a first marriage, the birth of a grandchild often brings about a reconciliation. In a remarriage this healing process does not have the chance to occur. The children already exist and the new spouse may well feel like a threat to your beliefs. If the religious difference is very painful to you, ask yourself if it is creating an emotional coolness between you and the parents. If you withdraw emotionally from the couple, by the time the children are older you may be too distant from them to have any influence over their religious education. In contrast, by staying in contact despite your discomfort, you can find ways of sharing your heritage and beliefs in ways that do not conflict with the parents' choices.

In one family, the Christian grandparents were very close to their divorced daughter and had participated in the religious education of her children, who had been baptized in their religion. Then she married a Jewish man. Her parents were biased against Jewish people and worried that he would influence their grandchildren's religious beliefs. Although based in prejudice, this kind of conflict is a real concern. You cannot ignore it and hope it will go away. Strong religious differences must be addressed before they pull your family apart.

It has been my experience that when grandparents get to know the new spouse as a person, preconceived prejudices abate.

Cultural and racial differences can be just as difficult. A woman was married to a Middle Eastern man who, from an American perspective, had extremely chauvinistic beliefs and values. His culture taught that the man should be in complete control of the family and make all the child raising decisions. In our more liberal society, this created a painful situation for all of them. Working with the husband and wife, we reestablished the underlying values that had drawn them together, so that they could find common ground to reconcile their differences.

A wealthy WASP couple once came to see me, disturbed about their daughter's remarriage to a Jamaican man of mixed race. "What can we *do* about this marriage?" they asked me. I discovered that they had never fully accepted their daughter's husband or her coffee-colored baby. "If you don't change your attitude, you're going to lose your daughter as well as your grandchild," I told them, and added, "The world is multicolored! Get with it!" Nothing is more important than continuing a relationship with your child and grandchild.

Same-sex liaisons are becoming increasingly common. This may be the most difficult challenge of all for grandparents. However, the reality is that your adult child's sexual choices are beyond your control (and should be), and that same sex couples can provide a very stable, nurturing environment for children. As in all families, your children and grandchildren need your love and support. Whatever you do, do not withdraw from your grandchildren or refuse to accept the new family. Both of these moves could be far more damaging to your grandchild in the long run than having same-sex parents.

No family conflict is so bad that you can't talk about it. It is not helpful to take the position that you know what is better for your children than they do. When many family members are bothered by a particularly difficult issue, it can be helpful to organize family meetings. By getting together and hearing everyone's side of the story, you can learn to manage what may initially appear to be unresolvable, emotionally laden situations.

I frequently recommend regular family meetings of one hour (or less with younger children) on a weekly basis to discuss differences between family members. The children should definitely be part of the group. When family members are conscientious in their commitment to work through their differences, these meetings are very successful. In some cases, after the issue that brought the extended family together is resolved, the group continues using the meeting time for a family sharing time. When grandparents live in a different community than the family, family meetings can be programmed into their visits. While there is less continuity, the agreement to meet is a commitment by all members to use verbal communication and group process as a way of resolving differences. The hardest part of these meetings may be assigning an ongoing regular time. However, if something is really important, the time can always be found.

Grandparent Gift-Giving

Despite the potential for heated conflicts over religion, race and culture, some of the trickiest issues in blended families are associated with gift giving. Who should you give gifts to, and why? Now that the family is larger, you may wish to give more generous gifts to your biological grandchildren than to your stepgrandchildren, for all kinds of reasons. Is that fair? And what if the two (or more) sets of grandparents are able to afford very different levels of gifts?

In most families, it is too rigid to spend the same amount on everyone under all circumstances. Approach these issues with creativity, flexibility and sensitivity as to how your gift-giving decisions will affect the family.

Talking about presents with the parents *can* help to resolve gift dilemmas, but this may be a much lower priority for the parents than for you. The parents may well say, "Look, we've got so much to think about, just do whatever you think is right." Yet to you, this may be a highly charged subject that cannot be so easily dismissed. It usually means you will have to work it out yourself.

In making gift decisions, the first consideration should be, "What is in the best interest of the grandchildren?" Children in the same home are very competitive with each other. Although there may be extenuating circumstances, a basic guideline is to treat everyone about the same for group gifting occasions such as Christmas and Hanukkah. It would usually be inappropriate to give your biological grandchild a new bicycle, and then turn to your stepgrandchild of the same age and give him a game. That kind of discrepancy hurts both children. It sends them confusing messages about their self-worth, and fans the competitive pressure between them, which the parents will have to deal with later.

You may be able to arrange with the other grandparents to give an equivalent gift to their grandchild. On the other hand, your stepgrandchild's grandparents may have very different ideas from yours, making cooperation difficult. It is obvious how important it is to avoid giving one child a much nicer gift than the other will receive. Children in most blended families are very alert to any different or preferential treatment by relatives. You know how ruthless children can be with each other; you want to give them as little competitive ammunition as possible.

Birthday gifts, in general, can be more flexible and personalized. There is usually less competition because you only give gifts to one child at a time. This is not to say that the general guideline to avoid competition and jealousy should be ignored for birthdays, just that there is more leeway for flexibility when it comes to preferring a biological grandchild.

When children do not live in the same household, they are usually not in direct competition for your love and attention. Unless the children are very close and likely to compare notes, you can choose to spend whatever you like on each one.

In my case – four different families in four different locations – we may spend more on one grandchild than another in a different home if the need is greater. But in a blended household that includes both grandchildren and stepgrandchildren, you will want to be very sensitive to the fact that inequities in how you treat the children will result in fights, teasing, hurt feelings and low self-esteem.

Holiday and Family Events with the New Family

Holidays and important family events can be stressful in any family, but particularly so after remarriage. Who will spend the holidays with whom? We already know what a struggle this can be with only two sets of grandparents. What happens when we are talking about, say, *four* families instead of two? As a grandparent, you have a vital investment here. Yet trying to respond to everyone's wishes and expectations adds to the already considerable stress on the parents. Even if you find a solution that feels fair and balanced to you, they may not want to do it that way. Holidays can become *hell-idays.*

Gracefully accept the fact that you have little control over the final outcome. Even if you feel slighted, realize just how many people your children are trying to please. When you acknowledge the difficulty of their choices, they will feel your understanding and perhaps find it more desirable to spend time with you in the future.

Deciding who is part of the family group for holidays and special events is an issue in itself. What if the noncustodial parent does not want his parents to attend family events to which he is not invited? With each addition to the family, the dilemma becomes more complex. One woman could never convince her mother to come to the house when *that man* was there. Since *that man* was her second husband, this turned every holiday and birthday celebration into a power struggle. Her mother was so fixated by an unreasonable dislike that she was oblivious to the pain she was causing the rest of the family.

Decisions about who goes where and for how long are often complex and fraught with emotional baggage. Even after those tough decisions are made, getting everyone where they belong is an arduous task in itself. The complications of hosting four (or more) sets of grandparents for an already stressful holiday or family event can be daunting to even the strongest stepfamily.

Although the final outcome may not be up to you, you'll still want to determine your own preferences and priorities:

- Whose interests are most important: yours, your childrens', or your grandchildrens'?
- Do not be afraid to stand up for yourself to avoid getting pushed into a corner by the rest of the family, and finding yourself suffering through an unpleasant time as a result.
- Exercise caution hosting a holiday event for more people than you can accommodate to avoid hurting anyone's feelings.
- Set limits. Say, "This is all I can or want to do."
- Once in a while you may want to stretch your resources for a really special occasion, but do it because you really want to, not because you feel pressured into it.
- Be willing to compromise.

When Grandparents Remarry

Frankly, I have never heard of a grandparent who is considering remarriage ask, "How will this affect my grandchildren?" We become so preoccupied with our own concerns and busy lives that it does not occur to us that our grandchildren might be worried about our remarriage. Maybe we assume that it will not affect them, but if you're close to your grandchildren, they will be concerned when you remarry, even if they don't know how to express it. Don't assume that it won't affect them. Instead, bring them into the process. Sit down with them and tell them what is going on, then encourage them to share their feelings with you. Give them plenty of opportunities to spend time with your intended new spouse.

Often your remarriage *will* affect your grandchildren. After a divorce, both separating grandparents can stay in touch with the children. However, it may not feel the same, or be as easy to arrange, especially if you and your ex-spouse end up living in different parts of the country. Even more difficulties may begin when you remarry. Your new spouse will probably also have grandchildren, and you could end up spending more time with your stepgrandchildren than your own grandchildren. The grandchildren may end up with more *grandparents*, but less quality time with each of them.

Your remarriage can also benefit your grandchildren, especially if your spouse dies while the grandchildren are young.

George's wife died when their grandchildren were ages 2 and 4. After her death, George started dating Sharon. George's daughter Barb liked Sharon (although she complained at first that her father was dating too soon after her mother's death). Barb, her husband and her children lived abroad, so the grandchildren had only sporadic contact with these grandparents. When Barb's children finally met Sharon, they loved her, and soon they could not wait to see her again. Since these children only saw their paternal grandparents once a year, this *new* grandmother and maternal grandfather were very important to them.

My own father died when my children were young. When my mother remarried a few years later, they were thrilled to have a grandfather again. They grew up with him and did not think of him as a replacement, but as the *real thing*. He was kind and caring. My children were lucky to have such a grandfather, and his grandchildren seemed to feel the same way about my mother. Together, they had 11 grandchildren. They found creative ways to approach holiday visits. Sometimes they both spent the holidays with one side of the family, and sometimes they split their time and visited both sides. Sometimes they split up and each visited their own side of the family. Other times they hosted all of us. When their *grandfather* died, years later, my children really grieved and came from all over to be at his funeral. He was a very important person to them.

The Benefits of Remarriage

Building a happy, stable remarried family is a long hard process for everyone involved, including the grandparents. Yet it is possible, and it is worth the effort. Despite the prevalence of disrupted families today, there is no replacement for a complete, well-functioning family in a child's home. To make it work, every member of the family must be flexible, understanding and realistic in their expectations. When it works out, having a second father or mother, or four sets of grandparents, can benefit the child.

Although children can thrive in a single-parent family, it's better for them to have two caring parents in the home, if at all possible. When a child has lost a parent through death, remarriage can give her the opportunity to recover from the loss and resume a happy family life. When a child has been living in a tension-filled home, remarriage may be his only opportunity to learn that adults can live together without fighting. Two satisfied, loving parents are the primary role models from whom children learn about healthy relationships – the foundation and examples for their own future marriages.

The younger the child, the easier they will find it to adjust to a remarriage. Younger children seem readily able to enlarge their sense of the family to make room for three parental figures. One child had accepted his two fathers so well that when his therapist asked him, "Can we talk about your dad?" he asked, "Which dad do you mean?"

Remember Grandpa Barry, from the beginning of this chapter? Barry's grandson has six grandfathers, each of whom can have a unique relationship with the boy, based on their individual lifestyle, experiences and interests. Each grandfather can enhance the boy's understanding of life, enrich his self-esteem, and expand his capacity to form relationships. One grandfather might take the boy on trips, another might share an interest in baseball, while a third might live close by and see him regularly after school. Although Barry's dilemma made me realize just how complicated remarried families can be, a boy who has loving bonds with six grandfathers is a very lucky boy indeed!

Recommendations

- Even if you have serious concerns, work hard to accept the new spouse. A supportive attitude from you can go a long way to ease the pressures on the new family, allowing everyone to function at their optimum potential. Above all, don't assume that you *know better* and try to disrupt the new marriage.
- Your grandchildren may be members of two family units with different parenting resources and skills. It's important not to take sides by viewing one household as *right* and the other one as *wrong*.
- Anticipate that it will take one to three years for the new family to work through the adjustment period. Don't expect everything to go smoothly from *Day One*.
- Strive to maintain a close relationship with your biological grandchildren even if the custodial parents do not encourage your efforts.
- Don't be afraid to communicate with all members of the new family, including your new in-laws. Share your feelings and concerns as they come up. Ask the custodial parents for their input on any sensitive issues with your grandchildren.
- When it comes to gift-giving, holidays and family events, try to identify the options which will create the least stress for the new family. There is rarely a *perfect* answer, so look for flexible and creative solutions and be willing to compromise. Don't forget to consider your own limits.
- Don't assume that your own remarriage won't affect your extended family. Work to help everyone in the family understand your decision and its implications.

Reading List for Adults

Berman, Claire. *Making It as a Stepparent.* New York: Harper, 1986.

Raven, Linda. *Stepfamilies: New Patterns of Harmony.* New York: Julian Messner, 1982.

Visher, Emily and John Visher. *Stepfamilies: A Guide to Working with Stepparents and Stepchildren.* Brunner/Mazel, 1979.

Visher, Emily and John Visher. *Stepfamilies: Myths and Realities.* Carol Publishing Group, 1990.

Wallerstein, Judith S. and Joan B. Kelly. *Surviving the Breakup.* New York: Basic Books, 1996.

Reading List for Children

Berman, Claire. *What Am I Doing in a Step-Family?* Lyle Stewart, 1992. Honest answers, advice and suggestions for children on adjusting to life in a stepfamily. Positive message, but tells children that it takes time to learn to live together. Ages 5 to 10 years.

Burt, Mala S. and Roger B. Burt. *What's Special About Our Stepfamily? – A Participation Book for Children.* Garden City: Doubleday, 1983. Excellent for age 6 years and older.

Delton, Judy. *Angel's Mother's Baby.* Houghton Mifflin, 1989. Angel's been happy since her mother remarried *(Angel's Mother's Wedding,* Houghton Mifflin, 1987), but now her mother announces that she's going to have a baby! Angel is angry – she doesn't want her family to change again.

Leach, Norman and Jane Browne. *My Wicked Stepmother.* Macmillan, 1993. When Tom's dad remarries, Tom thinks his stepmother is a wicked witch who tricked his dad into marrying him. Tom isn't nice to her, even though she's nice to him. But when Tom sees that his stepmother can cry and be hurt, she changes from a wicked witch into a fairy godmother. Ages 4 to 8 years.

9

It *Can't* Happen in My Family: Abuse and Teen Pregnancy

*There is no more fundamental test of a society
than how it treats its children.*
– Ronald Reagan

Elsie thought her son-in-law Charlie was unusually punitive to his son Chris. He smacked the 8-year-old whenever the boy raised his voice or talked out of turn. Besides being physically abusive, Charlie was verbally abusive. If Chris failed to catch the ball in a game of catch with his father, Charlie yelled at him for being clumsy and lazy.

Elsie and her husband Mike watched in silent horror until their daughter Brita confessed to them that she could not convince her husband that his behavior toward Chris was wrong and damaging to him. She asked for her parents' help.

This was all the encouragement Elsie needed to become involved. First she spoke to her son-in-law's parents, reasoning that they might be the best people to talk with him. To Elsie's frustration and dismay, Charlie's parents saw nothing wrong with his behavior. Most likely Charlie's behavior was *normal* in his family of origin. Next, Elsie tried talking with Charlie, thinking some child development insights from an experienced grandmother might be all Charlie needed to recognized how harmful his behavior was to Chris's sense of self and his self-esteem. Unfortunately, the only result from this encounter was that Charlie grew cool to Elsie. He continues to treat his son badly, and barely tolerates his mother-in-law.

Is there anything more Elsie and Mike can do?

- They need to remain vigilant. If they find the abuse is more serious (details below) than what they initially observed, they should call their county social service agency and report Charlie.
- They can try to empower their daughter to help Charlie learn better parenting skills – perhaps parenting classes or marital or family counseling.
- They can be actively supportive with Chris, so he knows he has some strong allies in his corner.

Abuse Alert

It is indeed unfortunate that the topic of child abuse must be addressed in *Grandparenting: A Survival Guide,* but the incidence of this societal affliction is much higher than was previously believed, and affects all social classes and ethnic groups. It cannot be ignored. Because any grandchild could be a potential victim of child abuse, it is essential for grandparents to be informed about the most current thinking on this subject.

There are three major categories of child abuse:

1. *Physical Abuse:* A physical harmful action directed at a child which inflicts injuries such as bruises, burns, head injuries or poisoning.
2. *Physical Neglect:* Failure of a caretaker to act properly in safeguarding a child's health, safety and well-being. Neglect includes failure to provide medical care, and nutritional neglect.
3. *Child Sexual Assault:* Refers to a child being assaulted sexually by a family member (incest) or by an adult (other

than family). Child sexual assault includes exposure, fondling or sexual contact, intercourse (vaginally or orally), sodomy, and sexual exploitation.

The short-term *and* long-term effects of child abuse are devastating to their victims. Early child abuse may have a lifelong effect on a victim's ability to develop trust and form relationships. Other serious effects include: physical scars and deformity; learning dysfunctions; death; negative, aggressive or hyperactive behavior; stunted physical growth; or abuse of own children.

According to a nationwide poll conducted by *USA Today*, 43 percent of adults who were asked, "What do you do if you think a child is a victim of abuse?" said they did not know where to go for help. This chapter will prevent readers in need of information from being part of that statistic.

Throughout this chapter I recommend consulting with a counselor/therapist. I do this because I feel the issues presented here are beyond the realm of the *ordinary* grandparent/parent/child agenda, and therefore the help of a well- trained professional is necessary. It may require a professional's skill to push for the protection of a grandchild in an abusive situation.

Suspicious Grandparents

If your grandchild is being abused, you will likely be suspicious. However, there is a strong tendency to deny what you perceive and to rationalize it away – you are being overly suspicious; it is none of your business; your grandchild is not really being hurt; you do not want to accuse your child, their spouse, the babysitter, a relative or friend. *No Way!* It is far better to raise the issue and suffer the consequences than to fail to act on your suspicion.

Vera suspected that her recently divorced husband was sexually abusing their 4-and-a-half-year-old grandchild. At the time, Vera and her ex-husband shared care of Stacy while her mother worked. Stacy's mother was not convinced that there was a problem, but she agreed to let Vera bring Stacy in for an evaluation. To prepare

Stacy for her appointment, I told Vera to tell the child she was going to see a *worry* doctor – one who does not give any shots or medicine, but who instead talks and plays with kids and has lots of toys. Kids can talk with the Worry Doctor about things they would not talk about with anyone else. The Worry Doctor is there to help kids talk about their worries and help them feel better.

Child abuse evaluations are not easy, nor are they 100 percent conclusive. In this particular evaluation, I found nothing which led me to think that this child was being abused. Nevertheless, the grandmother was wise to arrange the evaluation, if only to set her fears at rest.

On another occasion, the paternal grandmother and her 4-year-old granddaughter Hanna were referred to me by the Victim/Witness Assistance Program of the county court for both an evaluation of sexual abuse and therapy. Her paternal grandmother had temporary custody of Hanna while her parents worked out custody arrangements and charges of sexual abuse against the father.

After six sessions with the child, I was highly suspicious of sexual abuse. It was clear that Hanna needed a period of psychotherapy to work through the very traumatic four years of her life. The court awarded custody to the maternal grandparents, and these grandparents discontinued contact with me. This was very sad for me and, I think, for Hanna, too. We had developed a positive therapeutic relationship, and Hanna used me and my office as a safe haven to play out her life traumas. Unfortunately, the family climate that allows abuse to occur is the same climate that makes meaningful therapeutic intervention often unsuccessful.

There are criteria grandparents can use to help them determine if their grandchild is in trouble. Consider these four basic questions which may indicate a child is having emotional problems; whether they are caused by abuse or a reaction to other stress factors is your judgement call.

- Have there been noticeable changes in the child's normal eating and sleeping habits?
- Is the child's behavior consistent or inconsistent in daycare or at school?
- Are the child's emotional responses and reactions, such as temper outbursts, sadness or joy, normal or inappropriate?
- Is the child behaving appropriately for his age?

Note your observations and follow up by listening closely the next time you visit with the child, or talk with the parents. If you see or hear something suspicious, keep your antenna up. Don't dismiss it. It may be helpful to maintain a written log with dates and behavior noted to consider symptoms over a period of time. Sometimes apparently isolated behavior reveals itself to be more persistent when observed over time. If a symptom persists and appears to be serious, this may be the time to consult with a professional counselor. They may be able to assess the situation and give you objective, professional guidance on how to proceed further.

A grandmother sought consultation with me because her daughter's new partner was using drugs. She was concerned that her granddaughter was being sexually molested by the boyfriend because she noticed such a dramatic negative change in the child's behavior. This could have been due to a number of different factors: the mother spending more time with the boyfriend instead of her child; appropriate behavior for her developmental stage; or, as grandma suspected, abuse. This was a serious issue, but before I could evaluate the child, the mother left town with her daughter.

As I have noted, it is frequently very difficult to get a clear picture of what is really happening to the child and to follow through with the much-needed intervention. However, in all three of the cases cited, I felt the grandmothers had done the right thing in consulting with me and, despite the outcome, I was able to be of significant support to these grandmothers.

What to Do?

According to current statistics, approximately 45 out of every 1,000 children nationally are reported as victims of some form of child mistreatment. In 1993, there were 20,000 substantiated cases of child sexual abuse in the U.S., and this alarming figure grows at the rate of 10 percent every year. The National Commission for the Prevention of Child Abuse and Neglect reports that 20 percent to 30 percent of all girls and 10 percent to 15 percent of all boys will be victims of some form of sexual abuse by age 17. The abuser may be anyone who has contact with the child: a parent, stepparent, relative, babysitter, friend, teacher, stranger, or even a grandparent. Usually the more contact a potential abuser has with a child, the more likely they are to act. This means that those in daily contact with the child are most often the source of the abuse.

Child abuse *must* be reported. Laws on child abuse differ from state to state, but certain generalities apply. In every state, professionals who work with children, as well as physicians, teachers, mental health professionals, and medical care workers including nurses and emergency medical service personnel, are required by law to report suspected child abuse. Police, county social service agencies or the child protective agency in all states will respond to reports made by *anyone* who is concerned about a child's safety or welfare. Often the agency guarantees confidentiality to the reporting party. Half of all reports are made by friends, neighbors and relatives, and anonymous callers.

If you suspect abuse and do not know who to call, you can contact the U.S. National Center on Child Abuse and Neglect, Washington, D.C. (1-800-394-3366), for referral to your state protective agency. One of the leading resources in the country for help, education and evaluation is the C. Henry Kempe Center for Prevention and Treatment of Child Abuse and Neglect, 1205 Oneida St., Denver, CO 80220 (303-321-3963).

Mom is Being Battered!

Something terrible is happening in your grandchild's home. Your son is battering his wife; your daughter is being battered by her husband. Although less common, the female in the marriage may be the batterer. You may know, you may suspect, or you may not know. You question your grandchild, but do not receive any answers. Children are protective of their parents and hesitate to disclose the violence that goes on *behind closed doors* in their home – it is a family secret. What can you do when you feel helpless to respond? Can you intervene for the sake of your child, the parent? Can you intervene for the sake of your grandchild?

You should certainly use whatever power you have to direct the adults involved to obtain help, such as counseling, AA, AlAnon, drug abuse programs, police intervention and women's shelters, and *please* do not ignore the grandchildren's well-being because of your concern for their parent! One-third of all children who witness their parent being battered demonstrate significant behavioral and emotional problems.

Children who live in a battering relationship experience the most insidious form of child abuse. Even if they are not physically abused by either parent, they bear deep psychological scars from witnessing the violence between their parents. They learn to become part of a dishonest conspiracy of silence. They live in a world of unhealthy make-believe.

Child Battering

Family secrets are not unusual in dysfunctional families. Once I treated a 7-year-old boy who was regularly battered by his father during alcoholic rage. Andrew had been referred to me by his school because of behavior problems. There was no indication of alcoholism or abuse when I met with his parents to obtain a family history. After a number of appointments with me, Andrew started sharing his secret. His dad often got drunk and hit him. Once he pushed the boy down the stairs, causing Andrew to bleed so badly that his mother took him to the emergency room. On the way to the hospital, he was carefully coached to tell the doctors he slipped and fell. As Andrew began to share accounts of the violence in his home, it became necessary for me to notify the authorities.

This often puts the therapist in a difficult position: a child has told you his *secret*, and now you have to report it. Andrew and I talked about how it was necessary for me to get help for his family in order to help him. He reluctantly understood. This case had a positive outcome. His father was able to resolve his drinking problem, the family underwent some family therapy sessions, while Andrew continued counseling with me for a year. His school problem abated, and by Andrew's eighth birthday, counseling was no longer needed.

Each situation has its own unique set of circumstances. Grandparents, seek professional advice on how best to intervene!

Too Young to be a Grandparent

You feel very fortunate – you have a well-functioning family! No abuse in your home. Then the bomb drops – your teenage daughter is pregnant and surprise, surprise, you're going to be grandparents. Your 4-year-old son is going to be an uncle.

Lucy, age 16, sought counseling at her grandparents' insistence. She was living with them because her parents – firm believers in *tough love* – had kicked her out of the house. Lucy was a model teenager during the first few months she lived with her grandparents, but five months later the *honeymoon* was over: Lucy announced she was pregnant. She wanted to have the baby and take care of it. She announced that she would show her parents that she could be a better parent than they had been to her – a typical teenage attitude.

The happily-ever-after fantasy rapidly disappeared as Lucy began to care for her new baby. She was too immature to be a good parent. She wanted to be doing what other kids her age were doing: hanging out, experimenting with relationships and developing autonomy from their parents. Instead, she was supposed to care for a baby. Guess who was called into action? The primary responsibility for child care of teen babies usually falls on the mother's parents, the grandparents. In this case it was the *great*-grandparents, who were still young enough to care for a baby.

Most pregnant teenagers live at home during the pregnancy as well as after the baby is born. The new mother is both a child to her parents and a parent to her child. The young grandparents-to-be, often still raising other children, first need to adjust to this crisis pregnancy and then face the dilemma of how much responsibility to take in caring for the new baby. Sometimes the baby begins to regard the grandparents as her parents, and the biological mother feels left out and resentful. In other situations, the grandparents resent this infringement on their lives. All three generations live under tremendous stress. Seeking counseling may help them find some relief and solutions to their tri-generational crisis.

There is a 1-in-5 chance of teen pregnancy occurring in your family. About 1 million teenage pregnancies occur in the U.S. each year, accounting for one-fifth of all babies born annually. This crisis pregnancy stirs up powerful and contradictory feelings. The options – abortion, adoption, marriage or single parenting – require some of the toughest decisions that teens and their parents (when they are included in the planning) can ever face. Conflicting emotions of denial, shock, anger, embarrassment, shame, guilt, resignation and joy make the choice even more difficult.

Studies show that a rapidly falling percentage of pregnant teenagers are opting for abortion. A 1992 study in seven southern states indicated the percentage of pregnant teens choosing abortion fell from 38 percent to 29 percent between 1986 and 1990. The social stigma of unwed motherhood is almost non-existent now, and teenagers consider having a baby a fantasy of unconditional love and living happily ever after.

As 16-year-old Lucy discovered , the *happily ever after* fantasy fades quickly with all the work and responsibility of motherhood.

As new grandparents, the following suggestions may help teenage mother and baby:

- You can best help your daughter learn good parenting skills by being good role models. The ideal is to facilitate the development of mothering skills while fostering the psychological growth appropriate for her age level – not an easy task!
- If you are willing to do it, an offer of extended child care for your grandchild may enable your daughter to return to school or work, improving future prospects for both mother and child.
- If your daughter wants you to be *the parents* and you agree, prepare yourself for the time when she decides to reclaim her child.

When Your Teen Son is the Father

According to estimates, one out of every 20 adolescent boys becomes responsible for a pregnancy. Since the boy's impending parenthood is not obvious, it is easier for the issues involved to remain hidden. He can keep the pregnancy secret from his parents. He is most likely to confide in them if he feels they will understand, provide helpful support, and not shame him or his girlfriend.

However, his parents may not understand that need for support and guidance. They may not want any part of the overwhelming decisions their son now faces:

- As the biological father, should he marry the mother, and if so, where will they live?
- Should he stay in school and complete his education, or drop out to support the mother and baby?
- What about his plans for higher education and career?

Many teen fathers remain involved throughout the pregnancy and childbirth, retain strong feelings for the mother and child, and contribute financial support. With paternal grandparent support, the birth father is more likely to bond with his infant, which can lead to a growth-producing father/infant relationship that benefits both infant and father.

A Tragic Case Study with a Happy Ending

Sonja and Gary were juniors in high school when Sonja discovered she was more than four months pregnant. She thought they had been practicing safe birth control because she had read an article about the rhythm method in a magazine. Sonja's parents had never talked to her about sex; her mother had said, "Ask your father," and her father said, "Ask your mother." She had wanted to remain a virgin until she married, but her attraction to Gary proved too strong.

Sonja and Gary considered marriage, but felt they were too young and still had important years of education ahead of them. They decided on abortion. Since Sonja was so far along in her pregnancy, this may not have been a realistic option. The night before the appointment, Sonja recalled, "I felt the baby move inside me. I could tell she was a little person! I couldn't do it. I told Gary, and he was relieved. We each thought the other one wanted to give up the baby, but neither of us truly did."

When Sonja was seven months pregnant, tragedy struck: Gary was killed in an auto accident. Following that traumatic event, Sonja described herself as functioning in *survival mode.* Her daughter was born the night before her senior year of high school was to begin. Six weeks later, Sonja returned to school. Her survival mode lasted for the next six months. She remembers little of that period except how great her parents and Gary's parents were. At first she hung out with her old friends, but soon realized she now had little in common with them. Her world no longer revolved around dating, drinking, dancing, and going to movies. Gary's death and the birth of Meredith had matured her far beyond her years.

When Sonja graduated from high school, she and the baby moved out of town so she could attend college. Gary's parents had already moved to this town and invited Sonja and Meredith to live with them, which they did. Sonja looked forward to marriage some day, but she wanted to know she could manage on her own first. She finally married when Meredith was 9 years old. In looking back at this period, Sonja says that it was only due to the support and understanding of the four grandparents that she and Meredith were able to survive under their very challenging circumstances.

Rapid Transition: Grandparents to Great-Grandparents

When your teen grandchild becomes a parent, you become a great grandparent. You look the same, you feel the same, but you are *different*. Your kinship is one generation farther away. In this unique situation of teenagers having babies and needing a lot of support, you may be needed by your child and their child and the baby in ways I cannot even outline here. My recommendation is to be calm, accepting and available if possible.

It *Can* Happen In Our Family

As we approach the 21st century, we are not leaving behind a culture of healthy social values that we can be proud of passing on to our children and grandchildren. As a society, we seem unable to harness or halt the negative energies destroying our ideals of family life. No one is immune. U.S. Attorney General Janet Reno recently noted, "Growing up as a child today is more difficult than raising a child."

Grandparents, what can we do to improve this situation for our grandchildren?

Here are some suggestions:

- The worst thing we can do is passively condone family misbehavior and acting out.

- We must calmly and rationally speak out against inap–propriate behavior, and suggest interventions and options.
- Our behavior should be contemporary and exemplary, and serve as a role model for our children and their children.
- As grandparents we must be able to forgive the past when our families learn to make changes for the future.
- It is urgent for us to find ways to *make a difference.*

Recommendations

- As painful as it may be for you, do not wear blinders when your antenna alerts you to possible child abuse.
- Be responsible and either report what you suspect to the proper authorities, or work with a counselor for guidance in reporting.
- Be supportive to your teenage daughter or son when a crisis pregnancy occurs. Help them with decision-making that suits their needs, rather than your preferences.
- View the crisis pregnancy as an event that draws your family into a closer relationship.

Reading List for Adults

Besharov, Douglas J. *Recognizing Child Abuse.* New York: Free Press, 1990.

Monahon, Cynthia. *Children and Trauma: A Parent's Guide to Helping Children Heal.* Lexington Books, 1993.

Owens, Carolyn. *Pregnant and Single: Help for the Tough Choice.* Zondervan Publishing House, 1990.

Walker, Lenore. *Battered Women.* New York: Harper Row, 1979.

Reading List for Children

Garbarino, James. *Let's Talk About Living In A World of Violence.* Erickson Institute, 1993. An activity book for children ages 7-11 years to help process feelings, thoughts and experiences as they relate to violence.

Subotnick, Leah S., *The Bird and the Buttons: Healing Stories for Children*. Kempe Center, 1992. Seven illustrated stories empowering children to survive crises and live happy lives. Includes a guide for adults.

White, Laurie A., and Steven Spencer. *Take Care With Yourself.* Daystar Press, 1983. Ages 7-11 years. A guide to understanding, parenting, and healing the hurts of child abuse.

10

Infertility Choices:
Pregnancy, Adoption or Child-free

So God created Man in his own image ...
And God blessed them, and God said to them,
'Be fruitful and multiply.'
– Genesis 1:27:28

"I'm glad you told me rather than my mother!" said Julie, divorced and age 40. I had suggested that she consult a specialist about freezing some of her eggs now to be used later. Current medical thinking is that after a woman reaches age 43, her eggs are old and not easily fertilized.

"My mom keeps bothering me about getting married and having a baby. She really gave me a guilt trip the other day when she said she wanted to be a grandmother before she died." Julie still hopes to marry and have a baby, but she knows that time is running short on her biological clock.

Based on a nationwide survey conducted by the National Center for Health Statistics (1995), of approximately 40 million couples of child-bearing age (including unmarried, cohabitating couples), some 3.3 million couples experience infertility. This rate of one infertile couple in 12 has not changed since the mid-1960s; the number has only increased with population growth.

The above example highlights some important issues we will examine in this chapter:

- Parents want to be grandparents.
- The timing of having babies and by what method they will arrive are subjects the younger generation avoids discussing with the senior generation.
- New techniques now available to help childless couples or singles have a baby may sound almost too incredible for potential grandparents to comprehend.
- Today, a woman of *advanced maternal age* (over age 35) can carry a healthy baby to term as successfully as a younger woman, as long as she is healthy and is still producing eggs.

When having a baby is an overriding priority for couples (or singles), the emotional impact this endeavor exerts on potential parents *and* potential grandparents concerns us. Would-be parents can invest a huge amount of time, money and energy in having a child. Natural conception by a husband and wife is certainly the ideal preference. Any departure from that ideal is experienced as a *loss* by those who want the baby. For those whose biology has let them down, non-conception is a real loss.

Whether the baby is eventually born though the mother's pregnancy, or adopted with no biological relationship, or the choice is child-free living, the process may be the most stressful experience your children ever encounter. It is important for potential grandparents to be sensitive to the crisis, and to be empathic, nonjudgmental and as supportive as possible regarding this difficult decision for your adult children.

Infertility: An Unanticipated Crisis

Have you heard these *charming* remarks from friends and relatives? "Isn't it about time your kids started a family?" "Are your children going to have children?" or "You're so lucky you're not asked to baby-sit all the time."

You want your children to have babies. You *want* to be grandparents, but perhaps they have not discussed the subject with you. After all, this is a very private matter, and you don't ask because you don't want to interfere. However, you can't resist subtle little suggestions like, "Isn't it nice you bought a house with so much room?" or "It's great you're taking vacations now – you won't be able to do that when you have kids."

Most married couples assume that conception and giving birth are their choice. The average age for marriage is much higher now than it used to be. The typical age for a first marriage has climbed to age 27 for men and age 24 for women, as reported by the Census Bureau in 1996.

Teena and Gary married when they were in their mid-20s. They planned to attend graduate school, become established in their careers, have a house and a little money set aside before starting their family – a common pattern. When Teena and Gary reached age 35, they felt ready to have children. After one year of trying, they had not conceived.

Infertility is defined as the inability to conceive a pregnancy after a year of sexual relations without contraception, or the inability to carry pregnancy to a live birth. Gary and Teena were shocked and surprised to discover that after all their careful planning, things were not working out. Teena began tests with her doctor, and Gary reluctantly went in for a semen analysis.

As they entered their second year of being unable to conceive, they began to avoid friends who had children. Each month they grew more unhappy. They became unable to discuss their infertility with anyone – even with each other! Infertility speaks to the most intimate aspect of a couple's relationship. Partners become frustrated, angry, hostile and anxious. Infertility can become the greatest stress factor in their lives.

Most couples report that infertility causes stress in their marriage. Some research reports that women react more intensely and show greater distress over infertility problems than men. That does not mean the men are not suffering, too. One man expressed his frustration: "I never know the right thing to say every disappointing month after month."

Why not discuss the problem with their parents? In this case, Gary and Teena were both close to their own parents and shared many things with them, but they were not able to share this. This reluctance and inability to discuss infertility issues with the couple's parents is typical. This subject is taboo, *especially* with one's parents. The couple know how much their parents want grandchildren, and admitting their infertility problem to their parents only intensifies their feelings of shame and failure. The issue is too painful, and the couple are too proud to face a frank conversation about it.

Some suggestions for potential grandparents that may help:

- Go along with your kids – don't pry.
- Don't shame them.
- Don't let your feelings of helplessness cause you to retreat from them.
- Become more informed about infertility issues on your own, including emotional stresses and possible solutions.
- Let your kids know that you are there for them, care for them and love them, regardless of conception.
- Avoid offhand remarks and comments about your desire for grandchildren.
- Show support and understanding, which can help reduce emotional stress and pressure on your children in dealing with infertility.

Gary and Teena were referred to Northwestern University Center for Assisted Reproduction (CFAR). At CFAR and similar facilities throughout the country, specialists in reproductive endocrinology and reproductive surgery work diligently to turn the disappointment and devastation of infertility into the excitement and elation of pregnancy. The center's goal is to discover and, when possible, correct mechanical failures of the reproductive system that prohibit the female egg from joining with the male sperm to produce a healthy embryo. The procedure consists of initial testing resulting in a diagnosis and a prognosis.

After two visits and approximately four months of initial tests, more than 90 percent of the couples will receive a diagnosis and prognosis. Achieving pregnancy will take longer, perhaps 12 to 18 months, and may involve medications, surgery or more high-tech procedures. Many excellent assisted reproductive programs are available throughout the country. The best source for information on these programs is often a couple's gynecologist.

In approximately 40 percent of infertility cases, the problem is solely female; in another 40 percent it is solely male; the remaining cases involve both partners. Infertility causes will never be fully understood in 3.5 percent of cases. About 95 percent of the time, infertility may be resolved.

Infertility is often perceived as a blow to a couple's self-esteem, a violation of their privacy, and an assault on their sexuality. Taking positive action almost always helps. Once Teena and Gary made the commitment to work with a fertility specialist, they became less depressed and withdrawn. Their doctor insisted the problem was one they needed to work on *together*. After a series of stressful tests and procedures, they were among the fortunate couples. Three years from the time they decided to get pregnant, they gave birth to a fine healthy baby boy.

Nontraditional Baby Making

Two of the most common and effective treatments for infertility today are *In Vitro Fertilization* (IVF) and *Gamete Intrafallopian Transfer* (GIFT). These procedures are described in a guide for couples published by the American Society for Reproductive Medicine. Presented here is a summary from *IVF and GIFT: A Guide to Assisted Reproductive Technologies.* For additional information, contact the American Society for Reproductive Medicine, 1209 Montgomery Highway, Birmingham, AL 35216-2809; tel. 205-978-5000.

- *In vitro* literally means outside the body. IVF is a method of assisted reproduction in which the man's sperm and the woman's egg are combined outside of the body in a laboratory dish. If fertilization occurs, the resulting embryo is transferred to the woman's uterus, where it will hopefully implant in the uterine lining and mature. IVF is a reasonable treatment choice for couples with various types of infertility.
- A *gamete* is a male or female reproductive cell (a sperm or an egg). During GIFT, sperm and egg are mixed and injected (transferred) into one or both fallopian tubes. Fertilization can then take place in the fallopian tube as it does in natural, unassisted reproduction. Once fertilized, the embryo travels to the uterus by natural processes. Women with normal, healthy fallopian tubes are candidates for GIFT, including women who have unexplained infertility, and couples whose infertility is caused by male, cervical or immunological factors.

The main difference between IVF and GIFT is that GIFT requires healthy fallopian tubes, while IVF is appropriate for women with tubal disease or even absent fallopian tubes. In IVF, fertilization takes place in a laboratory dish and can be visually confirmed. In GIFT, fertilization is unconfirmed. There are other more complicated and more expensive procedures which are variations of IVF and GIFT, known as *ZIFT, PROST* and *TET*.

In Vitro Fertilization (IVF) or Gamete Intrafallopian Transfer (GIFT) cost between $7,000 to $10,000. Some health insurance plans will cover one-third to one-half of the cost. The procedure is expensive; *too* expensive for some couples. The cost of ZIFT, PROST or TET is usually greater than IVF or GIFT because additional procedures are needed.

- *Artificial Insemination*: In this case, the woman is fertile, but the man is infertile. The woman can be artificially inseminated with another man's sperm. Within the sterile confines of an examining room, a physician instills precollected sperm into the woman's vagina with an instrument resembling a turkey baster.
- *Surrogate Mothers*: If a husband is fertile, but his wife is not, the couple may decide to hire a woman to be artificially inseminated with the husband's sperm and carry the baby to term. The agreement is that the surrogate mother will relinquish the baby to the couple at birth.

Parents Want to be Grandparents

As the couple become involved in active pregnancy intervention, they may share information with you about what they are doing. Some of the procedures may sound so alien in terms of medical and scientific procedures that would-be grandparents are unsure how to respond. When the couple finally reveal this most sensitive secret, they want their parents' understanding and support to bolster their beliefs, their decision and their sense of self-determination. This can be a most delicate situation. It is imperative that your reaction does not allow this to become a no-win situation for everyone involved. Some important points to consider:

- New reproductive technologies may raise deep and profound questions for you and jolt your fundamental values. Try your best to remain open-minded, and keep your focus on the end goal – a healthy grandchild.
- Because of discomfort in talking about sexual matters with your adult children, you may withdraw due to embarrass–ment. Examine your boundaries within this subject and find a comfort level between your child's need to discuss sexual matters and your personal reluctance. This might

also be the time to try pushing beyond your previous comfort level if you are willing.

- You may resent the possibility that the couple may decide on a baby that does not have a genetic connection to both families. Try talking about this with your minister, priest or rabbi, and with other friends and family members who may have experienced this situation firsthand.
- Avoid the reverse situation: would-be grandparents who grow so excited about their grandparenting opportunity that they become overly involved and intrusive in *nontraditional baby making*.
- Be aware that your strong wish for grandchildren may create an additional sense of failure, guilt or shame for the infertile couple.
- The legal dilemmas associated with nontraditional baby making have been about *other* people – but now, all of a sudden, they may apply to *your* kids!
- If your children are not already aware of Resolve, Inc., suggest this as a valuable resource offering support groups across the country and helpful literature pertaining to coping with and mastering infertility. (Resolve, Inc., 1310 Broadway, Somerville, MA. 02144-1731; tel: 617-623-0744.)

Single-Parent Conception

Sally has not had great success with men. Now her biological clock is running out and she wants to be a mom. Jill, a lesbian, is in a comfortable long-term relationship and feels she has everything except a baby. Sally and Jill represent an ever-increasing number of women who want to give birth to babies where the biological father will have no role in parenting or support. Prospective grandparents may already have a whole range of feelings about their daughter's choice of lifestyle. Now, added to that, comes the daughter's wish to become a single parent. As the saying goes, *Little children, little problems; big children, big problems.*

Many prospective grandparents are ambivalent about their child's decision. It is wonderful to contemplate becoming a grandparent, and it is wonderful for one's daughter to become a parent. Yet certain unavoidable practical questions arise. Whose sperm will she use? Can she manage parenting in her chosen lifestyle? As in so many difficult personal family issues presented and discussed in this guide, the decisions ultimately belong to our children. Our role is to support them in their choices.

Let us review some hypothetical questions and answers:

Q: If she asks our help in this decision-making process, what should we say? It's nice to be a mother, but is she aware of all the obstacles – and how much help does she want from us?

A: There is no single answer to this concern. Your concerns are valid, and acting on them depends on your previous relationship with your daughter.

Q: Our daughter's outlook on life is so different from ours. What should we do if this turns out to be just another of her irresponsible whims?

A: That may happen, but if she is already pregnant, remember that she is presenting you with a grandchild, and it is your joy and responsibility to accept this child with love and support!

Q: Is she living in a *safe* community that will accept her lifestyle and her child?

A: This is a *very important* consideration, and one I suggest you raise with your daughter.

Q: Can this child develop appropriately without a male in the home?

A: The important issue is parenting style, rather than family configuration.

Q: What happens if the biological father re-enters the scene
        later on and requests visitation or custodial rights?
A: Encourage your daughter to consult a lawyer for the most
        current rulings before she pursues conception.

As yet there is little research on *donor* conception. We do
know more and more women are using this as a means to
parenthood. There is no question that we are treading on shaky
territory. My overall recommendation is to have confidence in
your daughter's decision.

The Adoption Option
Eventually a couple may decide to end attempts to achieve a
pregnancy. When parenting remains a top priority, adoption
becomes a consideration. This option may feel more *familiar* to
would-be grandparents – but don't be so sure. Adoption
procedures are changing dramatically:

* The traditional form of adoptions, with most decisions made
  by professional counselors and the adoptive parents, and
  birth parents turning over all decisions to them, is a thing
  of the past. In these adoptions, all information about all
  parties was kept secret and no contact before, during or
  after the adoption was permitted.
* Secrecy between the relinquishing parents and the adopting
  parents has been replaced by open adoptions with a variety
  of arrangements between the birth mother and the adopting
  parents.
* Fully open adoption is when the birth parent and the
  adopting parents select each other. They have the option
  of ongoing contact over the years, either in person or
  through correspondence.
* Some programs offer a limited version of open adoption,
  sometimes called semi-open. In these adoptions, the
  secrecy of the past is avoided, but there are some limitations

in contact between birth parents, adopting parents and the
child before, during and after the adoption.
- Also different today are the unanticipated and sometimes
monumental legal problems resulting from our litigious
contemporary society.

Some years ago, Lorna came to see me about her son and
daughter-in-law's problem. Mark and Trudie badly wanted a
baby. They had tried to get pregnant for many years. They were
not interested in pursuing nontraditional methods of conception,
and were now thinking about adoption. Lorna, the would-be
grandmother, was exploring resources for adoption to share with
them. Could I help her?

This was a new experience for me. I had never experienced
the mother of an adult son quite so involved with what I had
always viewed as a rather private issue. I carefully considered
whether I might be fostering inappropriate behavior on Lorna's
part by giving her suggestions and information. Counseling
revealed her to be a caring, supportive mother trying to be helpful
to her son and his wife, rather than attempting to interfere or
exert control. We discussed some of the options presented here.

Lorna felt the couple wanted a Caucasian infant and were
willing to wait until a child became available. I shared
information on agencies I knew about and she took it from there.
This story ends happily. The agency accepted the couple on
their waiting list, which in itself is not easy. This was only the
beginning of the process. The couple had to be evaluated for
age, health, stability and finances, followed by a home study.
After waiting three more years, a pregnant woman reviewing a
number of information sheets on prospective adoptive parents
chose them as the parents for her baby.

Trudie and Mark accompanied the expectant mother to her
last two prenatal appointments and were with her in the delivery
room along with her mother when she gave birth. For Trudie
and Mark the hardest part was the 72 hours following delivery –

the period of time in their state in which the biological mother may change her mind. Six months later, when they had completed all the necessary legal procedures, a healthy female infant was finally theirs!

The procedure in legally finalizing an adoption differs from state to state. Healthy white American infants are difficult to adopt. Ninety percent of single mothers are raising their babies – often with help from grandparents (see Chapter 2). Very few married couples give up their babies. Only a small fraction of adopting parents find healthy Caucasian infants available. For many prospective parents, the desire to raise a family leads them to consider other options. Grandparents, here are some of your kids' choices:

- Special needs children – those with emotional, physical and mental disabilities – are usually available. They are often older, ages 5 to 17 years, and have spent time in foster care before becoming available for legal adoption.

  The adopting parents need a very strong commitment to developing trust and attachment with older foster care children. Frequently these children have been deprived of ongoing healthy experiences and are very cautious about committing to yet another relationship. It can be done, but it is not easy.

- Adopting attractive youngsters *advertised* on TV as needing a home, such as *Wednesday's Child* featured on many local TV news programs. I hope your children exercise extreme caution if they are considering this avenue. The children are so appealing that potential parents respond emotionally before sorting out the practical details.

  On the other hand, if parents are sure they are tempera-mentally suited for this child, it may be the right fit for the parents and child. The skill in evaluating placement varies with the various agencies that participate in the TV feature.

To bring a child into your home and then find it is the wrong placement is heartbreaking for the child and adults.

- Enlisting the help of a lawyer, clergyman or doctor who may know personally of a special case in which a mother is planning to give up her unborn baby. As long as the adopting couple pays only the legitimate costs of the mother and the professionals that help them, this form of adoption is legal. Be aware that independent adoptions are less ironclad than agency adoptions, and arrangements can evaporate overnight if the mother changes her mind.

- Adoption of foreign orphans, particularly children from Third World countries, is legal and is handled through American adoption agencies.

  For more information, consult the *Report On Foreign Adoption*, International Concerns Committee for Children, 911 Cypress Drive, Boulder, CO 80303; tel. 303-494-8333.

- African-American parents can easily adopt African-American babies, but African-American social workers have been reluctant to allow these children to grow up in white homes, citing difficulties the children have adjusting as they grow up. This restriction seems to be relaxing at present; biracial children are placed in white homes where they are wanted after a concerted search has been made for an appropriate African-American home first.

Each adoption option has its advantages and disadvantages. The mother of three adopted special needs children came to talk to me about her children. In working with her, I learned what a remarkable family this was and what wonderful opportunities for growth and development a nurturing environment can offer special needs children.

One of the babies was born to a woman with a crack cocaine addiction. The mother did not want the baby, so my client and her husband adopted Frank when he was one week old. Everyone around them discouraged them from taking a *crack baby* because the prognosis was so bad. At that time they were experienced parents of two special needs girls who were doing quite well, and they wanted to round out their family with a boy.

They fell in love with Frank, who was age 3 when I had contact with Jan, his mother. He was the easiest and least disabled of the three children. More recent research has confirmed what this couple must have felt when they first saw Frank: crack babies raised in a warm, supportive, loving environment work through their addiction quite rapidly and have the capacity to develop normally. This is quite a different story than the couple were told when they adopted Frank.

On the minus side, I recall the case of an attractive youngster *advertised* for adoption on a TV show that caught the attention of a couple who thought it might be nice to have one more child. Unfortunately, this impulsive response in no way qualified these parents to deal with this particular child's emotional problem. The resulting situation was a disaster for the whole family, who were referred for counseling by their minister after James, an African-American age 11, had lived in their home for three months.

The presenting complaint was frequent fighting that verged on violence between the two older biological brothers and James, the new addition to the family. In my brief contact with the family, they revealed that they had received family counseling a few years earlier for disruptive behavior by the two boys and their inability to set limits. This biological family, barely able to function as a family unit, was complicated by the addition of James, who had lived in five different foster homes before joining them. James' needs were considerable, and this family completely lacked the skills to help him and integrate him into their family.

The Emotional Impact of Adoption on Parents and Grandparents
The setting in which an adopted child arrives is frequently one of mourning rather than celebration. An adoption is the result of a *loss*. It is the recognition by a couple that they are unable to conceive or carry to term their biological child. The couple can often blunt this loss with the joy of their new child, but the loss has to be worked through eventually. While grandparents may be more removed, they also feel the loss of a biological child, and must find ways to deal with it through recognition, awareness and resolution. Parents and grandparents feel cheated of an option they had long taken for granted. (Chapter 7 provides a detailed discussion of loss and mourning.)

Grandparents should be aware of these unique emotional qualities of adoption:

- The adoptive mother does not experience pregnancy, delivery or lactation.
- The adoptive mother does not have the physical, psychological or hormonal changes that are *normal* preparation for motherhood.
- The adoptive father, not having gone through the natural pregnancy period with his wife, misses the growing experience of developing his emotional identity of fatherhood.
- The adoptive couple is especially sensitive and vulnerable to their parents' acceptance and approval – or criticism.
- Single-parent adoptions, which are increasing, offer additional emotional stress due to the unique parenting situation, which can include additional stress on the mom and sometimes a lack of community acceptance.

Grandparent Stress – As Heard in a Clinical Setting
It can be difficult for grandparents to understand and cope with some of the choices their children make that will directly affect them as grandparents, but over which they have little or

no control or input. The following remarks are a sampling from clients that illustrate this emotional gray area. It is easy to empathize with these grandparents' concerns and sincere feelings, and also tempting to chide them gently for carrying such objections to the happiness of their children and their children's family.

- "We don't want our son to marry Helene – she can't have children!"
- "I understand Mike had cancer and the radiation destroyed his chances of having children. I wish our Margo would go with someone else!"
- "The baby isn't of *our* bloodline. How can I feel the same about him as I do about our biological grandchildren?"
- "Why would they want to adopt a Chinese girl? She won't fit in with the rest of the family."

Adjusting to Alternative Choices

Your children can surely sense how you feel about their decisions involving nontraditional conception and adoption. Even when you try to hide it, they know. If they sense you are not on their team, they will likely withdraw and avoid involving you in any part of the process. This is most unfortunate, because there has never been a time when they need your understanding and support more.

Try to sort out what bothers you most about the issue. Is it fears about genetic background? Risks in raising adopted children? Perhaps the fact that they didn't talk over their decision with you before they acted? Are you concerned that they acted too quickly? If you can get a handle on what is bothering you most, you may be better able to work through your feelings. Your genuine acceptance is so important for these new parents.

On the other hand, perhaps you are so excited about becoming a grandparent that you are insensitive to the unique experience that is being played out in your child's life. Adoption is different, and it impacts parents differently than a biological birth.

After Adoption

When a new child comes home, all couples face a sudden role change: now they are parents for the *rest* of their lives. When the child has been adopted, the couple becomes two things at once – parents and adoptive parents. Their child has four parents: two biological parents and two adoptive parents. For the single parent it is even more convoluted – two biological parents and one adoptive parent – three parents.

Adoption presents unique conditions and circumstances for your grandchild. The adopted child brings with him or her a sense of loss of the biological parents. Even children adopted in very early infancy who never knew their birth parents may still experience a sense of loss, and will later question, if only to themselves, why their biological parents relinquished them.

Implicit in this emotional self-examination are questions such as, "What could be wrong with me for my parents to give me away?" "If nothing was wrong with me, what was wrong with my parents? Will the same thing be wrong with me?" One of the most difficult things for adoptive parents to accept is that nothing can change their adopted child's genes, early life experiences, or ties to another family.

Peter was 23 years old when he located his birth father. It was an incredibly wonderful experience for him, as it was for his biological father, who had never known he existed. In therapy, Peter explained that the parents who raised him were good, loving and caring. Adoption was never discussed in his home, although he knew he was adopted. People always told him how much he looked like his mother. Peter describes the insights that changed his life:

> *"I always felt like there was a hole in me. I never understood it, because my parents gave me everything I wanted. I had*

a recurring dream about me being in the middle of a room with a family on my left side and a family on my right side and feeling stuck in one spot, not knowing which way to go. Now that I have found my father, I don't love the parents that raised me any less, but I don't have an empty hole anymore. I know who I am and what my roots are. I didn't realize how much I wanted to know until I found my father and began to ask him questions. I guess my dream was about not fitting in. Now I do!"

For more information about locating birth parents, try:

* Adoptees' Liberty Movement Association, P.O. Box 727 Radio City Station, NY, NY 10101; tel. 212-581-1568.
* Adoption Reunion Registry Tracers, 183 Waverly Avenue, Medford, NY 11763; tel. 516-654-0091.

The Shared Fate Theory

It is vital in such families that there be an *acknowledgment* of the differences rather than a *rejection* of differences with the adoptive child. H. David Kirk, an authority on adoption, writes about the *Shared Fate Theory* of adoptive children and their families. Kirk's investigation found two significant themes: families that *did not* view adoptive parenthood as significantly different from natal (birth-based) parenthood (rejection-of-differences); and families that *did* view adoptive parenthood as different in some ways (acknowledgment-of-differences.)

From his data, Kirk found that acknowledging differences allows more empathic communication between parents and the child, and enables parents to be more understanding of the biological, genetic and emotional influences their child brings to the family.

Kirk put his theory of Shared Fate into practice while raising his two adopted children. In his book, *Shared Fate,* he recounts a poignant comment made by his son, then age 11:

"The child who is born into his family is like a board that's nailed down from the start. But the adopted child, him the parents have to nail down, otherwise he is like a loose board in midair."

My clinical work with adopted children and adults strongly supports David Kirk's theory. The need is very real for parents – *and grandparents* – to emotionally and intellectually accept the adoptive child's differences. When the child resembles his adoptive parents in skin color and size, it can be tempting to *pretend* the baby is their birth child, blinding themselves to accepting differences.   School-age and adolescent children in therapy may acknowledge that they are adopted, and then typically go on to talk about something else. If the adoption issue is pursued as perhaps being at the root of the referral, they generally respond by saying, "My parents are my real parents and I never think about being adopted." This is accurate in the sense that in their home it is not permissible to think about biological parents or any of the issues of adoption because these parents reject the differences. After working together for a time, a child may eventually feel safe enough to share their questions and fantasies related to being adopted.

Is There an Ideal Adoptive Situation?

The family that accepts its differences in a positive way knows that an adoptive family is different from a biological family. This acknowledgment of reality impacts family life and makes it easier for the child. As child development specialists, we know from experience that any family secret has a destructive impact on a child's healthy development. Parents may argue that no one knows the secret except them, so how can it possibly affect the child? Research proves them wrong! Honesty is the best policy.

Even in the most ideal situation, grandparents need to be reminded that *adoption is different* – not better or worse, just different. Among these differences:

- Adoption is a lifelong condition.
- Adoptive families are different from biological families. Adoptive children are unique in that they have the present parents and the *other* parents which always plays a role in their development.
- Adopted children bring their own genes, birth experience, biological family ties, and perhaps even an extensive history, to their adoptive family.
- Both adoptive parents and adopted children tend to feel they have less control over their situation than other families.
- Adoptive parents and adoptive children are likely to experience a sense of loss.
- For all children to be *given up for adoption* is a blow to their self-esteem.

Adoption *is* Different

A colleague who read this manuscript admonished me for making adoption sound so high risk. I hope this has not been the case. My effort has been, as in other areas in this survival guide, to alert grandparents to issues they may not have previously considered. I certainly believe adoption fills the needs for many children and many families. I wholeheartedly encourage thoughtful adoption, and I know numerous successful adoptive families.

When Child-Free is the Choice

Infertile couples who decide to live child-free must also come to terms with their grief and loss. As their parents, you may be empathic to their pain in making this decision, and experience your own pain or sorrow at this choice at the same time. It is possible the couple may finally feel relief and closure, while you remain sad and disappointed for them. It may help for you to be reminded that we only truly learn how wonderful it is to be a parent when we ourselves are parents. It is possible that your adult children who have not or will not experience parenting can never feel the loss that you, as an experienced parent, may so acutely feel.

Their decision not to have a baby may deprive you of being a grandparent. This can be a real disappointment. As I have stated before, becoming a grandparent is never your decision. For people who need to be in control, it is truly difficult at times to accept your child's decision. It may be wise for you to contact your clergy or a counselor to work through feelings of grief and loss, to enable you to be comfortable with the couple's decision. Regardless of your own feelings, this vulnerable couple needs you to support their lifestyle decision.

Here are some *alternative grandparenting* suggestions for those who feel this loss acutely:

- Become more invested with other grandchildren, or with great-nieces and nephews.
- Become involved in Adopt-A-Grandparent programs (such as those described in Chapter 5.)
- Share time and activities with the children of a friend or neighbor who may not have grandparents in their lives.
- Volunteer to help out at your local school, library or day care to share your knowledge, skills and caring in programs with kids.
- Offer to be a mentor to a child who shows an aptitude or interest in a skill you possess and enjoy, such as photography, sewing, cooking, woodworking, fishing, or computers.

In conclusion, I hope this discussion of nontraditional baby making and current adoption practices, as well as the non-baby option, has provided some insight into the ways in which your kids may be dealing with these issues. As the great sage Yogi Berra once said, "Never expect to find what you expected."

Recommendations

- Read this chapter before you become a grandparent. It will help you prepare for the choices your children *may* have to face – including some unexpected ones.
- Remember: dealing with unanticipated infertility is a life crisis of huge proportion for your child.
- Try to stay current on nontraditional ways of conceiving children. This will keep you and your children on the same wavelength if they choose this route. Keep an eye out for news stories on this subject in newspapers and magazines and for segments on television that you might ordinarily skip because they do not apply to you.
- Adoption is not a substitute for having a biological child, nor does it erase the loss or pain.
- Adoption is an intergenerational endeavor. A successful outcome is enhanced when there is understanding and support within the entire family.
- Every family member benefits (including grandparents) when the whole family can *acknowledge the differences* and love the adopted child for those differences, rather than pretending they do not exist.
- If the infertile couple chooses to remain childless, you can turn to your nieces and nephews and enjoy taking a more active role as grand-aunts and grand-uncles to their children. Every child benefits from more loving attachments. *Never* make the childless couple feel guilty for not providing you with a grandchild.

Reading List for Adults

Berger, Gary S., et al. *The Couple's Guide to Fertility.* Doubleday, 1995.

Bourguignon, Jean-Pierre, and Kenneth Watson. *After Adoption.* Illinois Department of Children and Family Services, 1987.

Kirk, H. David. *Shared Fate.* Revised edition. Port Angeles, WA: Ben-Simon Publications, 1984.

Melina, Lois R., and Sharon K. Roszia. *Open Adoption Experience.* HarperCollins, 1993.

Menning, B. *Infertility: A Guide for the Childless Couple.* Englewood Cliffs, New Jersey: Prentice Hall, 1988.

Register, Cheri. *Are Those Kids Yours? American Families with Children Adopted From Other Countries.* New York: Free Press, 1991.

Sebel, Mackelle M., et al. *Infertility: Your Questions Answered.* Carol Publishing Group, 1995.

Watkins, Mary, and Susan Fisher. *Talking with Young Children About Adoption.* Yale University Press, 1995.

Reading List For Children

Freudberg, J., and T. Geiss. *Susan and Gordon Adopt A Baby.* Random/Children's Television Workshop, 1992. Ages 2-8 years.

Koehler, P. *The Day We Met You.* Aladdin Paperbacks, 1997. Ages 2-5 years.

Krementz, Jill. *How It Feels To Be Adopted.* Knopf, 1988. Ages 8-14 years.

Livingston, C. *Why Was I Adopted?* Carol Publishing Group, 1997. Ages 4-8 years.

Stein, S. *The Adopted One: An Open Family Book For Parents and Children Together.* Walker & Co., 1986. All ages.

Turner, A. *Through Moon and Stars and Night Skies.* Harper & Row, 1990. The story of a small boy adopted from a faraway country. Ages 4-8 years.

Walker Livingston, C. *Why Was I Adopted?* Lyle Stuart. Ages 4-8 years.

11

The *Nonperfect* Child

*We are vulnerable because of our very intricacy
and complexity.*
– *Lewis Thomas,* The Medusa and The Snail

Everything appeared to be progressing smoothly with Martha's pregnancy. She was into her seventh month when her parents received a frantic telephone call from Tom: they were at the hospital, and birth was imminent. A premature birth – why? What went wrong?

The minute Joan and Dick saw their new baby son's face, they knew something terrible had happened. His lip was split and his pug-like nose was pushed to the side. Joan freaked out. Baby Simon had a cleft-lip and palate.

Beth and Ron loved to party, even when Beth became pregnant. Beth's drinking was much more serious than anyone realized. The grandparents have learned their grandbaby has Fetal Alcohol Syndrome (FAS).

Another set of grandparents expressed concern that their granddaughter Pamela was not gaining weight. In fact, she continued to lose weight. Pamela was hospitalized. When the medical staff could find no organic cause for her condition, they diagnosed it as *failure to thrive.*

This chapter examines the risks, disabilities and weaknesses that may accompany our grandchildren's birth. Once having experienced the birth of a *nonperfect* baby, we can really appreciate the miracle of a *perfect* baby!

As parents and grandparents, we expect normal, healthy babies. When our pregnant daughter or daughter-in-law passes her ultrasound, AFP screening, amniocentesis or Chronic Villius Sampling (CVS) with flying colors, we assume that everything is fine with the pregnancy. The AFP screening is a simple maternal blood test performed between the 16th and 18th weeks of pregnancy. A normal result for women under age 35 suggests the absence of some brain and spinal abnormalities, and some chromosomal abnormalities. For women over age 35, or those who produce an abnormal AFP, either an amnio or CVS is recommended.

Amnio and CVS both reveal the baby's sex – privileged information which the parents-to-be may or may not choose to share with us! However, the primary purpose of these tests is to conduct a chromosome analysis which can diagnose Down syndrome and other similar but rarer disorders. It is important to be aware that 3 percent of babies born at term have some type of significant abnormality, and that the amnio or CVS rule out only 0.5 percent, leaving 2.5 percent undetected.

Diagnosis of a disorder is infrequent, but when it does occur, what can be done when the tests results are affirmative? There are basically two options available: anticipate a nonperfect baby, or terminate the pregnancy. In the not too distant future, these abnormalities may be corrected interuterine. At present it is a difficult dilemma and a painful decision for expectant parents, who must choose to carry a nonperfect fetus to term, or abort.

To discover during pregnancy that the fetus is nonperfect is a horror that nobody wants. The choices that a couple needs to make may profoundly affect and change the family's life forever. Grandparents may or may not be included in the decision making. As always, you need to wait to be included. If you are included, how would you respond?

Recently, I learned about a case that touched on these issues. It was the mother's first pregnancy and she was carrying fraternal twins (not fertility induced). The amnio revealed a rare and serious disorder in one of the babies. The prognosis for aborting only one baby was poor.

The dilemma was shared with the four grandparents. Each grandparent-to-be dealt with this trauma differently, as would be expected. The maternal grandmother researched the condition and found information on the impact of the disorder on children, and what medical and psychological interventions were available.

After reviewing the information, the couple chose to continue the pregnancy. They have found that with aggressive medical intervention, the nonperfect child (now age 7) is managing reasonably well.

In my opinion, this was a very mature group of people. They supported each other, they looked at their options, made a choice, and are now doing all that is medically possible to help the child. A different group might have made a different decision, which would have been the right decision for them.

At birth, babies are routinely tested for a number of genetic disorders, most of which can be treated successfully with immediate intervention, thus preventing serious consequences. In Colorado, all newborns are tested for eight genetic diseases by drawing a few drops of blood from the baby's heel and sending it to the lab. Testing programs vary in the 50 states, so families may want to explore this and perhaps arrange for private testing.

Once we consider all that can conceivably go wrong with a developing embryo, we realize how truly fortunate we are when there are no problems. The nonperfect fetus may miscarry (a natural process which is sometimes a blessing), or the baby may be born blind, deaf, autistic, stillborn, cleft palate, retarded, FAS, or cerebral palsy. These are some of the possibilities seldom anticipated – and with no prenatal diagnosis available at the present time.

The nonperfect baby is certainly not the expected baby. Parents are shocked and disappointed. How could this happen? In many cases, parents feel they did everything *right* – the pregnant mother did not smoke cigarettes or consume alcohol, she ate healthy foods, she watched her weight, and she avoided medication even with early nausea and later headaches. The parents' grief is actually double; they grieve for what happened to them, and they grieve for their nonperfect baby. Grieving parents need a great deal of support, especially from their parents and close family members, and they are not always able to find the support they need.

The loss of what was expected – a perfect baby – needs to be mourned as a *loss*, but the loss never ends for some parents. (A more in-depth discussion of mourning can be found in Chapter 7.) As one mom reacted angrily about her autistic baby, "Not only did I not get the baby I wanted, but now I have one that rocks all day and who acts like he hates me!"

Denial and guilt are typical reactions to the birth of a nonperfect child, followed by depression, anger and shame. While the parents struggle to cope with their loss, these special babies need even greater amounts of love and nurturing to enable them to develop the attachment and trust that is so essential for their ongoing development. This makes for a very hard time for parents.

Grandparents are affected by this situation as deeply as their children. Instead of sharing an anticipated joy with their children, they share sadness, anxiety and disappointment. Yet there are important ways we can help our children, in spite of our own sadness:

- By drawing on our own life experiences of facing major crises, we are often able to offer the new parents the benefit of our ability to see the crisis in perspective, rather than becoming overwhelmed by the immediacy of the event.

- Although we may not have parented a nonperfect baby, we can be a supportive, understanding sounding board for many of the emotions and conflicts our children are experiencing.

- If we *have* lived through a similar experience, we may be very helpful at this time!

- We need to keep our *antenna* finely tuned to anticipate how best to help.

- We may be able to assist in the self-education, research and awareness aspect of our family's situation. This is a fine way to show support. First make an initial effort in this direction to gauge whether your efforts are appreciated and further solicited, or politely but firmly discouraged.

- Be patient. As one young mother said, "I wish my dad wouldn't keep asking me how things are going. I know he is concerned, but I wish he wouldn't ask during every conversation, and instead wait until I volunteer the information."

- Our most important role may be to reassure our children that we really do care for them, support them fully and unconditionally, and are willing to help in any way we are asked.

Some grandparents may become so upset and distraught by the situation that a role reversal occurs. Grandparents are unable to be good comforters, and the grieving parents are further compromised by having to provide comfort to their parents as well. If this sounds like you, please try to work through your feelings with family and friends, so you can turn things around and become available to help the parents. Reminders:

- Your grief is secondary to your children's.

- For the sake of your grandchild's optimal growth and development, she needs to become integrated into her family, and your role is to foster that, rather than interfere with it.
- If you believe that it is better to give than receive, this is a prime time to put that principal into practice.
- Allow yourself to experience the sadness you feel, but avoid sharing it with your adult child.
- Build the parents up whenever possible, admiring all that they are doing well with their difficult child.
- For goodness sake, don't withdraw from them and their child.
- Don't try to take over – grandparents don't always know best!

My Nonperfect Baby

One of my children was born with an imperfection that was corrected during the first two years of her life. We were fortunate that it was a correctable condition.

Bob and I were young and perhaps a bit naive. We had never talked to each other about the risks of anything being wrong with *our* baby. What a shock, then, when at birth our young obstetrician told us, "You have a fine, healthy baby girl – but I'm not sure she will ever walk." This may have been the first case of clubbed feet this particular doctor had ever seen. A more experienced doctor might have been more supportive and reassuring in informing us of our baby's condition and the possible treatments.

Enter my concerned parents, who fell into the group of grandparents that try to organize their children's lives before they are even asked. They had a plan of action for us: (1) Don't tell *anyone;* and (2) Consult with a specialist *immediately*.

Their ideas had merit, but it was *our* problem, and *we* had to make the decisions. In their effort to make everything better for their children, these over- involved grandparents needed to tell their adult children how to feel *and* act. In addition, my parents stirred up all kinds of doubts and uncertainties about whether or not we were making the right choice for our baby. They interfered because they loved us and felt bad for us and for their grandchild – not to mention the emotional upset they experienced themselves about their eagerly awaited and now nonperfect first grandbaby.

This was a very hard time for Bob and me. Not only were we stressed out over our baby, but equally stressed out in handling my parents. Cognitively we understood their concern and wish to help us, but emotionally we could not deal with them. Our way was to ignore them and operate on our own. That was not easy for a young inexperienced couple, and in retrospect, I am sure it was not easy on my parents. Fortunately, all went well and our child developed into a happy, healthy, running and jumping youngster who was well loved and cared for by her grandparents.

The lesson grandparents can learn from this experience is to be more introspective about yourself, and realize how your grief influences your behavior towards your children. Be aware of the impact your emotions are having on the young family. I offer this advice often because it is sound advice and it works: *Wait until you are asked! Be available, but not controlling.*

The Preemie

Labor is premature if it occurs well before the expected date of delivery. The more premature the birth, the greater the risks for survival. Martha and Tom, mentioned at the beginning of this chapter, had nothing unusual happen in their lives that might bring about premature labor, but their 28-week fetus was suddenly about to be born.

Tom telephoned their parents from the community hospital, since both families were concerned and anxious for news about Martha's condition. The hospital's obstetrics staff tried to stop Martha's contractions without success. Kevin was delivered by cesarean section, and at a critically low weight of 1 lb., 8 oz., he was immediately airlifted to a neonatal intensive care unit (NICU) in Denver, 150 miles away.

Sometimes there are indications that premature labor may be expected and anticipated; other times, premature labor begins unexpectedly. Certain drugs and procedures may delay the delivery, but not always. With the advent of advanced medical technologies in NICUs, 85 percent of the babies now survive premature birth, according to the 1995 U.S. Bureau of Statistics.

Premature birth creates a psychological situation in which hope competes constantly with fear of death. The crisis atmosphere intensifies when conditions warrant transporting the *preemie* to a distant hospital equipped with a NICU.

This was the situation in Kevin's case. As soon as Martha was able to travel, she and Tom joined Kevin in Denver. Many weeks later, when Kevin was strong enough to come home, the pediatrician referred them to me because he felt strongly that mother, father and baby were in crisis.

Though still very small, the baby was fine and the physical prognosis was excellent. The emotional impact of the NICU experience was the greatest cause for concern, as well as how the parents would care for a still very small and sensitive baby at home.

Kevin was a difficult baby, and his parents were having a hard time recovering from their NICU experience and the transition to caring for their baby on their own. They really needed a network of support. I saw them fairly regularly throughout Kevin's first year.

Our work together focused primarily on talking out what had happened to them, and how scared they still were that their preemie might not survive. I helped them understand that the early birth and all the stress surrounding it would probably slow Kevin's normal development. I assured them that he would likely catch up completely in time, but urged them not to compare him to their neighbor's full-term baby. Our work together allowed them to relax and bond with their precious child.

In many communities, there is often not enough in the way of support systems for families stressed by unexpected or traumatic birth situations. Martha and Tom's many friends had understandably quite busy lives, and their availability was limited. Both sets of grandparents traveled to Denver to be with the couple and Kevin, but their visits were shortened by their own commitments back home. Had the grandparents lived in Martha and Tom's community and been more available, perhaps the couple's visits with me might have been less necessary.

The Premature Baby Experience

Everything is different when the baby is born prematurely. Mothers often feel the pregnancy is unfinished and something is missing. They express feelings of being *cheated* because they were not emotionally prepared to give birth. Tension and anxiety mount during the delivery. Will the baby live? If the baby survives, will he or she be perfect? What will we do if there are problems? Financial as well as emotional concerns add to the stress.

Preemies are usually kept in NICU until they are eating and gaining well. Parents may spend days to weeks visiting their baby in the nursery. The nursing mother finds the situation complex and stressful. Often the baby is not strong enough to nurse when mother visits, so she must express milk at home, freeze it, and bring bottles to the hospital, knowing that it is unlikely that her tube-fed baby will receive her milk at all. If she plans to nurse when she brings the baby home, it is essential for her to empty her breasts to stimulate the milk supply. The new mother who has done her homework knows how important mother/infant bonding is in enabling healthy child development, yet now she must pump milk that may not be used. This can be very discouraging and depressing to the bonding process.

The premature baby, in contrast to a full term baby, experiences a much different beginning. Physical surroundings of the NICU, such as constantly rattling and humming monitors and machinery, and an atmosphere of urgency – factors which saved the baby's life in the first place – are not especially soothing and comforting for the baby or the parents. Parents need to be encouraged to hold and soothe their babies, despite tubes, monitors and other medical equipment. NICU nurses are as sensitive to parent's needs as the preemie's needs, and they are quite wonderful in helping parents bond to their tiny babies. This primary care nurse is just what the name implies – the primary person that provides care for baby and parents during the NICU stay.

Grandparents, be prepared when you visit – and *do* visit! The NICU is like some strange realm out of science fiction: flashing lights, metallic machinery stacked close together, strange noises and smells, beeping alarms, cramped spaces, too many people, and little calm or quiet. As for the baby, preemies are not only smaller than other babies – their bodies are not yet fully developed, so they may look different and act different from the baby you were expecting to see. All the drama and tenseness of the situation can affect grandparents as it does parents, making them withhold natural feelings of bonding until they are sure the baby will survive. However, *this* is the time when the infant needs warmth, expressions of comfort and support, and soothing, loving touches from parents, grandparents and other family members.

Coming Home

When Kevin was finally ready to leave the NICU and come home, it was a major transition for everyone. The longed-for homecoming was fraught with anxiety. Martha and Tom were on their own with Kevin: no nurses, no machines, no medical experts standing by to answer every question. Kevin had a hard time adjusting to *his* home: a new environment, a new routine – even different smells. Everything felt different.

Kevin's nervous system was raw from not having a full nine months to mature and overstimulated from the hospital nursery. Because of this, NICU preemies are usually hypersensitive and acutely vulnerable to overstimulation. Any tension the preemie senses from his parents may cause him to withdraw from well-meaning parental care and effort. This behavior then becomes circular: the baby withdraws, and then the parents feel they have failed, and they respond by withdrawal. The stage is set for misattunement.

More education is needed for parents to better prepare them to care for and understand the infant that has spent time in NICU. Child development specialists are learning that the develop–mental outcome of preemies is much less dependent on the particular events of the infant's medical history than it is on the infant's ability to successfully negotiate the major challenges of the first few years of life. Technology keeps preemies alive, but nurturing makes them thrive. We are talking about the close emotional connection between infant and parents – bonding, attunement and trust (discussed in depth in Chapter 3). Expert *baby watchers* have found that the support system parents have during that first year becomes an important predictor of a healthy outcome for preemie development.

I believe grandparents might make themselves more available during the preemie's early weeks and months if they knew how much the parents need their help and support. Some suggestions:

- Stroke your grandbaby as much as possible. Recent research reports that stroking babies encourages growth and reduces stress. Findings also suggest that infant massage significantly fosters growth and development in preemies (according to Tiffany Field, Ph.D., director, Touch Research Institute, University of Miami School of Medicine).
- Offer to baby-sit. Parents are reluctant to leave their preemie, yet they need time off, and they may be only willing to trust a family member.

- Be patient. Your baby will catch up with your friends' grandbabies eventually.
- Be involved emotionally and *present* as much as you possibly can for the struggling family. Dealing with a preemie, with or without mitigating circumstances or more serious conditions, can be tough duty. Resist the tendency to put distance between yourself and the painful situation. It is better for everyone involved – parents, baby and grandparents – if you can participate, be supportive and share emotionally.

A caring grandmother of a preemie told me with great confidence, "I told my kids that it's a big world, and don't you worry – Hannah will grow in the world," and indeed she has!

Down Syndrome

Doctors do not know how Down syndrome occurs, or how to prevent it. They do know there is an increased risk of occurence with older mothers and fathers. Parents do not cause Down, and it is not hereditary. A few facts about Down syndrome babies:

- About one in 166 newborns has a chromosome ab– normality, with Down syndrome being the most common among live births.
- The baby has one extra chromosome in each of its millions of cells.
- Down occurs as frequently in boys as in girls.
- Down is one of the most common birth defects.
- Down children are usually moderately or mildly retarded and educable.
- Few people with Down are severely retarded.
- Today's prognosis for Down is much more positive than it was 20 years ago.

Medical problems occurring with Down syndrome that not too long ago meant premature death are now treatable. With improved medical care and close monitoring by parents and professionals, there is every reason to expect children with Down to lead full, healthy lives. Down kids can do most everything other kids can do; it just might take them longer. They may be mildly retarded. They tend to have a shorter life span than other children. Usually Down kids are very affectionate, and for that reason it is rewarding to be around them.

Megan, the younger sister of Max, age 6, was a Down child. Their mother was age 27 when Megan was born. A year later, she gave birth to another child who was perfectly healthy. Mother often brought all three children with her to the mental health clinic for Max's appointments. When I needed to meet with Mom, she brought Megan with her.

Until then, I had almost no experience with Down children. True to an outdated and inaccurate stereotype, I expected a severely retarded and unattractive child with a large head. To the contrary, Megan was a sweet, happy, attractive little girl, slightly undersized for her four years and developmentally a little slow. I learned from her mother that Megan's special education and therapeutic intervention offered by the public school system was exceptionally good, and Mother felt very optimistic about Megan's future. As can happen, many of the emotional problems Max was having were reactive to the impact this nonperfect child had on the family and his unresolved feelings about himself.

Mom was a single mother; the marriage broke up when she was pregnant with her third baby. Max's father was somewhat involved in the course of Max's treatment. Raising three children close in age, including one with Down syndrome, was simply too much for this young man. He had wanted his wife to abort the third pregnancy, which she had refused. Unfortunately, this scenario is not too unusual. A nonperfect child can put a great strain on the marriage, and quite frequently (although there are no statistics on this) the marriage breaks up. Educating pediatricians to recommend preventive counseling for families with a nonperfect child might help reduce this occurrence.

Hopefully, grandparents now have a more current under–standing of Down than I did when I first met Megan. Whatever the disability, it is tempting for some grandparents to avoid accepting it. When the child lives out of town, grandparents may *forget* the problem and resist sharing it with their friends. Sometimes they avoid having the grandchild visit because the disability is shaming to them. This can be devastating to parents who are struggling to cope and accept their nonperfect child. If I am describing *you,* shape up! Your acceptance is essential to your grandchild and his parents!

It may be natural to have these feelings, but it is not productive or useful to become stuck over feelings of guilt and shame when parents and grandchild need your support.

- Every child needs and deserves love and support from his or her family members, including grandparents, regardless of any disabilities. Every child brings love, warmth and joy to families. Move off of concerns about yourself to ways you can help and enjoy your new grandchild.
- If you have concerns about how your Down grandbaby may develop, consider arranging to meet with a family with a Down child. You may need to readjust or modify your expectations slightly, but you may also better realize that Down grandchildren have full, rich lives to share with you.
- Visit or volunteer some time at a school where Down children attend. Down children are routinely accepted and befriended by their peers, and sharing this experience may help you, too.

Cerebral Palsy

Many cases of Cerebral Palsy (CP) go unrecognized until well into the baby's first year. The main symptoms of abnormal muscle tone and lack of coordination can cause either stiffening of limbs or floppy limbs which are the first visible manifestations of the disorder. Additionally, some CP babies may have difficulty sucking and swallowing. These behaviors are usually not apparent until the baby is at least 6 months old. The impact here is quite hard on the family. The perfect baby turns out to be nonperfect.

CP is a general term applied to any motor problem caused by a brain injury. How brain damage occurs can be difficult to determine, and potential causes are numerous. Damage may result from:

- Abnormal brain development due to a serious illness suffered by the mother during pregnancy.
- The fetus may have suffered a stroke.
- Brain damage may occur at the time of delivery.
- Damage may be caused by an injury after birth.

Frequently the precise cause cannot be determined. As with many other infant imperfections, CP is definitely *not* inherited. CP brain damage does not worsen with time, nor can it be improved. However, other parts of the brain can be trained to take over some of the functions of the damaged parts. Though Cerebral Palsy typically applies to a physical disability, some CP children may have some degree of mental retardation; others may be highly intelligent. Caring for a CP child is very demanding, and involves teamwork between parents, physicians, physical therapists, occupational therapists and teachers.

My friend Patrice loves children, and although she never had children of her own, she is now surrogate grandmother to Ryan, a CP child. Knowing my interest in children, she invited me to join her and Ryan, age 5, at her home.

Ryan sat slumped in Patrice's lap, his leg braces across the room. He had finished his *walking work* and was now playing with Patrice. Playing for Ryan took the utmost concentration to make his fingers seize a Lego piece to place onto the tower they were building. Patrice and Ryan were settled in for the afternoon, sitting on the floor by her sunny picture window overlooking a lush green field. Beside them were Ryan's music, his books and Legos, and a portable telephone, so Patrice had no need to leave him abruptly. Patrice is Ryan's loving caretaker when Ryan's parents, Corrine and Bill, need a break. This surrogate grandmother's loving, positive and shining personality is one of the many interventions that has made the doctor's words of "hopelessly retarded" untrue. Ryan has an intact, active, alert mind, matched with an uncontrollable motor system.

The relationship between Ryan and Patrice has grown and flourished, serving both their needs. How fortunate Ryan is to have this kind of love from a nonfamily member – and how fortunate Patrice is to have Ryan as an outlet for her grand maternal caring. Patrice is experiencing the dependent, innocent love that is the joy of parenting; Ryan is the baby she never had.

The unanswered question is how will Ryan cope with life apart from his primary caretakers, now that he is entering kindergarten? Will Patrice continue to be as emotionally responsive as Ryan grows and changes? It really does not matter. The chemistry that exists between this child and adult has been growth-producing and nurturing. This experience was not planned; it simply happened. Patrice, for a time, regardless of how long or short, has her grandchild, and Ryan has a special adult in his life that has provided complete attention, affection and acceptance.

Ryan's parents cherish the special love between the two. They are wonderful, loving parents, committed to providing as enriching an environment as possible for Ryan. While Ryan will have his share of lifelong problems, he has the benefit of a strong, coping family to help him manage.

Cleft Lip and Palate

Mary Jo, the expectant grandmother, had been invited to participate in the delivery. At the moment of birth, she saw Simon's cleft palate. The delivering mom asked her rather routinely, "Mom, does everything look all right?" Mary Jo answered, "Yes," feeling she was not the one to inform her daughter of the imperfection. She went home with a very heavy heart. She later told me, "I don't think I've ever had as much to drink as I had that night." The awful realization that the baby was not perfect and she had no one to talk to about it was a terrible burden for her.

Although early surgery corrected the defect with a minimal scar, the early days of Simon's life were terrible for everyone. Simon was unable to nurse, so feeding became a nightmare for Joan and Dick; an adult had to squeeze the bottle nipple to allow milk to drip into his mouth. The much anticipated experience of holding her baby close to give nourishment did not work. Joan, quite shaken by her baby's appearance, found herself unable to look at Simon or to hold him close. The risk here, as with other disabilities, is that the unresolved rage, grief, blame, guilt and disappointment on the part of the parents and grandparents may interfere with their interaction with the baby and disrupt the all-important infant/caregiver bonding and attunement.

Failure to Thrive

Pamela, the failure to thrive infant described at the beginning of this chapter, did not begin life with any disability. For this nonperfect baby, we know both the cause and the correction. The initial indication of problems began when Pamela failed to gain weight appropriately, and exhibited developmental delays such as not smiling or making sounds. Hospitalization followed to check her for organic causes.

To her family's surprise, Pamela immediately began to gain weight and develop when hospitalized and cared for by a nurturing primary care nurse. When organic factors are ruled out, it often becomes evident that problems exist between mother and baby. This is particularly true when the baby responds so dramatically to hospital nursing care.

This response is the result of a psychological misattunement between mother and baby. Unfortunately, fathers of these infants are relatively uninvolved with their babies. As we have seen, bonding with the father can emotionally sustain a baby when the mother is unavailable. Failure to thrive infants have no one! This condition may have been brought on by Mom's post partum depression, which has not abated. Additionally, mothers of these infants often have experienced early deprivation in their own childhoods, and are likely to have a poor relationship, if any, with their own mothers now. This same mother may have mothered another infant successfully, but this particular infant's temperament and personality displeased the mother in such a way that she responds to the baby with displeasure, rejection or neglect.

I bring this problem to the attention of readers to alert you to the need for immediate intervention by professionals trained in infant psychiatry if this situation arises. Though the infant may be kept alive by its family, without real effort made to change the psychological conditions of her environment, *serious psychopathology* may result. The failure to thrive infant, lacking appropriate intervention, becomes a person unable to form attachments and who lacks trust in others and himself or herself. Theirs is a high-risk life.

Fetal Alcohol Syndrome

Fetal Alcohol Syndrome (FAS) affects children in a wide variety of ways. Some have mental retardation, growth deficiency, facial malformation and central nervous system dysfunction. The majority of FAS children are affected more subtly, with low average intelligence, mild delays and facial characteristics that may appear normal to the untrained eye.

It is widely known that expectant mothers can improve their babies' chances for good health by reducing or eliminating alcohol consumption during pregnancy, and especially before delivery. In a recent study, 100 percent of the women who reduced excessive drinking before the third trimester delivered infants who were comparable to infants of nondrinking mothers. Statistically, about one-half of all heavy drinking mothers have normal children, 10 percent have children with full FAS, and 40 percent produce offspring with partial FAS, defined as having some developmental delay and/or neurobehavioral disorder.

Grandparents, this is one time I advise you *not* to wait to be asked! Intervene in any way you can to protect your unborn grandchild if you feel excessive alcohol consumption is a factor in your children's pregnancy. FAS is preventable. Some suggestions:

- Avoid the temptation to ignore the drinking problem, hoping the mother will stop on her own, or that the problem will simply *go away.* It won't.
- Address the alcohol problem directly with your adult children, whether they like you for it or not.
- Offer to fund any counseling intervention that may be appropriate.
- If an alcohol rehabilitation program is necessary, and the rehab is residential, offer child care for the other children.
- Be kind, but firm.

I have a friend who adopted an infant who turned out to be retarded, most likely from Fetal Alcohol Syndrome. After the diagnosis, the concerned grandparents asked, "Can you give her back?" The infant's parents replied simply, "She's our daughter."

When All is Not Right – Part II

We have examined several of the more common disabilities that may occur when your grandchild is born nonperfect. It is impossible to discuss all the possible disabilities or conditions here. Each situation requires treatment tailored to the child and his family. How you feel about it may be all out of proportion to the way it appears to others. A mild defect can be as distressing as a major one. Being challenged physically or mentally is a hard blow for a child. But it is even harder if those important to him become so involved in the disability that it becomes all they can see.

There is a normal three-stage process that most of us go through in reacting and adapting to *our* baby's birth defect:

1. Initially, a sense of shock and disappointment.
2. Anger, loss of self-esteem, "Why me?"
3. A gradual restoration of equilibrium.

The following example is an illustration of this process.

One mother explained, "My mother became so despondent over Nadia's problems that she was depressed for a year after Nadia was born. Now she feels like she has a very special grandchild in her life, and she says things like, 'She's marvelous! I'm so proud of her!' She talks about Nadia constantly. What a change I've seen in her. I'm so happy about this."

The nonperfect child, like the child without disabilities, is still *your grandchild*. There are a world of wonderful qualities about this special child to share and enjoy. Don't waste precious time and energy feeling sorry for him, or sorry for yourself. Be his grandparent. Help him grow up and feel good about himself.

Recommendations

- At a time of crisis, the most important role for grandparents is to reassure their children that their parents really do care about them and are available to help in a multitude of ways. You can offer to provide child care, an extra pair of hands at home, financial support, driving to appointments, emotional support, library research – whatever is needed that you can reasonably do.

- With the birth of a nonperfect baby, grandparents need to be introspective and assess whether or not their own grief is negatively influencing their behavior towards their children and their grandchild.
- Allow yourself to mourn the loss of the expected perfect baby. By working through this loss, you will be more available to your grandchild and her parents.
- Avoid comparing this child with your other grandchildren. Remember that each child is unique in his or her own way.
- Read up on your grandchild's disability. The knowledge may be comforting to you, and in turn you may be able to offer some helpful insights to the parents *(if they ask you)*.
- Remember: there are some things in life you have choices about, and there are other things you do not. It is more useful to make the best of the situation rather than dwelling on what cannot be changed.

Reading List for Adults

Dorris, Michael. *The Broken Cord.* GK Hall, 1990. Psychological problems of the FAS child.

Exceptional Parent magazine. Psy-Ed Corp, 209 Harvard Street, Brookline, MA, 021146-5005.

Geralis, Elaine, editor. *Children With Cerebral Palsy: A Parents' Guide.* Woodbine House, RI, 1991.

Jackson, John F. *Genetics and You.* Totowa, NJ: Humana Press, 1996.

Levitz, Mitchell. *Count Us In – Growing Up with Down Syndrome.* New York: Harcourt Brace & Co., 1994.

Klayman, Charles, editor. *American Medical Association Family Medical Guide.* Random House, 1994.

Marx, Russell. *It's Not Your Fault.* NAL-Dutton, 1996.

Reading List for Children

The Children's Disability Catalog lists children's books on a wide range of health topics. Contact the Disability Bookshop, P.O. Box 129, Vancouver, WA 98666-0129.

Krementz, Jill. *How It Feels to Fight for Your Life.* Boston: Little, Brown & Co., 1989. Age 8 years and up.

Lafferty, Litta. *Born Early: A Premature Baby's Story for Children.* Songbird Publishing, Grand Junction, CO, 81502, 1995.

Wanous, Suzanne. *Sara's Secret.* Carolrhoda Books, Inc., 1995. A story for schoolage children who have a sibling with CP.

12

WE SURVIVED – *AND THRIVED!*

*The life which is not examined
is not worth living.
– Plato*

My friends who are grandparents themselves ask me, "When are you going to finish your book? We need it!" My younger friends say they can't wait to be able to give this book to their parents: "They need a grandparenting guide to understand us better." My own children tell me, "Mom, finish your book so you can spend more time with *your* grandchildren!"

Well, we have reached the end – or the beginning, for many of you embarking on the great adventure of grandparenting for the first time. We have examined our new developmental stage of *grandparenthood,* a state of emancipation and an opportunity for great joy. Our focus has been on an effort to better understand ourselves, our children and our children's children. The end result is the reward of enriching their lives and our own in the process. I hope I have been able to convey to you my belief, both personal and professional, that grandparenthood is a time of great personal growth.

What, you may ask, will *that* personal growth be? Let's take a historical look back for a moment. Until the mid-1970s, most developmental theorists believed developmental change ended with adulthood. According to accepted theory of the day, the developmental stages that infants and children passed through solidified at adulthood. After that, they told us we did not change. I guess they thought we stagnated after age 21!

In the 1970s, sociologists such as Roger Gould, Daniel Levinson and others began researching *adulthood,* and through their work dispelled the stagnation theory by postulating developmental stages of adult life. You may be familiar with journalist Gail Sheehy's popularization of these notions in her books *Passages: Predictable Crises of Adult Life* (1977) and more recently *New Passages: Mapping Your Life Across Time* (1995). While this historical review does not define our growth, it does give us permission to acknowledge that developmental changes can occur during *grandparenthood.*

Our Developmental Stage: *Grandparenthood*

The uniqueness of being a grandparent is that we have an emotional distance from the young children we love so much. We can be part of their lives in varying degrees, as we have discussed throughout this guide, but our grandchildren were not born to us, and psychologically this is significant.

Our relationship with them does not become as distorted by emotions and expectations as it likely did with our own children, now their parents. You might say that, as grandparents, our ego and narcissism are much less involved in their development. *If asked* by their parents, our view of the overall picture may offer clarity and assistance. For many of us, grandparenthood is a *second chance.* This is particularly true for those of us that had to balance working and parenting to materially provide for our families. Now that urgency *may* be gone, freeing us in time and psychic energy to really enjoy parenthood, once removed.

As with all stages of life, grandparenthood has its unique joys and sorrows. We have considered this subject at length in the previous pages. In my opinion, grandparenthood can offer adults a second opportunity to become part of a new life. We can enjoy this experience in a different, less conflictual way this time around, while at the same time we fill other segments of our lives in creative new ways. Grandparenthood may be the most fulfilled freedom we have yet experienced. Life may not work quite this way for all of us, but I believe it is a worthwhile ideal to which we can aspire.

Into the 21st Century

Whether you chose to use this book as a guide and turned first to the section of immediate interest to you, or whether you preferred to read it from the beginning, I think you will agree that life has changed dramatically for this generation of parents. I think you will also agree, as I have pointed out, that it is much harder to be a parent today. My own children, all parents now, say with some awe, "You and dad raised four children – how did you do it?" My answer to them is, "I am glad we're not doing it today."

Great-Grandparenthood

Let's conclude with a look forward to the 21st century. Here are some amazing statistics:

- In 1980, 25 million Americans were over age 65.
- In the year 2000, 35 million Americans are projected to be over age 65.
- In 1980, 2 million Americans were over age 85.
- In 2000, *5 million* Americans are projected to be over age 85.

What does that mean to us? It means we not only need to find ways to survive and thrive as grandparents, but we need to anticipate *great*-grandparenthood. In our inner cities and the rural South, this is already common. In these areas, the teenage mother's grandmother often has the primary responsibility for taking care of the baby. When there have been three generations of teen mothers, the great-grandmother is often the matriarch who cares for the offspring of the entire extended family.

The new idea here is that it does not require a teenage mother for us to become great-grandparents. Consider this hypothetical case: Mildred married Joe when both were age 25. They had their first child at age 27. This child, Judy, married at age 30, and had a baby at age 31. This baby, Austin, married at age 22 and had Dane at age 25. Mildred and Joe are great-grandparents at a vigorous age of 83.

As we have noted throughout this guide, the more support the new parents and baby receive, the better they are able to cope with the pressures of an increasingly stressful society. Strong, healthy 83-year-old great-grandparents have a vital role to fill!

If great-grandparents are able and willing to play an active role, they can be an invaluable resource for the young family. This is especially true when the relationship between mother and daughter is strained. In that case, the great-grandmother can step in and be the supportive advisor the young mother needs.

Laura, the mother of a toddler, related that when her mother offers a parenting suggestion, she typically rejects it out of hand. "But when my grandmother tells me the same thing, I take her advice!" she added. Her grandmother is less intimidating to her than her mother, since the two do not share the emotional conflict of the two adjacent generations.

It is also less likely that great-grandparents will be working full or part time, like so many of today's grandparents are. This may place them in a better position to reach out to the young family, but ultimately we can only speculate on this potential.

My mother and her husband were often available for daytime baby-sitting for my oldest daughter's children while my husband and I, the grandparents, were working.

Another likely scenario is that our increased lifespan will require us as great-grandparents to need more care and support from our children – thus putting our children in the middle between their parents' needs and their children and grand–children's needs. In this situation, the new family may suffer because of our longevity.

Great-grandparenting: A Survival Guide is the book that needs to be written 20 years down the road.

To Conclude: The *Real* Experts Speak Up

Grandparents are very special people. Here is how some children responded when they were asked, "What is *really* special about your grandparents?"

- "They're warm when I sit on their laps." – *Charles, age 7.*
- "They taught me how to walk on stilts." – *Amanda, age 10.*
- "They're mine and not everybody else's." – *Chris, age 10.*
- "They make me laugh so hard my jaw feels like it's going to fall off!" – *Olanda, age 8.*
- "I like to hear their corny jokes." – *Bethany, age 9.*
- "They took care of me when my mom and dad got a divorce." – *Nikky, age 10.*
- "They taught me I can do anything I want if I put my mind to it." – *Danny, age 10.*

(Above quotes excerpted from *Modern Maturity* magazine, December 1990-January 1991; *"We thank teachers and students of California's Lincoln Alternative School, Corona; Stowers Elementary School, Cerritos; Alta Loma Elementary School and Belmont High School, Los Angeles; and of Central Missouri State University."*)

INDEX

Index